P9-DGK-236

Victors and Vanquished

Spanish and Nahua Views of the Conquest of Mexico

Edited with an Introduction by

Stuart B. Schwartz

Yale University

BEDFORD/ST. MARTIN'S   Boston • New York

María Victoria, para tí

For Bedford/St. Martin's
Executive Editor for History and Political Science: Katherine E. Kurzman
Developmental Editor: Charisse Kiino
Editorial Assistant: Chip Turner
Production Supervisor: Cheryl Mamaril
Marketing Manager: Charles Cavaliere
Project Management: Books By Design, Inc.
Text Design: Claire Seng-Niemoeller
Indexer: Books By Design, Inc.
Cover Design: Richard Emery Design, Inc.
Cover Art: Plate from *Lienzo de Tlaxcala,* c. 1560s
Composition: G&S Typesetters, Inc.
Printing and Binding: Haddon Craftsmen, an R. R. Donnelley & Sons Company

President: Charles H. Christensen
Editorial Director: Joan E. Feinberg
Director of Editing, Design, and Production: Marcia Cohen
Manager, Publishing Services: Emily Berleth

For information, write: Bedford/St. Martin's, 75 Arlington Street, Boston, MA 02116 (617-399-4000)

ISBN: 0-312-39355-5 (paperback)
      0-312-22817-1 (hardcover)

Acknowledgments appear at the back of the book on page 260, which constitutes an extension of the copyright page.

Foreword

The Bedford Series in History and Culture is designed so that readers can study the past as historians do.

The historian's first task is finding the evidence. Documents, letters, memoirs, interviews, pictures, movies, novels, or poems can provide facts and clues. Then the historian questions and compares the sources. There is more to do than in a courtroom, for hearsay evidence is welcome, and the historian is usually looking for answers beyond act and motive. Different views of an event may be as important as a single verdict. How a story is told may yield as much information as what it says.

Along the way the historian seeks help from other historians and perhaps from specialists in other disciplines. Finally, it is time to write, to decide on an interpretation and how to arrange the evidence for readers.

Each book in this series contains an important historical document or group of documents, each document a witness from the past and open to interpretation in different ways. The documents are combined with some element of historical narrative — an introduction or a biographical essay, for example — that provides students with an analysis of the primary source material and important background information about the world in which it was produced.

Each book in the series focuses on a specific topic within a specific historical period. Each provides a basis for lively thought and discussion about several aspects of the topic and the historian's role. Each is short enough (and inexpensive enough) to be a reasonable one-week assignment in a college course. Whether as classroom or personal reading, each book in the series provides firsthand experience of the challenge — and fun — of discovering, recreating, and interpreting the past.

Natalie Zemon Davis
Ernest R. May
David W. Blight

Preface

The story of the Conquest of Mexico has captured the imagination of readers since the sixteenth century. The last agonies and fall of the great "Aztec" empire and its island capital city, Tenochtitlan, is a story of epic proportions, still generating strong emotions even today. The tale of a great civilization conquered and destroyed by a determined and ruthless band of Spanish conquistadors led by Hernando (Hernán) Cortés, enthralled contemporary Spanish chroniclers, fascinated nineteenth-century historians like the American William Prescott, and continues to demand the attention of present-day scholars. The conquest is a history of courage, treachery, and of cultural shock whose relevance has not diminished with time.

While the outlines of the story are familiar, the interpretation of events, of rights and wrongs, and of the personalities of the major actors has changed radically over the years, especially following the process of decolonization after World War II. To some extent this movement has been due to changing attitudes toward European expansion, a fuller appreciation of Native American civilizations, and more critical attitudes about the conquest of the Americas. But it also has been the result of increased accessibility to new sources, many of them produced by the indigenous peoples of Mexico.

The primary objective of this volume is to introduce students to the Conquest of Mexico and through it to the clash of European and Native American cultures by a reading of excerpts from two of the classic sources of this story: From the Spanish side, the account of the conquistador Bernal Díaz del Castillo entitled *The True History of the Conquest of New Spain;* from the "Aztec" side, testimony gathered shortly after the conquest from survivors and recorded by the Spanish Franciscan friar Bernardino de Sahagún with the help of young Native American assistants. Additional alternate texts paint a broader, richer canvas, fleshing out the narrative and conveying to the reader a sense that there was not simply a "Spanish" or an "Indian" view. Rather, there are a variety of visions and opinions, influenced and mediated by personal interests, class and ethnic biases, political considerations, and many other factors. Native American accounts were no less influenced by such considerations than were European ones.

The conquest also raises the question of how to judge who are the winners and losers historically. I have chosen the title "Victors and Vanquished" because in military terms clearly the Spaniards won and the "Indians" lost. However, some indigenous peoples were militarily on the winning side even though subsequently they too fell into a dependent status. And although defeated militarily, indigenous cultures demonstrated considerable ability to accommodate, adapt, and resist the challenges that a new religion and political system imposed. Historians of colonial Mexico are continually faced with the dilemma of what to emphasize; the resilience of indigenous culture or the disruption and exploitation that the conquest represented. The title then is as much a question as it is a description of a permanent condition.

This book begins with an introduction outlining the major features of the indigenous civilizations of central Mexico as well as the background of the conquistadors. It also discusses the major sources from which selections have been chosen. The book then presents these historical documents divided into eight chapters, proceeding chronologically. Beginning with Native American accounts of omens that preceded their encounter with the conquistadors, the following chapters cover the early Spanish contacts with Yucatan, the first encounter of Spaniards and the Mexica peoples, Cortés's landing and march to the Mexica capital, Cortés's flight and defeat, and the bitter last struggles. While the book is about the conquest itself rather than the subsequent colonial history, a final chapter discusses the aftermath of the military conquest, the subsequent attempts to impose a colonial regime, and the creative resistance of indigenous peoples to those efforts. A short introduction precedes each chapter setting the historical context of the selections and discussing their relevance to the overall story. Each chapter includes both indigenous and European sources. Sometimes it is difficult to separate these sources by such labels since cross-cultural influences were already at work in the years following the conquest. Each selection has an accompanying headnote. Notes have been kept to a minimum and are intended to serve as an introductory guide to sources, primarily those in English. A chronology of events, study questions for students, a listing of the principal individuals mentioned in the texts, a glossary of both Spanish and Nahuatl terms, and a bibliography as a guide to further research are also included.

ACKNOWLEDGMENTS

Books like this one are always collective projects in some way. A number of people helped me at various stages in the preparation of this volume. My friends and colleagues James Lockhart and Serge Gruzinski through their work provided me with the inspiration to do this book and also with too many hours of reading pleasure to ever count. Sarah Cline (University of California, Santa Barbara), Susan Deans-Smith (University of Texas at Austin), Kevin Gosner (University of Arizona), Robert Haskett (University of Oregon), and Matthew Restall (Pennsylvania State University) gave the manuscript a careful reading and made substantive suggestions that improved it. Mary Miller, my colleague at Yale, gave me the benefit of her extensive knowledge of Mesoamerican art and culture and access to her own collection of pictorial sources. At Bedford/St. Martin's, Developmental Editor Charisse Kiino worked with me to polish this book and Executive Editor for History and Political Science Katherine Kurzman was the guiding hand through the publication process. I also wish to thank the students in my 1998 Junior Seminar at Yale on the Conquest of Mexico. Sometimes unknowingly, in their questions and discussions they did much to shape this book. Manuel Berrelez, a student in that course and later my research assistant, contributed his own extensive knowledge of early Mexico to the project.

Finally, I wish to make clear that this volume is born out of my experience as a student of the Early Modern World, of cultural encounters, and as a teacher of Latin American history for over thirty years. My classroom experience has taught me that there are few stories as fascinating or as troubling as the Conquest of Mexico. I am not a *Nahuatlato* (speaker of Nahuatl) nor a research specialist in Mexican ethnohistory. As a Latin American historian, however, I have tried, over the years, to keep abreast of developments in that specialized field. My main objective in this volume has been to bring some of those recent discoveries and approaches to the attention of a wider audience. They raise significant methodological and epistemological questions that are important not only to those interested in Mexico, but to all of us fascinated by the past and hopeful of understanding cultures different from our own.

Stuart B. Schwartz
Yale University

Note on Sources and Conventions Used

The question of sources needs to be confronted continually. Nahuas and Spaniards differed not only in what they chose to record and remember about these events, but also in the form of how they recorded them. This matter of representation is addressed by including a number of indigenous sources of a pictorial nature so that readers can begin to understand the Nahua perception and interpretation of events and some of the conventions used to record them. The story of the Conquest of Mexico presents an opportunity to consider heroism, greed, and despair, but it also challenges us to think about problems that confront all historians: Can we understand and interpret other cultures? How can we evaluate conflicting sources? How can we read and understand such differing styles of representation?

A few words are in order about some of the conventions used. First, the term "Aztec" is infrequently used by modern scholars. It was never used by the indigenous people themselves. The Spaniards first heard of these people as Culhua or Mexica but that too was somewhat inaccurate. Most of the peoples of the great imperial state of central Mexico were speakers of Nahuatl and culturally it is accurate to refer to them as Nahua peoples. However, they were divided into a number of separate political units and different ethnicities. Thus while both the people of Tenochtitlan and Tlaxcala spoke Nahuatl and shared many cultural attributes, they were bitter enemies. The occupants of the great capital city Tenochtitlan, and of its neighboring island community of Tlatelolco, were the core of the empire. They referred to themselves not as "Aztecs" but as "Mexica," and modern scholars now use that term to designate them, recognizing that many groups, Tlatelolcas, Iztapalapas, and those of other cities often associated with them and fought alongside them. I shall use the term "Mexica" to refer specifically to the residents of the island capital and try where possible to use the ethnic designation of other groups when they are mentioned.

There is considerable variation in the texts as to the spelling and pronunciation of names and terms. Spaniards wrote what they heard or thought they heard. Sometimes Spanish could not reproduce Nahuatl sounds and so variations abound in the sources. Take for example the various forms used for the name of the Mexica ruler — Montezuma, Moctheuzoma, Moctezuma, and so forth, or for his successor Cuauhtemoc (Guatemoc, Guatemoctzin, etc.). I have chosen to standardize the forms used in the introductions, but to leave the original selections alone to retain their flavor. To clarify matters, I have indicated in parentheses the standardized form after the first appearance of a variation. This problem of course is not only encountered in the writing of indigenous names and terms. Sixteenth-century Spanish usage also presents its own set of difficulties. Accents were often left "in the inkwell" and orthography was not standardized. Bernal Díaz referred to Diego Velásquez, yet the modern spelling of his name would be Velázquez. Hernán Cortés was usually called Hernando or Fernando by his contemporaries. I have used Hernán, which is more familiar to English-speaking readers. In obvious cases, I have not altered the selections and only where necessary have I tried to standardize according to modern usage. Finally, footnotes that appeared in the original versions of the texts are asterisked, while those I have written are numbered.

Contents

Maps and Illustrations

PART ONE

Introduction:
Civilizations in Conflict

The history of European expansion includes few stories of drama and tragedy equal to the Spanish conquest of Mexico and the fall of the great indigenous empire that controlled its heartland. In 1519 Hernán Cortés and a small contingent of Spanish adventurers arrived on the Mexican coast, and eventually encountered a great imperial state that was heir to a long tradition of civilization that dominated the land and held sway over millions of people. Within only three years that empire was destroyed, its ruler captured, the foundations of its cultural traditions toppled and hundreds of thousands of its people dead from warfare, famine, and disease (see Figure 1). Those who remained struggled to survive and adapt to the new Spanish colonial regime and to a new religion, Catholicism. In many ways the conquest represented both the death of a political state, or more exactly states, and much of their way of life and the birth of a new colonial regime in its place.

A LONG TRADITION: THE INDIGENOUS PEOPLES OF MESOAMERICA

The Mexica were not the only people who occupied the lands of central Mexico, but they were the most powerful. Their story has come to symbolize what happened to all the indigenous peoples of Mesoamerica (the cultural region that extended from north central Mexico southward to modern Nicaragua). One of the reasons for their representative role

Figure 1. Moctezuma in shackles next to a broken crown and broken weapons. Cortés holds the crucifix and his translator, doña Marina, supports the symbol of Tenochtitlan-Mexico.
Source: Relaciónes geográficas del Siglo XVI: Tlaxcala, ed. René Acuña (Mexico City: UNAM, 1984). The original manuscript is in the Hunterian Museum Library, University of Glasgow. Glasgow University Library, Department of Special Collections.

surely has been the survival of a Mexica version of these events that parallels, confirms, and contradicts the Spanish accounts. The Mexica and the related peoples of Mexico had their own system of recording and remembering events through a combination of pictographic representation and oral history. It was after the conquest that they learned to write both in Spanish and in their own language, Nahuatl, using the Roman alphabet. Because of these traditions and skills, there exists, perhaps more so than for any other indigenous people of the time, a written record of Nahua views and perceptions.

The Mexica who ruled central Mexico from their island capital, Tenochtitlan, were the inheritors of ancient cultural traditions. Agrarian societies based on the cultivation of maize and other crops had developed in Mexico and Central America in the centuries before the birth of Christ and had reached an apogee of cultural attainments between 600 and 900 C.E. in what has been called Mesoamerica's Classic Era. In southern Mexico, the Yucatan peninsula, Guatemala, and other regions of Central America, the Maya peoples created a number of flourishing city-states. At places like Tikal (Guatemala), Copán (Honduras), and Palenque (Mexico) great advances were made in architecture, sculpture, mathematics, and astronomy. A complex writing system was developed that only recently has begun to yield to researchers the content of the inscriptions that cover Maya buildings, monuments, and pottery. At roughly the same time, farther to the north, beyond the Maya-speaking area, the great city of Teotihuacán, not far from modern-day Mexico City, developed its own distinctive culture that spread through conquest, trade, and missionary activity to other regional centers in Mesoamerica. For reasons still not fully understood, the classic Maya cities were abandoned (ninth century C.E.) and Teotihuacán first fell into decline and then to invaders around 750 C.E. By about 900 to 1000 C.E., the Classic Era had ended and a period of instability followed. (See Map 1.)

Although the reasons for the end of the Classic Era are much debated, pressure from outside forces was an important factor, especially in central Mexico. For example, nomadic peoples or those who had been brought under Teotihuacán's influence constantly exerted pressure from the north on the stable agricultural areas in order to secure more resources. After Teotihuacán's fall, one of the invading groups, the Toltecs, established their capital at Tula (Tollan) in the modern state of Hidalgo. By military means, the Toltecs established control over much of central Mexico and their influence eventually reached as far as the Maya cities of Yucatan. Yet by 1175 C.E. the Toltecs succumbed, apparently once again to new waves of peoples from the north.

During these cycles of imperial formation and dissolution, the Toltecs were especially important for the subsequent history of Mexico. The historical memory of the peoples who came after the Toltecs extended back to Tula and its glory but did not reach back to Teotihuacán. For the Mexica and others who came later, the Toltecs were transformed into the legendary creators of all the good things of civilized life: agriculture, crafts-

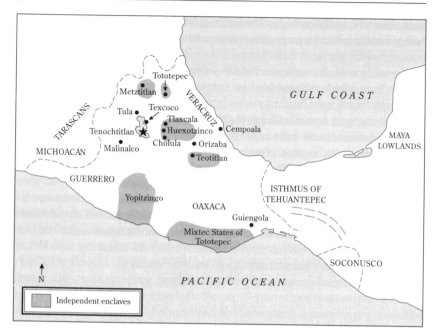

Map 1.   The Mexica Empire and the independent enclaves, c. 1519.
Source: Adapted from Figure 11 in *Religion and Empire: The Dynamics of Aztec and Inca Expansion* by Geoffrey W. Conrad and Arthur A. Demarest (Cambridge: Cambridge University Press, 1984, 1995), 45. Reprinted with permission.

manship, the arts, the calendar, and so forth. Claiming descent from the Toltecs, as the families in some of the later cities did, gave their descendants legitimacy, authority, and political advantage. The legends of the Toltecs and their gods became a crucial element in the way later peoples viewed their world and their place in it.

After the fall of Tula, central Mexico was without a central authority. Many peoples lived there, speaking a variety of languages — Otomí, Tarascan, Totonac, and especially Nahuatl, apparently also the language of the Toltecs. The Nahua shared many cultural elements, but they were divided politically into a number of separate peoples or ethnicities, each organized around a city-state or *altepetl,* only a few of which could claim descent from the Toltec nobility. By the twelfth century, the population had concentrated around Lake Texcoco, a series of brackish and freshwater lakes in the central valley of Mexico. Larger cities like Azcapozalco and Texcoco clashed and struggled for regional dominance and control of the agricultural lands around the margins of the lake. It was into this turbulent and competitive world that another Nahuatl-speaking group, probably immigrants from the northern frontiers, arrived. These were the Tenocha or Mexica, a group of perhaps 10,000 people who, according to their legends, followed their patron deity Huitzilopochtli, the Hummingbird of the South — a form of the sun god — to the shores of the lake.[1]

The story of the Mexica's rapid rise to power is a mixture of legend, myth, and history. From their mythic home, Aztlán, somewhere to the northwest, the Mexica migrated to the world of the lake around the year 1250 C.E. Driven to marginal lands, they were despised by the settled peoples of the lake, but they were sometimes used as mercenaries in the internecine fighting. Eventually, around 1325 C.E., they settled themselves on adjoining marshy islands in the midst of the lake. There, according to legend, they saw an eagle perched on a cactus devouring a snake, a sign from the gods, and so established their capital city, Tenochtitlan. From the security of this base, they established a political foothold in the surrounding area, first as dependents of Azcatpozalco but increasingly on their own. By the early fifteenth century, the Mexica had emerged from a subordinate role to one of increasing power. Under their ruler or *tlatoani* (speaker) Itzcoatl (1426–1440) and later under Moctezuma I (1440–1468), the Mexica controlled much of central Mexico and neighboring peoples like the Totonacs on the Gulf coast and the Mixtecs to the south in Oaxaca. By 1470 the Mexica had become the dominant power of central Mexico, extracting tribute from peoples who lived hundreds of miles away.

The process of Mexica imperial expansion was accompanied by increasing centralization and by changes within Mexica society itself. Perhaps under the influence of Tlacaelel, who served as a sort of prime minister under a number of rulers over a sixty-year period, the cult of warfare and sacrifice became part of the Mexica way of life as society was militarized. Victories were celebrated with great pomp and display and with the ritual sacrifice of many captives. The old clan or *calpulli* system that survived from their nomadic days continued, but was transformed as the division between the nobility or *pipiltin* and the mostly peasant commoners (*macehualtin*) grew ever wider. Politically, Tenochtitlan conquered and then integrated the neighboring island city of Tlatelolco. Its people were also Mexica but they continued to maintain a separate local identity as Tlatelolcans. Tenochtitlan then created an

---

[1]Some good introductions to Mexica society and history can be found in Inga Clendennen, *Aztecs* (Cambridge: Cambridge University Press, 1991); Miguel León-Portilla, *Aztec Thought and Culture,* ed. Jack E. Davis (Norman: University of Oklahoma Press, 1963); Burr Cartwright Brundage, *The Fifth Sun: Aztec Gods, Aztec World* (Austin: University of Texas Press, 1979); Nigel Davies, *The Aztec Empire* (Norman: University of Oklahoma Press, 1987).

alliance with the lakeside cities of Texcoco and Tlacopan. Despite the alliance, Tenochtitlan always remained the predominant power. Some neighboring peoples remained politically independent and hostile to the Mexica. The Tarascans in Michoacán to the north were never conquered, and other Nahuas to the east in cities such as Tlaxcala, Huexotzinco, and Meztitlán remained bitter enemies. In the beginning decades of the sixteenth century the Mexica empire had reached its greatest extent but its power, while real, was also fragile. Subject peoples were restive and occasionally rebelled; traditional enemies continued to pose a formidable threat to their rule. The stability of the ruling alliance itself was precarious as court factions and ruling families jockeyed for advantage in each of the cities where Tenochtitlan's partners looked with envy and fear on its power.

TENOCHTITLAN: THE FOUNDATION OF HEAVEN

In these years, prior to the arrival of the Spaniards, Tenochtitlan grew in status and size. This city, a backdrop to much of the story of the conquest, was in comparative terms a world-class city. To the Mexica it was "the foundation of heaven," the political, symbolic, and ritual center of their universe. From humble beginnings as the marginal settlement of a marginal people, Tenochtitlan became a mighty metropolis covering approximately five square miles with a population estimated to be as high as 150,000 people. Its core was a central complex of palaces and temples surrounded by an enclosing wall. This central temple precinct was dominated by a sixty-meter-high great pyramid with twin temples, one to Tlaloc, the rain god, and one to Huitzilopoctli, the patron god of the Mexica. Around it were grouped some seventy to eighty other palaces and temples, including the ruler's residence and the school for the priesthood. Beyond the enclosing wall were other palaces, temples, markets, and the adobe residential buildings, some of them two stories high with gardens on their roofs. The architecture and craftsmanship, especially of the public buildings was remarkable. "It could not be bettered anywhere," noted one Spanish eyewitness. Tlatelolco, at first a separate city on an adjacent island was eventually incorporated as part of greater Tenochtitlan. It too had palaces, temples, and markets, but was most famous for its great marketplace.

Because of its location in the midst of the water and its maze of canals, a number of the first Spanish visitors to Tenochtitlan compared the city to Venice. The island location gave the city its peculiar character with the constant traffic of canoes carrying goods to and from the city. Fresh

Map 2. The valley of Mexico.
Source: Adapted from Figure 12 in *Religion and Empire: The Dynamics of Aztec and Inca Expansionism* by Geoffrey W. Conrad and Arthur A. Demarest (Cambridge: Cambridge University Press, 1984, 1995), 12. Reprinted with permission.

water was supplied by aqueducts, and away from the city center many families farmed "floating gardens" or *chinampas,* rectangular plots of silt on which multiple harvests could be made in a single year in a kind of hydroponic agriculture. A dike had been constructed to hold out the brackish waters of the eastern side of the lake and protect crops near the city. Four great causeways extended from the lake shore to connect the city to the other cities and towns that surrounded the lake. Bernal Díaz, the young soldier who saw the city in 1519 gave voice to the awe that many of his companions felt:

> Gazing on such wonderful sights, we did not know what to say, or whether what appeared before us was real, for on one side, on the land there were great cities, and in the lake ever so many more, and the lake was crowded with canoes, and in the causeway were many bridges at intervals, and in front of us stood the great city of Mexico.

But Tenochtitlan was much more than Bernal Díaz perceived. In many ways it was also a plan of the Mexica social and religious universe. Its causeways represented the four cardinal directions. Neighborhoods were organized in pairs of twenty communal corporate groups or *calpulli* and in temple-maintenance groups, each with its own temple and school to look after. Thus, the cosmology and calendar were physically represented by the city's organization and by the placement of different sectors of the population.

The *tlatoani* of Tenochtitlan was in theory just another ruler of an *altepetl,* like the rulers of the fifty or so other city-states, but the Mexica's swift rise to power had made their *tlatoani* far more powerful and important than the others. Tenochtitlan had become a great urban center rivaling Venice, Seville, or Paris in complexity and size. The Tenochtitlan of 1519, in the autumn of Mexica greatness, seemed to be an impregnable fortress and a symbol of the very favor of the gods. Little did the Mexica suspect that in three short years it would be mostly destroyed. Bernal Díaz reflected on the loss of the city as he wrote his account in the 1560s, "today all is overthrown and lost, nothing is left standing."

MEXICA CIVILIZATION AND SOCIETY

Certain aspects of Mexica culture repeatedly emerge in the story of the conquest and deserve close attention. Mexica religion was a powerful and uniting force that penetrated every aspect of life and shaped their world in innumerable ways. Like many other religious traditions, the Mexica were concerned with the basic issues of human existence: What is life? What constitutes moral behavior? Is there life after death? What is the proper relationship between human beings and the gods? Religious thinkers and philosophers wondered if the pleasures of this life were transient or if life was simply a "veil of tears." As part of the great Mesoamerican tradition, Mexica religion had a complex cosmology and mythology that sought to explain the existence of the universe and the relationships within it. For the Mexica, little distinction was made between the natural and the supernatural world. They knew and honored the ancient Mesoamerican gods: the deities of the sky, the earth, the corn, and the sun. Although there was recognition of a unifying life-giving force, there was a vast pantheon of gods and goddesses. Often the same basic force could manifest itself in male and female forms. Xochipilli, the god of sport and leisure, for example, was really the male form of Xochiquetal, the goddess of beauty and eroticism. This extensive pantheon was honored through the yearly religious calendar by complex ritual and ceremonial activities of feasting, fasting, dancing, penance, and sacrifice.

The many gods and goddesses can perhaps be grouped into three major categories. As an agricultural people, the Mexica gave particular devotion to the gods of the earth and of fertility, to gods like Tlaloc, god of rain, or his sister Chicomecoatl, the goddess of maize. A second group consisted of the creator deities who had brought the universe into being and whose actions formed the core of Mexica cosmology and mythology. Tonatiuh, the sun god, and Tezcatlipoca, god of the night sky, were especially important. Finally, there were the deities who formed part of the cult of war and sacrifice. Chief among them was the Mexica's main patron, a form of the sun god, the Hummingbird of the South, Huitzilopochtli.

The great deities of the imperial cult were the first to be recognized by the Europeans. The Spaniards looked with fear and horror at the great temple of Tenochtitlan dedicated to Tlaloc and to Huitzilopochtli, whom they called Huichilobos. But above all, in the story of the conquest, Quetzalcoatl, the feathered serpent, god of the wind, of creation, and of civilization, figures most prominently.

Quetzalcoatl, an ancient god of the sky and wind, had been worshiped by the Toltecs. Apparently one of their kings or priests, Topiltzin, also had taken his name; from that point forward, god and man became confused in legend and history. Eventually, Topiltzin-Quetzalcoatl left or was forced from Tula in a power struggle with the followers of another deity. With his followers, Topiltzin migrated down to the coast where according to legend he departed on a raft made of snakes for "the Red Land," or Yucatan. In fact after 990 C.E. evidence of a Toltec presence and the cult of the Feathered Serpent are widely found in Yucatan. The god Quetzalcoatl came to represent the arts and civilization and he was supposedly opposed to human sacrifice. Because of his special importance to the Toltecs, he also was worshiped by the Mexica who wished to claim legitimacy not only based on their military prowess but as cultural descendants of the ancient Toltecs. To that end, Moctezuma Xocoyotzin (Moctezuma II) built a great temple to Quetzalcoatl in Tenochtitlan.

Two aspects of the feathered serpent legend bear special notice. First, there was a belief that Quetzalcoatl would someday return to reclaim his position and lands. He had been born in the year Ce Acatl one-Reed and had supposedly left in the year one-Reed as well, exactly fifty-two years later, or one cycle of the Mexica calendar. Curiously, the year of Cortés's arrival, 1519, also corresponded to the year one-Reed in the Mexica calendar. Second, in some of the legends Quetzalcoatl was described as white or bearded. In fact, it is difficult to know whether these legends were truly part of Mexica mythology before the conquest or whether they were developed afterward to explain events. In the indigenous accounts of the conquest, the idea that Cortés might be the returning Quetzalcoatl is used to explain Moctezuma's seeming inaction, confusion, and failure of his leadership. Yet the Mexica claimed to be the successors of the Toltecs and they believed Tenochtitlan to be the new Tula. This may have made their ruler particularly susceptible to prophecies about the ancient deity-ruler who would someday return to claim his throne.

Here the knot of legend and history becomes even more difficult to untie because of the embroideries and glosses that Nahua commentators added to the story after the conquest. Perhaps in an effort to please Spanish overlords and missionaries, Nahua informants and later historians claimed that the Quetzalcoatl of the myths was a bearded white man who opposed human sacrifice and the cult of war. Seeking to explain Moctezuma's vacillation in the face of the Spanish challenge, the Nahua historians claimed that he truly believed Cortés to be the returning god-ruler that the prophecies foretold. Cortés's letters contain no mention of this theme, but the later Nahua accounts and those of the Spanish chroniclers like Bernal Díaz usually mention it. Cortés's arrival in the year one-Reed is either the fulfillment of prophecy, extraordinary coincidence, the later Nahua construction of a tale to fit the circumstances, or the intentional use of the Mesoamerican calendar and legends to bolster Spanish claims.

When the Spaniards arrived in central Mexico, they encountered a great civilization with a powerful political and military force. Warfare for the Mexica served as a political tool but it was also a way of life with deep ritual and religious meaning. The Mexica mobilized large armies and sent them long distances despite logistical problems caused by their lack of wheeled vehicles and beasts of burden. Mexica armies usually campaigned in the dry season from December to April when the roads were better and the peasants who comprised the bulk of the troops were free from labor in the fields. This was also the time when food was available to support the army along its march. The armies were led by distinguished warriors whose accomplishments were recognized by specific uniforms, decorative clothing, hairstyles, and other symbols. There were military organizations of distinguished warriors, the Eagle warriors, the Jaguar warriors, similar in some respects to the medieval European orders of knighthood. Although sometimes a simple threat of force was often enough to gain submission, faced with resistance, the Mexica were an implacable foe. From the comments of their hostile neighbors and from the Spanish observations it is clear that the Mexica were a powerful and dreaded military threat.

This was a society geared toward warfare. Boys were prepared from birth for a warrior's life and death and inculcated with military virtues. Military accomplishment was the measure of manhood and a means of social mobility. While campaigns had political goals, there was also a strong individual component. While the Nahua peoples had projectile weapons like slings and bows and arrows, their preferred weapons were those for close combat where individual skill and bravery could best be demonstrated. Their primary weapon was a kind of wooden sword set with obsidian blades designed for slashing and incapacitating rather than killing an enemy. In this way battle was a scene for personal demonstrations of bravery where the individual taking of a captive was the greatest achievement. These were formidable weapons. Spanish accounts tell of a horse's head lopped off by a blow from one.

The Mexica believed that the gods, especially the sun god, required "precious water," or human blood, to nourish them. The best and most noble sacrifice as a messenger to the gods was that of a warrior taken in battle. Thus the presentation of captives for sacrifice was a main goal of battle and an occasion of great religious significance surrounded by ritual obligations and responsibilities. These sacrifices were usually accompanied by a strict set of observances including forms of ritual cannibalism. As the Mexica and their allies controlled more and more of the country and subjected additional neighbors to their control, it became difficult to find suitable warrior opponents. "Barbarian" nomads from the frontiers were held in low esteem and were not viewed as worthy opponents or sacrifices. Therefore, war with other Nahua peoples who were political opponents but who shared the same culture as the Mexica was considered best. Sometimes they fought in arranged battles or *xochiyaoyotl* ("flower wars") designed for each side to demonstrate its valor and to have the opportunity to take appropriate captives for sacrifice. The cities of Tlaxcala, Huejotzinco, and Cholula, all of which joined Cortés as allies, were traditional opponents in these flower wars.

Despite the Mexica's experience in warfare their military objectives, weapons, tactics, and experience put them at a decided disadvantage in the face of Spanish steel and Spanish objectives even though they outnumbered the Spaniards. The Mexica could not compete with Spanish artillery, steel weapons, crossbows, and firearms, although they quickly learned to adjust their tactics. They sought terrain that neutralized the advantage the Spaniards gained with horses, and they learned to avoid the firearms' line of fire. Transforming their concept of battle and the goals of warfare itself, however, was a more difficult change to make.

RENAISSANCE CONQUERORS

The Spaniards themselves represented a society no less impressive or interesting than the Mexica, a society of transition from the late Middle Ages to the Renaissance. The Iberian peninsula had been part of the Roman Empire, and that experience was reflected in its language, laws, and customs, as were the Germanic traditions brought by later invaders. Above all, perhaps more so than any other place in Western Europe, Spain had been for some seven centuries a multicultural region where Muslims, Christians, and Jews had lived in close and continuous if often hostile contact and proximity. At the close of the fifteenth century, however, that coexistence was ending. In 1492, Granada, the last Muslim kingdom, fell to Catholic arms. A few months later the Jews were forced to either convert or leave the country. With these events, the Christian kingdoms of the peninsula — independent Portugal to the west, Aragon to the east, and the largest of all, Castile, in the center — were now free of internal religious challenge. In 1485 the unification of Aragon and Castile under the same monarchs created the political basis of modern Spain.

Religious unification was seen as a necessary element in the same process. Spain had undergone considerable religious reform, and in 1479 Spain established the Inquisition to insure and enforce the orthodoxy of society, especially of those recently converted from Judaism and Islam.

The last two decades of the fifteenth century had been a time of political and religious consolidation and of war. The final struggle against the Muslim kingdom of Granada was primarily a war of small-scale raids and the seizing of booty and captives. Campaigns had mobilized thousands of young men and convinced them to make their fortune through military prowess, courage, and skill. Throughout Europe the use of arms and horses was a privilege of the nobility, but in Spain many young men of common birth knew these skills and used them to their advantage. By the early sixteenth century, through Aragon's interests in Italy, Spain also had become involved in further conflicts and these wars provided additional military experience.

Meanwhile, the voyages of Columbus beginning in 1492 had opened up a new outlet for Spanish interest and activity. The conquest, colonization, and exploitation of the Caribbean was fully under way by 1500. The Spaniards explored the islands and coasts of their territories and established control of the major islands along with a few places on the mainland: Española or Hispaniola (1493–1508), Puerto Rico (1508), Jamaica (1509), Cuba (1511), and Panamá or Castilla de Oro (1509–13). The indigenous populations were quickly defeated, suffering rapid decline as a result of war, exploitation, and the impact of Old World diseases. Each conquest further raised individual Spanish hopes of fame and fortune, and all were justified as expeditions that extended the sovereignty of the Spanish crown and the truth of the Roman Catholic faith. With each conquest a few, usually the leaders and their close associates — friends, relatives, or those from their home province in Spain — reaped the rewards, but many others were left unsatisfied. There never seemed to be enough treasure. The crown always received its 20 percent and the "Indians" assigned to the control of the conquerors often resisted imposed control or disappeared quickly in the face of disease, mistreatment, and social disruption. Cortés's expedition to the mainland of Mexico was in no way unusual. It followed two earlier ones which had gone westward from Cuba to nearby Yucatan, about 120 miles away, in search of new islands and new kingdoms to conquer. The difference was not in the expedition's leadership, composition, or goals, but in the nature of the indigenous peoples encountered. In Yucatan and Mexico the Spaniards encountered for the first time ancient civilizations that were structured in hierarchical societies, organized in large kingdoms, and willing to defend their way of life.

In many ways the Spaniards and the Mexica were well-suited opponents. Both were the heirs of a long process of cultural development and fusion, both had a warrior ethos, both held fervently to a religious faith, and both justified their imperial expansion in terms of theological ideals. However, despite all their remarkable achievements, the peoples of

Mesoamerica, like the Mexica, remained essentially Stone Age civilizations. Metallurgy was limited, the wheel had no practical applications, there were no large beasts of burden, and other technologies known in the Old World like the milling of grain by mechanical means were unknown in the Americas. Nothing like the great semitheocratic imperial state of the Mexica had been seen in Eurasia since the time of Babylon or Assyria, yet even those empires had the wheel, livestock, horses, and metal tools and weapons. In confrontation with the Europeans, the New World civilizations, for all their size and power, remained at a great technological disadvantage.

Great controversy exists over the size of the indigenous populations when the Europeans arrived. In all estimates, however, central Mexico is usually considered to have been the most densely populated region of the Americas. Most estimates place the population of Tenochtitlan somewhere between 150,000 to 200,000 in the early 1500s. Historical demographers Woodrow Borah and S. F. Cook have estimated that central Mexico alone had a population of about twenty-five million people in 1519. Not all scholars agree and some have placed the estimate at half that figure, but almost all concede that central Mexico was densely populated at the moment of conquest. By 1580, after the conquest and colonization of Mexico, only about one million indigenous people remained. Thus, the process of conquest implied a terrible demographic disaster.[2]

The size of the invading force of Spaniards is easier to calculate. Various participants spoke of the numbers involved. Bernal Díaz himself noted that Cortés's original expedition had 550 men. Later, with the addition of other Spaniards including a few Spanish women after 1520, Cortés's forces swelled to perhaps over 1,500, but many were lost in subsequent fighting. Before the final siege of Tenochtitlan on April 28, 1521, Cortés reviewed his troops and counted 86 horsemen, 118 musketeers and crossbowmen, and 700 foot soldiers, as well as perhaps another 400 men who manned the ships he built to sail on the lake.

The disparity in numbers makes the Spanish victory particularly impressive, and so the great mystery remains as to the number of indigenous allies that supported the Spaniards. In the first entry into Tenochtitlan, Cortés's forces included perhaps 2,000 Tlaxcalan allies. In the final siege of the city, not only Tlaxcalans, but troops from Huezotzingo, Texcoco, Cholula, and many other towns and cities fought alongside

---

[2]There is an ever-growing bibliography on this topic. Woodrow Borah and Sherburne F. Cook, *Essays in Population History,* 3 vols. (Berkeley: University of California Press, 1971–79), contains the classic arguments for high figures. Doubts have been raised. See David Henige, "Counting the Encounter: The Pernicious Appeal of Verisimilitude," *Colonial Latin American Review* 3 (1993): 325–61.

the Spaniards in the last battles. Cortés himself noted 50,000 Tlaxcalans alone at the final siege and over 75,000 indigenous allies supporting the Spanish units. Bernal Díaz mentioned 100,000 indigenous allies in the engagements. Such figures emphasize the fact that in many ways the conquest of Tenochtitlan and the fall of the Mexica Empire was as much a struggle among indigenous peoples as it was a clash of the Old and New Worlds. Moreover, in terms of scale, the battle for Tenochtitlan was a major military effort, equal to the great contemporaneous battles of the Old World.

THE SPANISH SOURCES

We know a great deal about the conquest of Mexico because participants and observers on both sides recorded their impressions, opinions, and stories. There are a variety of sources from Spaniards who participated directly in the conquest. These accounts reflect the personal, political, economic, and social interests of their authors. Hernán Cortés, the leader of the Spanish expedition wrote a number of reports or "letters" which were sent back to Charles I, the Spanish king. These were quickly published and became the basis of the "official" story of the conquest. Cortés's observations were realistic and direct, lacking the fantasy found in other, earlier European observations of the New World. Naturally, Cortés's reports tended to justify his decisions and actions and placed him always in a positive light.[3] Later, Francisco López de Gómara, a distinguished author met Cortés and was hired by him to write a history of the conquest. Using Cortés's letters, notes, and personal papers, López de Gómara produced in 1553 a laudatory biography, very favorable to his patron.[4] Luckily, these official versions written or paid for by Cortés

[3] See *Hernán Cortés: Letters from Mexico*, trans. and ed. Anthony Pagden (New York: Orion Press, 1971); *Hernando Cortés: Five Letters, 1519–1526*, ed. J. Bayard Morris (New York: Norton, 1991). Cortés's letters have been subjected to analysis since they were published. There are a number of works by historians and literary scholars that examine them from various viewpoints. See, for example, the critical analysis in Beatriz Pastor Bodmer, *The Armature of Conquest* (Stanford: Stanford University Press, 1992), 50–100; José Valero Silva, *El legalismo de Hernán Cortés como instrumento de su conquista* (Mexico City: UNAM, 1965). Francis J. Brooks, "Motecuzoma Xocoyotl, Hernán Cortés, and Bernal Díaz del Castillo: The Construction of an Arrest," *Hispanic American Historical Review* 75, no. 2 (1995): 149–84, suggests that Cortés fictionalized certain events in order to fit his actions into the framework of Spanish legal and political theory. Rolena Adorno, "The Discursive Encounter of Spain and America: The Authority of Eyewitness Testimony in the Writing of History," *William and Mary Quarterly* 49, no. 2 (1992): 210–28, demonstrates how Díaz's account represents the fusion of eyewitness and authoritative or official accounts.
[4] Francisco López de Gómara, *Cortés: The Life of the Conqueror by his Secretary*, trans. and ed. Lesley Bird Simpson (Berkeley: University of California Press, 1966).

were not the only accounts from the Spanish side. A few of the participants and eyewitnesses also wrote down their experiences. One of these stands out above all the rest and is drawn on extensively for this volume.

It is generally agreed that the great chronicle of the Spanish conquest of Mexico was written by Bernal Díaz del Castillo. Like many of the conquistadors he was not a soldier by profession but he knew the use of arms and he served as a common foot soldier. He had actually gone to Mexico prior to Cortés in two earlier expeditions and later participated in subsequent campaigns, finally settling down in Guatemala where he died around 1580, respected but not very wealthy.[5] The events of his youth marked him deeply and Díaz del Castillo had a remarkable memory and eye for detail which he used effectively in his narrative. By the time he began to write down his version of the conquest he was an old soldier, veteran of the great campaigns of the conquest, and frustrated by the hopes of his youth. He wished to set the record straight about the efforts of the common men like himself who with their blood and steel had delivered heathen souls to the Church and a mighty empire to their king. Here is how Bernal Díaz introduced himself and his book:

> I, Bernal Díaz del Castillo, citizen and *regidor* (alderman) of the most loyal city of Santiago de Guatemala, one of the first discoverers and conquerors of New Spain and its provinces . . . a Native of the very noble and distinguished town of Medina del Campo, and son of its former *regidor,* Francisco Díaz del Castillo, who was also called, "the graceful" (may his soul rest in glory), speak about that which concerns myself and all the true conquistadors my companions who served His Majesty by discovering, conquering, pacifying, and settling most of the provinces of New Spain, and that it is one of the best countries yet discovered in the New World, we found this out by our own efforts without His Majesty knowing anything about it.

Here in this introductory paragraph we see some of the motives that drove Díaz and his companions: localism, pride in their lineage and origins, a great sense of self-worth and accomplishment, a hope for recognition (and reward), and a desire to set down a "true" story of their deeds and triumphs.

---

[5] There are a number of studies of Díaz and his book. See, for example, Carmelo Saenz de Santa María, *Historia de una historia: Bernal Díaz del Castillo* (Madrid: Consejo Superior de Investigaciones Científicas, 1984), and his *Introducción crítica a la "Historia verdadera" de Bernal Díaz del Castillo* (Madrid: Consejo Superior de Investigaciones Científicas, 1967). There is a biography in English: Herbert Cerwin, *Bernal Díaz: Historian of the Conquest* (Norman: University of Oklahoma Press, 1963).

We know relatively little about his early life. Born in Medina del Campo about 1496, of honorable but not titled family, he received some education. As a teenager he left home and made his way to Seville, and in 1514 at the age of nineteen he joined a great expedition under Pedrarias Dávila which sailed for Castilla del Oro, modern-day Panama. The expedition was something of a disaster. Disgruntled and disappointed, many men, Bernal Díaz among them, abandoned the region. From Panama he made his way to the island of Cuba where he settled for a few years. Then in 1517, he signed on to a new expedition under Francisco Hernández de Córdoba which explored the coast of Yucatan, and after some stiff fighting, Díaz returned to Cuba with reports of a densely populated land where people wore fine cotton garments, lived in stone dwellings, cultivated fields of maize, and possessed gold. The Spaniards had encountered the Maya civilizations of Yucatan. The governor of Cuba, Diego Velázquez, impressed by these reports, immediately organized another expedition under a nephew named Juan de Grijalva, and Bernal Díaz signed on yet again. More fighting and exploration up the coast as far north as modern-day Vera Cruz was the result. By this time the Spanish, through trade and plunder, accumulated more gold and, through their indigenous translators, learned of the existence of a great empire that lay in the interior of the country. Grijalva returned to Cuba where the gold and reports moved the governor to immediately start plans for yet another, larger expedition to the west. Thus by 1519 when this third expedition set sail under Hernán Cortés, Bernal Díaz was a young man of twenty-three with military experience in three expeditions, and, as he liked to point out, he had been to Mexico twice before Cortés.

The events of the conquest of Mexico are the core of Bernal Díaz's account. Subsequently, frustrated in his hopes for wealth in Mexico, he participated in the conquest of Guatemala and there he settled down with an *encomienda* or grant of native laborers to support him as a recognized if not particularly wealthy member of the local elite, a member of the local town council, and a man of some stature.

Garrulous and with a prodigious memory for detail, he must have been asked on numerous occasions to retell the stories of the conquest, of the glories of the Mexica capital, the hardships of marches and battles, the appearance of Moctezuma, and the exploits of Cortés and his men. When he began to write them down is unclear, but by the mid-1550s he had composed a number of chapters. Perhaps there was a political motive behind the origins of the work. The struggle for control of indigenous labor and the *encomienda* between the colonists like Bernal

Díaz and the crown during the 1540s may have motivated Díaz to set the record straight by pointing out what the conquerors had in fact accomplished. We know he had taken an active role in defending the colonists' behavior against the criticism of reformist clerics like Bartolomé de Las Casas who wished to remove native peoples from the control of the colonists.

Whatever the origins of the project, Bernal Díaz was shocked to learn that others had published first. The work of Francisco López de Gómara, a noted scholar and Cortés's private secretary, fell into his hands as did some of the other chronicles of the conquest. Although Gómara and the others wrote with an elegance that the old soldier could not hope to match and Díaz was tempted to give up the endeavor altogether, these were books by scholars who had not been eyewitnesses like him and they contained many factual errors. Above all, the work of Gómara like the letters or reports of Cortés himself celebrated the captain's role and gave little credit to the common soldiers, men like Bernal Díaz who felt they had been overlooked. He called his book *The True History of the Conquest of New Spain* because it was written against the "false" histories of Gómara and others (see Figure 2). The old battler wished to set the record straight and, in doing so, bring his own accomplishments and those of his companions to the forefront so those in authority might reward them.

Much of the book was written in the 1560s when Bernal Díaz was in his seventies. Friends who read the manuscript were impressed that he could remember so many details about the campaigns and his companions. Perhaps they doubted his accuracy. Here was his response:

> I replied it was not so remarkable, because there were only 550 of us and we were always together conversing before and after campaigns and following a battle it soon became known who were killed or who were sacrificed; when we came from a bloody and doubtful battle, we always counted our dead — I retained in my memories all the details about them and if I could paint or sculpt, I would fashion them as they were, their figures, their faces, and their manners — I would like to paint all of them, according to life, with the full expression of courage which was on their faces when they entered battle.

Díaz's "true history" was completed about 1567 and sent to Spain in 1575. There it remained unnoticed in the papers of the Council of the Indies until other historians began to make use of it at the beginning of the seventeenth century. It was not published until 1632, long after Bernal Díaz, the last of the Spanish conquerors of Tenochtitlan, had passed away.

Figure 2. The frontispiece of the first edition of Bernal Díaz's *Historia Verdadera de la Conquista de la Nueva España*. Cortés is on the left under the Latin word "manu" signifying "by his hand." He is faced on the right by the friar Bartolomé de Olmedo, under the Latin word "ore" or "by his word." Thus the conquest as deed and word is summarized on the title page.

Source: Bernal Díaz del Castillo, *Historia Verdadera de la Conquista de la Nueva España*. Madrid, 1632. Courtesy of John Carter Brown Library at Brown University, Providence, Rhode Island.

Later, years after the conquest in the following generation, a number of authors like the Dominican friar Diego Durán or the civil judge Alonso de Zurita wrote about Nahua society and what happened to it. These works often incorporated evidence from eyewitness accounts and sometimes provided new information, but they also reflected the interests of their times and their authors. They have been used only sparingly in this collection.

THE INDIGENOUS HISTORICAL TRADITIONS

Different peoples have different ways of thinking about, narrating, and recording the past. For the peoples of central Mexico, there was a profound belief in a cycle of time in which events repeated themselves and in which prediction was possible. For them, the past was essential and its recounting served both sacred and political ends. In 1427, the Mexica ruler Itzcoatl ordered that all historical accounts and manuscripts be destroyed so that only the "official" record would survive to guide the memory of the Mexica rise to power as the sun god's selected people. In this, the Mexica rulers like the ancient Egyptian pharoahs displayed a practical concern for how the past could be used to influence the future.

But history was also a sacred trust and remembrance of the past essential for the continuation of their identity. The postconquest historian Tezozómoc in his *Crónica Mexicayotl* captured the pre-Columbian importance of history in this verse:

> Thus they have come to tell it,
> thus they have come to record it in their narration
> and for us they have painted it in their codices,
> the ancient men, the ancient women.
> They were our grandfathers, our grandmothers . . .
> Their account was repeated,
> they left it to us;
> they bequeathed it forever
> to us who live now,
> to us who come down from them.
> Never will it be lost, never will it be forgotten,
> that which they came to do,
> that which they record in their paintings:
> their reknown, their history, their memory.
> Thus in the future
> never will it perish, never will it be forgotten
> always will we treasure it,
> we their children, their grandchildren . . .

we who carry their blood and their color,
we will tell it, we will pass it on
to those who do not yet live, who are to be born,
the children of the Mexicans, the children of the Tenochcans.[6]

The cadence or rhythm of such texts suggests that they were recited out loud. The drawings and symbols used to record the legends, myths, and events of history served as a basis for an accompanying oral tradition in which commentaries and analysis of the written or pictorial record created a composite kind of history that made up the indigenous form of presentation. The *tlacuilo* or artist-scribe, "the master of the black ink and the red ink," as the Mexica poetically referred to him, was a respected and essential figure in the preservation of indigenous culture. We should notice, however, that this skill and knowledge was socially limited. Only a few people, always boys, were trained to be a *tlacuilo* and the books or codices they produced became the exclusive possessions of the priesthood, rulers, and nobility.[7]

Prior to the arrival of the Spaniards, the peoples of central Mexico used a system of images that were ordered in patterns based on a number of criteria to record and transmit knowledge. Unlike the European tradition where writing and painting were discrete activities, for the Nahuas, Mixtecs, and others, the two activities were fused and often accompanied by oral explanation as well. These people had no alphabetic script, and so images were patterned and accompanied by symbols or icons that "readers" could readily identify. These were usually painted into books on deerskin or a paper made from the maguey plant and then folded into panels like an accordion. In certain instances it is not known exactly how a text was read, but the scale of objects, their position on the page, and their relationship to each other determined how they were interpreted. There were a number of genres or types of texts. Preconquest

---

[6] Miguel León-Portilla, *Pre-Columbian Literatures of Mexico* (Norman: University of Oklahoma Press, 1969), 117.

[7] On the Mesoamerican indigenous writing traditions, see Joyce Marcus, *Mesoamerican Writing Systems* (Princeton, N.J.: Princeton University Press, 1992); Donald Robertson, *Mexican Manuscript Painting of the Early Colonial Period,* ed. Elizabeth H. Boone, 2nd ed. (Norman: University of Oklahoma Press, 1992), is a classic starting point. Gordon Brotherston, *Painted Books from Mexico* (London: British Museum Press, 1995), makes excellent use of manuscripts in that collection. Best of all for its text and illustrations is Serge Gruzinski, *Painting the Conquest: The Mexican Indians and the European Renaissance,* trans. Deke Dusinberre (Paris: Flammarion/UNESCO, 1992). Although somewhat out of date, the best starting point for a study of the indigenous codices and manuscripts is the four volumes called "Guide to Ethnohistorical Sources" edited by Howard F. Cline, which are volumes twelve through fourteen of the *Handbook of Middle American Indians,* 16 vols. (Robert Wauchope, general editor) (Austin: University of Texas Press, 1964–76).

books recorded annals or the chronology of important events, prophecies, calendrical information, rituals, lists of merchant goods, boundaries, and tribute or tax records. Because the Spaniards later came to believe that these texts preserved the ancient religion of the conquered peoples, many were destroyed and few preconquest texts survive to this day. In fact, at present there are about five hundred Mexican codices in existence, but less than twenty of these pre-date the conquest and of those surviving, probably none is from the heart of the Nahua region. The vast majority of surviving codices, therefore, were created after the conquest and reflect some European influences.

Because indigenous writing systems had not developed an alphabet, had only a limited syllabic component, and had recorded a somewhat limited range of concepts, some authors have drawn a sharp distinction between the alphabetic writing of Europeans and the pictorial forms used by the indigenous peoples. They have argued that the limitations of symbols and images placed indigenous peoples at a considerable disadvantage.[8] This position may privilege writing too much and disregard the effectiveness of the composite nature of Mesoamerican texts. Contemporary European observers were not always convinced about indigenous disadvantage in recording what they wanted to remember. Fray Diego Durán believed that the Mesoamerican system was effective. He stated:

> they have written and painted it all in books and large sheets (*papeles*), with the count of the years, the months, and days in which things happened. They have written in these paintings their legends and laws, their customs, etc. all with great order and care. From this they have most excellent historians that, with these paintings, compose the fullest history of their forebearers.[9]

[8] The ways in which alphabetic languages were linked to power in the conquest of America have been emphasized by Tzvetan Todorov, *The Conquest of America: The Question of the Other* (New York: Harper and Row, 1984), and more recently by Walter Mignolo, *The Darker Side of the Renaissance* (Ann Arbor: University of Michigan Press, 1995). On indigenous literacy see Frances Karttunen, "Nahuatl Literacy," in *The Inca and Aztec States, 1400–1800,* ed. George Collier, Renato Rosaldo, and John Wirth (New York: Academic Press, 1982), 395–418. An argument which emphasizes the adaptability of the Nahuas and thus implicitly contests the idea of indigenous linguistic limitations is developed in James Lockhart, *The Nahuas after the Conquest* (Stanford: Stanford University Press, 1992). See also Miguel León-Portilla, "El binomio oralidad y códices en Mesoamerica," *Estudios de Cultura Nahuatl* 27 (1997): 136–53.

[9] Diego Durán, *Historia de las Indias de Nueva España e Islas de Tierra Firme,* ed. Angel María Garibay, 2 vols. (Mexico City: Editoral Porrúa, 1967). See also his *Book of the Gods and Rites and the Ancient Calendar* (1581), trans. and ed. Fernando Horcasitas and Doris Heyden (Norman: University of Oklahoma Press, 1971).

In the years immediately following the conquest, a curious double-headed process took place which transformed indigenous ways of perceiving and recording. The ancient tradition of the *tlacuilos* who had been specially trained in priestly schools underwent modification through their contact with Europeans. The old forms of symbolic representation and glyphs continued to be used but the artists were now influenced by images and techniques introduced from European art. Perspective, shading, and other techniques now were used alongside traditional methods of composition and presentation. But, at the same time, the indigenous peoples were also acquiring alphabetic writing. Through missionary instruction and schools, a generation of indigenous youth not only learned Spanish and Latin, but also began to write their native languages, Nahuatl, Mixtec, Maya, Purepecha (Tarascan), and others, in the Roman alphabet. The two traditions were combined sometimes as in the case of the *Florentine Codex* or the *Codex Mendoza* to produce a new "colonial" kind of writing. The mixture of the two traditions produced not just new texts, but a new kind of text altogether. A large number of these postconquest texts exist, reflecting various degrees of indigenous and European elements and presenting a variety of viewpoints.[10]

Among the various postconquest indigenous texts are a number that record aspects of the conquest itself. The peoples of Mexico did not form a single political entity, and these political and ethnic divisions contributed to the success of the Spanish conquest. Peoples subject to the empire of the Mexica used the arrival of the Spaniards to break free from Mexica control and to settle old scores. Traditional enemies of Tenochtitlan like Tlaxcala, after initial opposition, became loyal allies of the Spaniards, and even former allies of Tenochtitlan like the old cultural center of Texcoco abandoned the alliance during the war. These political and ethnic differences were also reflected in the later accounts of the conquest. Those narratives produced by native sons of Tlaxcala, Texcoco, Chalco, or other city-states told the story from their perspective and usually in a way favorable to their historical role and the glory of their city-state. We can note specifically the work of the Chalco historian Domingo Francisco de San Antón Muñón Chimalpahín, as an example.[11] In this volume short excerpts from Chimalpahín, from the pictorial Tlaxcala

---

[10] Gruzinski, *Painting the Conquest*, provides a beautifully illustrated discussion of the different kinds of writing practices by indigenous peoples and Europeans.

[11] On Chimalpahín see Susan Schroeder, *Chimalpahín and the Kingdoms of Chalco* (Tucson: University of Arizona Press, 1991).

canvas (*Lienzo de Tlaxcala*), Diego Muñoz Camargo from Tlaxcala, and a few other non-Mexica postconquest indigenous sources have been included. Readers should be aware that together these sources do not form an "indigenous" vision of events that can be placed in opposition to a "Spanish" view. The indigenous sources are often at odds with each other over details and interpretations of events, and just like the Spanish sources they reflect social, political, geographic, and other interests of their authors.[12]

Of all the indigenous accounts, one group or collection stands out above all the others. It was a collaborative effort, compiled by a Spanish Franciscan missionary who used indigenous informants. As early as 1533, some missionaries advocated recording and collecting information on the culture of the indigenous peoples of Mexico as a way of facilitating their conversion. Of these projects, by far the most ambitious and complete was that of Fray Bernardino de Sahagún, a missionary with interests in the language and culture of the Nahuas of central Mexico. To learn their language and to understand their traditions as a means to bring them into the Church, around 1547 Sahagún began to interview indigenous informants who had lived before and during the conquest. The work was done with the help of young Nahua men of noble birth who had been trained in the *calmecac,* the Mexica school for the priesthood, and subsequently had been instructed by the missionaries and converted to Christianity. They collected information on the calendar, rituals, social organization, and philosophy of the Nahuas. This was done in three different locales: Tepepulco, Tlatelolco, and Tenochtitlan itself. The information was cross-checked in a method akin to what a modern anthropologist might do. Informants sometimes drew pictures illustrating their responses and then added commentary, which was then translated by Sahagún's young informants. The text that resulted was organized in parallel columns of Nahuatl and Spanish translation and commentary. The text went through a number of versions. The most famous of them is today called the *Florentine Codex* because it is located in the Laurenziana Library in Florence, Italy. Sahagún called his work the "General History of the Things of New Spain." It was not published in his lifetime but only in 1579. It has been called one of the greatest ethno-

---

[12]Arthur J. O. Anderson and Susan Schroeder, trans. and ed., *Codex Chimalpahin,* 2 vols. (Norman: University of Oklahoma Press, 1997); Fernando de Alva Ixtlilxochitl, *Obras históricas,* ed. Edmundo O'Gorman, 2 vols. (Mexico, 1975); Diego Muñoz Camargo, *Historia de Tlaxcala,* ed. Alfredo Chavero (Mexico City: Secretaria de Fomento, 1892). An excellent brief annotated listing of the indigenous codices that relate to the conquest of Mexico is presented in Hugh Thomas, *Conquest: Montezuma, Cortés, and the Fall of Old Mexico* (New York: Simon & Schuster, 1993), 774–84.

graphic works ever done, a remarkable encyclopedia of Nahua culture which is simultaneously a dictionary and a grammar as well.

There are two aspects of Sahagún's work which merit special attention. The conversion of the indigenous peoples of New Spain (Mexico) was carried out in the sixteenth century primarily by missionary orders: the Franciscans, Dominicans, Augustinians, and after 1574, the Jesuits. The first generation of these missionaries were often men of considerable ability and fervent beliefs, but the deep divisions and factions within each order mirrored the profound differences between the orders on how best to convert the indigenous peoples. The Dominicans tended to take a more formal position in terms of theology and were less willing to look for parallels in indigenous religions which might lead native peoples to convert more easily. The first Franciscans were often moved by a messianic belief that the New World was God's gift to the Church and would restore the souls that had been lost in the Protestant Reformation. Many of them emphasized the learning of indigenous languages and an understanding of local custom and behavior as a way to bring converts to Christianity.[13] This was Sahagún's position. He was sympathetic toward the people he was studying. As he put it, "These people are our brothers, descendants from the trunk of Adam like ourselves, they are our fellowmen whom we are obliged to love as ourselves."[14] Despite his horror at Nahua ritual practices, especially sacrifice, and his disgust at their "pagan" worship, Sahagún came to appreciate and even celebrate much of Nahua culture. Others did not share his enthusiasm. Both from the rival Dominican Order which was much less sympathetic to the integration of some indigenous beliefs into Catholic practice and from more conservative elements within the Franciscan Order itself, Sahagún's project encountered opposition. Fear that his work preserved too much of the ancient beliefs and thus preserved the works of the Devil led to opposition. At one point the manuscripts were taken from him,

[13] An excellent English language version of Sahagún's text exists. See Bernardino de Sahagún, *The Florentine Codex: General History of the Things of New Spain*, trans. and ed. J. O. Anderson and Charles Dibble, 12 vols. (Salt Lake City: University of Utah Press, 1950–82). On Sahagún himself, see Luis Nicolau d'Olwer, *Fray Bernardino de Sahagún, 1499–1590*, 2nd ed. (Salt Lake City: University of Utah Press, 1982). On Sahagún's research methods, see Alfredo López Austin, "The Research Method of Fray Bernardino de Sahagún: The Questionnaires," in *Sixteenth-Century Mexico: The Work of Sahagún*, ed. Munro S. Edmunson (Albuquerque: University of New Mexico, 1974), 11–150. On the goals of the Franciscans, see John L. Phelan, *The Millennial Kingdom of the Franciscans in the New World* (Berkeley: University of California Press, 1956), and more recently Georges Baudot, *Utopia and History in Mexico* (Niwot: University of Colorado Press, 1995).

[14] Bernardino de Sahagún, *Historia general de las cosas de Nueva España,* ed. Angel María Garibay, 4 vols. (Mexico City: Editorial Porrúa, 1956), Volume I: 31.

presumably because some missionaries and civil authorities believed that the old ways had to be completely eliminated. Although he regained his manuscripts in 1575, the project later encountered political difficulties in Spain.

Book Twelve of the *Florentine Codex,* "How the War Was Fought Here in Mexico," is essentially a Nahua account of the conquest, filtered through Sahagún and his informants. Due to its content and size, it is the most important Nahua version of the conquest. This account also has its biases and problems. First, many of the informants were from Tlatelolco, the junior partner of Tenochtitlan. Thus, the accounts tend to be highly critical of Tenochtitlan and especially of its leader Moctezuma, laying the blame for defeat on his indecision and weakness and viewing any successes as due to the bravery of the Tlatelolcans. Second, the accounts were written down some thirty years after the events described, and it is difficult to know to what extent the passage of time clouded memories and provided time for reflection on events. Also unknown is the extent to which the subsequent conversion of the informants to the Church may have colored their view of their historical past. Scattered throughout the texts are postconquest elements. The ancient deities are called "devils," and metaphors such as "lusting after gold like pigs" are used even though there were no domestic swine in Mexico before the Spanish brought them. It is difficult to tell how much the young Nahua translators, already tied to Spanish culture, shaded meanings, molded their informants' accounts, or even misunderstood what the elders told them. Nevertheless, these accounts provide the basis of our knowledge of Nahua views of the conquest and its aftermath. They are surely indigenous texts, but they are postconquest and they reflect the subject position and colonial situation of the Nahua peoples at the time they were recorded.

The Nahua accounts have been translated into English a number of times, but the most recent version and the one represented in this volume is that of James Lockhart. He was for many years a professor of Latin American history at the University of California in Los Angeles where he worked on postconquest Nahuatl texts and where he trained a generation of graduate students in the philological and historical skills needed to use and analyze these documents. His translations of Book Twelve directly from the Nahuatl are particularly important because they are sensitive not only to the literal meaning of the Nahuatl, but also to its common usage and the problems of converting it into idiomatic English. Lockhart has pointed out that Sahagún's original translation into Spanish was often a paraphrase in which the friar inserted commentary and other observations. To what extent Book Twelve of the *Florentine Codex* is Sahagún's interpretation or to what extent it is really a Nahua account is open to much debate, but Lockhart is convinced that these texts reflect "indigenous ideas, frameworks, and imperatives." In terms of language, narrative technique, and structure, Book Twelve presents an indigenous view of the conquest, albeit a partial one biased by the passage of time, localism, and the peculiar circumstance of its composition.

Finally, the Nahua and Spanish accounts also differ in their form, structure, and content. Both Bernal Díaz and Cortés, whatever their differences, sought to tell a connected story, linking events in chronological order, mixing discussions of personality with analyses of motives and actions. The Nahua accounts are more episodic, a series of vignettes in which feats of individual bravery and the designs of capes and uniforms receive as much attention as the decisions of leaders. This is typical of the indigenous tradition where visual images were often used alongside oral accounts. The fact that those pictures which accompanied Sahagún's manuscript lack the detail of the written texts seems to confirm their use as markers or aides and the composite nature of Nahua texts. Traditional Nahua ways of remembering depended on song, dance, and formal oratory as well as on images. It is difficult to know how the Nahua understood the symbols they saw, when metaphor replaced literal understandings, or when irony was used. With the adaptation of the Spanish alphabet to write Nahuatl, a whole new range of possibilities and cultural fusions opened up. The Nahua texts of the conquest provide a rich and complex vision of history but one that is opaque and complicated as well.

Finally, as important as documents are to historians, attention must be paid to the "silences" as well as to the documents. Certain groups or sectors of society are not represented in the surviving sources and may not have had access to the means of having their voices heard and recorded. First there is the bias of class. Literacy was limited among both Europeans and Nahua to certain groups in society. Although Bernal Díaz is seen as a representative of the common man, he was not from the lowest rungs of society but rather from the provincial middle class and, unlike many of his companions, he was educated. The indigenous accounts were written often by or for the nobility. How Mexica peasants or *macehualtin* saw these events remains open to question. Then there is the issue of gender. Although women are mentioned throughout these pages and one woman in particular, doña Marina or Malinche, Cortés's translator and mistress, figures importantly in the story of the conquest, no sources on the events of the conquest are written by women.[15] Surely, they witnessed these events through different eyes but we can only surmise what they thought. Unfortunately such absent voices are not uncommon in history. The story of the Conquest of Mexico presents not only an opportunity to consider moments of heroism, greed, and despair born of this clash of cultures, but challenges us to think about the problems that confront all historians: How can we understand and interpret other cultures? How can we evaluate conflicting sources? How can we read and understand such divergent styles of representation? And, how can we try to recapture the presence of those whose voices have been lost?

[15]The lack of sources by and studies about indigenous women is now being rectified. See the essays presented in Susan Schroeder, Stephanie Wood, and Robert Haskett, eds., *Indian Women in Early Mexico* (Norman: University of Oklahoma Press, 1997). An excellent collection in Spanish is Margo Glantz, ed., *La Malinche, sus padres y sus hijos* (Mexico City: UNAM, 1994).

PART TWO

The Documents

1

Forebodings and Omens

For the indigenous peoples of Mexico the conquest brought an end to the world they had created. In an attempt to decipher the miraculous nature of the unfolding events of the conquest, Nahua accounts emphasize signs and omens that preceded the Spaniards' arrival.

Although these omens appear pre-Columbian and indigenous in origin, a closer look raises some questions. There is evidence suggesting that the Nahua peoples were not alarmed by the arrival of the Spaniards, and rather than viewing them as an almost supernatural force, they saw them as simply another group of powerful and dangerous outsiders who needed to be controlled or accommodated. After the conquest, on the other hand, from the perspective of Tenochtitlan-Tlatelolco where the impact of the Spanish conquest was the most profound, the need for supernatural explanations was the clearest. Nahua emphasis on eight miraculous omens — the usual number when the Nahua considered sets of anything — and on Moctezuma's bewilderment in the face of invasion may be a postconquest interpretation by informants who wished to please the Spaniards or who resented the failure of Moctezuma and of

Figure 3. Moctezuma observes a comet, an omen of death.
Source: From the *Codex Duran,* in Serge Gruzinski, *Painting the Conquest* (Paris: Flammarion, 1992), frontispiece. Servico de Reprografia de la Biblioteca Nacional.

the warriors of Tenochtitlan to provide leadership. In the indigenous accounts of the omens, the story of the return of Quetzalcoatl begins to play an important role in explaining Moctezuma's behavior from the outset of events, but that too may be a postconquest gloss added to the story. Included here also are Nahua pictorial representations of the strange events that preceded Cortés's arrival (see Figure 3).

Omens announcing a cataclysmic change were not limited to the Nahua version of events as we see from the second excerpt drawn from *Chronicles of Michoacán,* a postconquest text based on information gathered from the Tarascan peoples, traditional enemies of the Mexica. They too believed that there were miraculous events that preceded the Spanish arrival. Finally, it became common for Spanish accounts after the conquest to incorporate a version of the omens, perhaps as a way of underlining the preordained nature of the conquest. The inclusion of such stories also made the beliefs of the indigenous peoples of Mexico appear even more exotic to European readers.

FRAY BERNARDINO DE SAHAGÚN

From the *Florentine Codex*

The following selection from James Lockhart's translation of the Nahuatl text provided by Sahagún's informants shows how miraculous and wondrous signs and events were set out at the inception of the story as indications of momentous events to come. Sahagún's informants came mostly from Tlatelolco, but similar stories were also included in the accounts that came from other Nahua communities.

Twelfth book, which speaks of how war was waged here in the altepetl of Mexico.

First chapter, where it is said that before the Spaniards came here to this land, and before the people who live here were known, there appeared and were seen signs and omens.

Ten years before the arrival of the Spaniards an omen first appeared in the sky, like a flame or tongue of fire, like the light of dawn. It appeared to be throwing off [sparks] and seemed to pierce the sky. It was wide at the bottom and narrow at the top. It looked as though it reached the very middle of the sky, its very heart and center. It showed itself off to the east. When it came out at midnight it appeared like the dawn. When dawn came, then the sun on coming out effaced it. For a full year it showed itself (it was in [the year] Twelve House that it began). And when it appeared there would be an outcry, and people would hit their hands against their mouths as they yelled. People were taken aback, they lamented.

The second omen that happened here in Mexico was that of its own accord the house of the devil Huitzilopochtli, what they call his

James Lockhart, *We People Here: Nahuatl Accounts of the Conquest of Mexico,* Repertorium Columbianum, UCLA Center for Medieval and Renaissance Studies (Los Angeles: University of California Press, 1993), 50–86, even pages only.

mountain, named Tlacatecçan, burned and flared up; no one set fire to it, it just took fire itself. When the fire was seen, the wooden pillars were already burning. Tongues and tassels of flame were coming from inside; very quickly they consumed all the building's beams. Then there was an outcry. They said, "O Mexica, let everyone come running, it must be put out, [bring] your water jars!" But when they threw water on it, trying to extinguish it, it blew up all the more. It could not be put out; it burned entirely.

The third omen was that a temple was struck by lightning, hit by a thunderbolt. It was just a building of straw at the temple complex of Xiuhteuctli, called Tzonmolco. The reason it was taken for an omen was that it was not raining hard, just drizzling. It was said that it was struck when the sun was shining, nor was thunder heard.

The fourth omen was that while the sun was still out a comet fell, in three parts. It began off to the west and headed in the direction of the east, looking as if it were sprinkling glowing coals. It had a long tail, which reached a great distance. When it was seen, there was a great outcry, like the sound of rattles.

The fifth omen was that the water [of the lake] boiled up; it was not the wind that caused it. It bubbled and made exploding sounds, rising high in the air. It reached the foundations of the houses; it flooded them, and they collapsed. This is the great lake that extends around us here in Mexico.

The sixth omen was that many times a woman would be heard going along weeping and shouting. She cried out loudly at night, saying, "O my children, we are about to go forever." Sometimes she said, "O my children, where am I to take you?"

The seventh omen was that once the water folk were hunting or snaring and caught an ash-colored bird, like a crane. Then they went to the Tlillan calmecac to show it to Moteucçoma; the sun was inclining, it was still full day. On top of its head was something like a mirror, round, circular, seeming to be perforated, where the sky, the stars, and the Fire Drill [constellation] could be seen. And Moteucçoma took it for a very bad omen when he saw the stars and the Fire Drill. The second time he looked at the bird's head he saw something like a multitude of people coming along, coming bunched, outfitted for war, carried on the backs of deer. Then he called the soothsayers, the sages, and said to them, "Do you not know what I've seen, something like a multitude of people coming along?" But when they were going to answer him, what they saw disappeared, and they said nothing more.

The eighth omen was that many times people appeared, thistle-people with two heads but one body; they took them to the Tlillan calme-cac and showed them to Moteucçoma. When he had seen them, they disappeared.

FRAY MARTÍN DE JESÚS DE LA CORUÑA

Popular Auguries and Prophetic Dreams

The Tarascan peoples who dwelled to the northwest of Tenochtitlan lived in a relationship of respectful hostility with the Mexica. They too believed that the arrival of the Spaniards was previewed by strange events. Their leaders (called the Cazonci*) had successfully resisted Mexica expansion into their area, the present-day Mexican state of Michoacán. After the conquest of this region by the Spaniards, Franciscan missionaries soon followed, and between 1539 and 1541, one of them, Fray Martín de Jesús de la Coruña, wrote a description of the province and its indigenous peoples. Like Sahagún's work it was based on interviews with indigenous informants although the author's own biases and commentaries appear throughout the text.*

These people say that during the four years before the Spaniards came to the land, their temples were burned from top to bottom, that they closed them and they would be burned again, and that the rock walls fell as their temples were made of flagstones. They did not know the cause of this except that they held it to be an augury. Likewise, they saw two large comets in the sky and thought that their gods were to conquer or destroy a village and that they were to do it for them. These people imitate parts of their dreams and do as much of what they dreamed as they can. They report their dreams to the chief priest who in turn conveys the information to the Cazonci. They say that the poor who bring in wood and sacrifice their ears dream about their gods who are reported as having told them that they would be given food and that they should marry

---

"Popular Auguries and Prophetic Dreams," *Chronicles of Michoacán,* trans. and ed. Eugene R. Crane and Reginald C. Reindorp (Norman: University of Oklahoma Press, 1970), 53–54.

such and such Christian girls. If this were a kind of omen they dared not tell it to the Cazonci. A priest related that, before the Spaniards came, he had dreamed that people would come bringing strange animals which turned out to be the horses which he had not known. In this dream these people entered the houses of the chief priests and slept there with their horses. They also brought many chickens that soiled the temples. He said he dreamed this two or three times in considerable fear for he did not know what it was until the Spaniards came to this province. When the Spaniards reached the city, they lodged in the houses of the chief priests with their horses where they held their prayer and kept their vigil. Before the Spaniards arrived they all had smallpox and measles, from which large numbers of people died, along with many lords and high families. All the Spaniards of the time are unanimous in that this disease was general throughout New Spain, for which reason it is to be given credence. The people are in accord in that measles and smallpox were unknown until the Spaniards brought them to the land.*

*This is not the contradiction it appears to be. The argument of the Indian is a good one. The Tarascan Indians maintained that these diseases came to Michoacán ahead of the Spanish, which would make the Spanish statement true as far as it goes. However, they point out that they were brought to Michoacán by Tarascans who, when they first went to Mexico City, contacted Spaniards and Aztecs with the diseases and then brought them back home with them. The *Relación,* as well as other sources, supports the contention that the Tarascans sent people to Mexico City in response to a plea from Montezuma, and, while there, they saw a great amount of death and destruction from war and disease.

DIEGO DURÁN

From *The History of the Indies of New Spain*

Soon after the conquest when European authors began to write about the peoples of Mesoamerica, they incorporated aspects of indigenous history. A number of Spanish authors, seeking to give their works a feeling of authenticity while admitting the possible divine hand of God in these events, included the indigenous accounts of omens. Diego Durán (1537?–1581) was one of those writers. Born in Seville, Spain, he came to New Spain (Mexico) as a child. He lived in Texcoco, a center of indigenous culture, and

Diego Durán, *The Aztecs,* trans. and ed. Doris Heyden and F. Horcantes (New York: Orion Press, 1964), 258–60, 268–71.

learned to speak Nahuatl fluently. He became a priest of the Dominican Order and eventually produced learned books on Nahua religion and history. His works were not published in his lifetime but they circulated widely in manuscript form. Many other contemporary authors used them. Included here is an example of the appropriation of omens into a Spanish explanation of indigenous actions which also touches on the importance of pictographic representation as a historical method.

Moteczoma was so disturbed that he was half desirous that the events which had been predicted take place immediately. In the midst of his preoccupation he called the chieftains of the wards, asking them if they had dreamed anything regarding the arrival of the strangers whose coming he so feared. He told them to reveal these dreams even though they might be contrary to his desires, since he wished to know the truth in this much-talked-of matter.

The heads of the wards told him that they had dreamed nothing nor had they seen or heard anything about this affair. He answered, "Then I beg you, my friends, to tell all the old men and women of the wards to inform me of whatever dreams they may have had, be they in my favor or against me. Also, tell the priests to reveal any visions they may see, such as ghosts or other phantoms that appear at night in the woods and dark places. Let them ask these apparitions about things to come. It will also be good to give this advice to those who wander about in the late hours; if they encounter the woman who roams the streets weeping and moaning, let them ask her why she weeps and moans."

Soon Moteczoma was notified that certain old people had dreamed strange things and they were brought before him. Said one old man, "Powerful lord, we do not wish to offend your ears or fill your heart with anxiety to make you ill. However, we are forced to obey you and we will describe our dreams to you. Know then, that these last nights the Lords of Sleep have shown us the temple of Huitzilopochtli burning with frightful flames, the stones falling one by one until it was totally destroyed. We also saw Huitzilopochtli himself fallen, cast down upon the floor! This is what we have dreamed!"

Moteczoma then asked the old women and received the following answer, "My son, do not be troubled in your heart for what we are about to tell you, although it has frightened us much. In our dreams we, your mothers, saw a mighty river enter the doors of your royal palace, smashing the walls in its fury. It ripped up the walls from their foundation, carrying beams and stones with it until nothing was left standing. We saw it reach the temple and this too was demolished. We saw the great chieftains and lords filled with fright, abandoning the city and fleeing toward the hills. This is what we have dreamed!"

Moteczoma listened attentively to what the old men and women had described. When he saw that it was not in his favor but that it confirmed the earlier ill omens he ordered that the dreamers be cast in jail. There they were to be given food in small measures until they starved to death. After this no one wished to tell his dreams to Moteczoma.

Moteczoma also consulted the people of the provinces about their dreams and as they refused to reveal anything they were jailed also. One of the old men who had been incarcerated exclaimed, "Let Moteczoma know in one word what is to become of him. Those who are to avenge the injuries and toils with which he has afflicted us are already on their way. I say no more."

When the sovereign heard this prediction he said to his attendants, "Go there and question him again! Ask him what kind of men are those who are coming, what road they will follow and what their intentions are!" However, when the messengers tried to comply with his command they found that all the prisoners had disappeared from the jail. The jailers, fearful of the wrath of the king, prostrated themselves before the sovereign, telling him of their innocence. They claimed they had not been responsible for the escape but that it had been achieved through the prisoners' own magic. Moteczoma ordered the jailers to rise and go to the towns of all those who had prophesied evil things. "Tear down their houses," he cried out, "kill their wives and children and dig in the places where the houses had been, until you reach water. All their possessions are to be destroyed. And if any one of them is ever seen in a temple he is to be stoned and his body thrown to the wild beasts!"

All of this was done and the wives and children of the offenders, with ropes about their necks, were dragged through the city, though the sorcerers and magicians were never seen again.

From that day on the heart of Moteczoma was filled with such sadness and affliction that he was never seen with a smiling countenance. He fled from all contact with others and locked himself up in his secret chambers with Texiptla to whom he communicated all that the prophets and magicians had told him.

. . . Moteczoma became even more worried and attempted to discover what kind of people had come to his land, their place of origin, lineage and, above all, whether they planned to return. For this reason he called Teoctlamacazqui and conversed with him in private. He said that he wanted to know more about those who had just departed and that he wished to have a painting made of them. He wished the picture to be drawn in his presence but said that it must be done secretly.

Teoctlamacazqui answered that he was willing to have this picture made, whereupon he ordered that the best artist of Mexico, an old man, be brought. Moteczoma told this man that he should not reveal anything that might happen, under pain of death. The painter was cowed, exclaiming that he was not a man to uncover secrets of such a great and mighty lord. His paints were brought to him and Teoctlamacazqui began to tell him what he should depict. The artist drew a picture of the ship in the way it had been seen, showing the Spaniards with their long beards and white faces. He painted their clothing in different colors, their hats upon their heads and their swords in their belts. When Moteczoma saw this he marveled and gazed upon the painting for a long time. Having looked, he said to Teoctlamacazqui, "Were these things as they have been painted here?" The answer was, "Yes, O lord, they are exactly so; I have not lied or added anything!"

Moteczoma paid the artist for his work, saying, "Brother, I beg you to answer me this question: by any chance do you know anything about what you have painted? Did your ancestors leave you a drawing or description of these men who were to arrive in this land?" The painter answered, "Powerful lord, I will not lie to you or deceive you — you are the image of the god. Therefore I will tell you that I and my ancestors never were occupied with any arts save those of painting pictures and other symbols. My ancestors were merely the artists of past kings and they depicted what they were ordered. Therefore, I know nothing of that which you ask me; if I tried to answer your question my answer would be a lie."

Moteczoma then ordered him to question the other artisans of his profession, asking if they possessed some picture coming down from their ancestors regarding those who might come to this land and possess it. The artist agreed to do so and for several days he inquired. But the painter was unable to find out anything certain and therefore returned to Moteczoma and told him that he had discovered nothing exact regarding these things.

Seeing that his attempts had been ineffectual, Moteczoma called all the oldest painters of books from Malinalco, the hot country to the south, together with those of Chalco. When they arrived he begged them to tell him if they knew anything about strangers who were to arrive in the land, asking them what kind of men might come, from where, and what they looked like. He also wished to know if the ancestors of the painters had left information regarding these things, or painted manuscripts or pictures.

When these things had been asked of them, the Malinalca brought a picture and showed it to him. It portrayed men with a single eye in their foreheads like cyclops. They said that their forebears had told them that these were the ones who were to come to this country and possess it. Other men in this picture were one-legged. The painters of books from the south displayed a drawing in which there appeared men who were fish from the waist down, explaining to Moteczoma that those were the ones who were to come to this land. Others showed the king beings which were half man, half snake. But in the end, none were able to present anything that looked like the painting of the Spaniards.

Having gotten rid of those painters, Moteczoma sent for others from Cuitlahuac and Mizquic, reminding them that they were descendants of the Toltecs, great wise men, and that they should be able to answer his questions. These men informed him, through their ancient paintings, that their ancestors had left a tradition that the sons of Quetzalcoatl were to come to these lands and that they were to possess them and recover that which had been theirs in ancient times. They were also to acquire again that which they had hidden in the hills, in the woods and in the caverns. They showed the monarch what kind of men they were but they did not look like those in his painting and therefore he bade them depart, thanking them for what they had told him and described.

Moteczoma was about to call the painters of books from Xochimilco, but the noble Tlillancalqui Teoctlamacazqui said to him, "Powerful lord, do not tire yourself or waste time in questioning so many men. None of them will be able to tell you what you desire to know as clearly as an ancient man from Xochimilco whom I know well. His name is Quilaztli and he is well informed in all matters which concern ancient history and painted books. If you wish I will bring him to you; I will tell him what you wish to know and he will produce his antique paintings." The king thanked him, commanding him to bring the old man immediately. When the latter appeared he brought with him his painted manuscripts. He appeared before Moteczoma, Angry Lord, who received him well because he was a venerable old man and of fine appearance.

Said Quilaztli to the sovereign, "O mighty lord, if because I tell you the truth I am to die, nevertheless I am here in your presence and you may do what you wish to me!" Before showing him the papers, he narrated that mounted men would come to this land in a great wooden house. This structure was to lodge many men, serving them as a home; within it they would eat and sleep. On the surface of this house they would cook their food, walk and play as if they were on firm land. They were to be white, bearded men, dressed in different colors and on their heads they would wear round coverings. Other human beings were to arrive with them, mounted on beasts similar to deer and others on eagles which would fly like the wind. These men were to possess the country, settle in all its cities, multiply in great numbers and be owners of gold, silver and precious stones.

"So that you may see," continued Quilaztli, "that what I say is the truth, behold it drawn here! This painting was bequeathed to me by my ancestors." He then took out an ancient picture on which were depicted the ship and the men dressed in the same manner as those which the king already knew through his painting. There he also saw other men mounted on horses or on flying eagles, all of them dressed in different colors, wearing their hats and swords.

Moteczoma, seeing the similarity between what the old man described and what appeared upon his painting, almost lost his senses and began to weep and to show anguish. Uncovering his chest to the elder, he cried out, "O brother Quilaztli, I now see that your ancestors were verily wise and well informed. Only a few days ago the men that you have shown me on your painting arrived in this land from the east. They came in the wooden house that you have described, dressed in the same colors and manner that appear in your drawing. I will show you how I ordered that they be painted: behold them here! However, one thing consoles me; I have sent them a present and begged them to go away in peace. They have obeyed me, departed, and I doubt if they will return."

"It is possible, O mighty prince," exclaimed Quilaztli, "that they came and went away again! Listen to the words I will say to you, and if I lie I am willing to have you annihilate me, my children and my descendants! Behold, before two years have passed, or at the most three, the strangers will return to these lands. Their coming was meant only to find a convenient way to return. Even though they said to you that they were returning to their native country, do not believe them! They will not go that far but will turn back when they have gone half way!"

Three years later, when Moteczoma had almost forgotten these things, news came from the sea that a hill was moving to and fro upon the waters again.

2

Preparations

The selection included here from Bernal Díaz traces the course of early Spanish contact with the mainland and the narrative begins as Díaz describes the events of the Grijalva expedition (1518) along the coast of Yucatan. Relations and fighting with Maya peoples comprise the heart of the account. At the outset of his narrative, Díaz chooses to mention the legend of Topiltzin Quetzalcoatl, the ancient god who the indigenous peoples believed someday would return to reclaim his throne, and their belief that the Spaniards might be returning gods.

Díaz then moves chronologically, writing of Grijalva's return to Cuba, the organizing of a new expedition under Hernán Cortés, whom Díaz often simply calls "the General," the return to Yucatan, and then the progress of the expedition up the Gulf coast of Mexico (see Figure 4). Included here are sections describing the first battles with the Maya peoples of Tabasco and Cortés's methods of negotiation and intimidation. Included also are sections that introduce some of the major personalities: Aguilar, the rescued Spaniard who becomes Cortés's translator; doña Marina, the Nahua woman who becomes Cortés's mistress, translator, and advisor; and the captains and men like Cristóbal Olid and Pedro de Alvarado. Finally, this selection ends with the founding of the town of Vera Cruz. The following selection from Cortés's first letter to the king gives his (favorable and self-serving) interpretation of these events.

Four themes are emphasized in these excerpts. First, is the importance of translators and of language itself in the process of encounter and conquest. The Spaniards seem to have understood this from the outset. They also had incredible luck. Their first contacts with the Maya had been facilitated by a Taino woman from Jamaica who had been a castaway on the Yucatan coast and who thus spoke Maya. Since Díaz and other Spaniards who had lived in the Caribbean spoke some Arawak (Taino), she served as a translator for the Spaniards. Later, two Maya youths who the Spaniards had taken with them to Cuba were brought

Figure 4. A portrait of Cortés by Christopher Weiditz done in 1529 after Cortes's return to Spain.
Source: Adapted from Norte: *Revista de Hispano America,* 242, July–August 1971. Courtesy of Norte.

back to serve as translators in Cortés's expedition. The major stroke of luck was Cortés's discovery that two Spanish shipwreck survivors were living among the Maya. Díaz recounts the story of the two: Aguilar, who returned to become Cortés's Mayan translator, and Guerrero, who refused to return and instead "went native" and remained with his wife, children, and adopted people. He later died leading Maya resistance against the Spaniards. Finally, Díaz tells in detail of the young Nahua noblewoman, a captive among the Maya, who was given to Cortés and who became his translator, advisor, mistress, and eventually the wife of other Spaniards. Doña Marina or Malintzin or Malinche, as she was called, is always treated with great respect in Díaz's account. The importance of language as a tool of conquest was never lost on Díaz.

A second theme that the old soldier emphasized continually — and logically so — were the military aspects: weapons, equipment, logistics, tactics. Díaz was a soldier with a soldier's interests and he went beyond others in noting how Cortés often used demonstrations of European technology, horses, and weaponry for their psychological impact.

The third theme is demonstrated by Díaz's awareness of the indigenous culture. He remarks on their system of writing or painting and communication, on their political system, and, of course, negatively on their sacrifices and idols. His descriptions of the first interviews with Moctezuma's ambassadors bear direct comparison with the Nahua accounts that appear in chapter 3. While Díaz and his companions often misunderstood what they observed, they began to differentiate between the various ethnicities and political loyalties of the indigenous peoples. This was an ethnography in the service of conquest. It is at this time that the expedition begins to hear about "Culua" and "Mexico." These are the first references to the Mexica Empire.

Finally, in the description of the founding of Vera Cruz, the fourth theme of rivalry and political struggle represented by the enmity between Cortés and the governor of Cuba, Diego Velázquez, emerges clearly. Cortés having learned that there was a rich empire to conquer broke away from the authority of Velázquez (just as Velázquez himself had earlier broken from the authority of the governor of Española). This was a relatively common pattern among the conquistadors. The foundation of the municipality of Vera Cruz (to establish a new basis of authority) and the sending of a representative directly to Spain for royal approval by Cortés was typical of practices in such struggles. The theme of conflict between the Cortés and Velázquez factions reemerges again and again in the story of the conquest of Mexico. Díaz was a member of the Cortés faction at this point, but he also notes with bitterness that the soldiers agreed to give Cortés too large a share of the spoils. The common soldiers' frustrations are also apparent here. It was one of the principal reasons why Díaz wrote his narrative.

The second selection includes excerpts from Cortés's first and second letters to the Spanish king, Charles V, explaining the events leading to the foundation of Vera Cruz and the scuttling of Cortés's ships. This was a tricky business. Cortés had created a new municipality (staffed with his loyal followers) which abrogated his authority as granted by the governor of Cuba, but established him as its representative. It was all a legal sleight of hand. Cortés knew that this maneuver would be opposed by Diego Velázquez, governor of Cuba, and by his supporters back in Spain, particularly Bishop Fonseca, head of the Council of the Indies. For this reason, Cortés gathered all the treasure acquired up to that point and dispatched it to the king along with his letter and two trusted representatives to plead his case. The decision to scuttle (not burn) his ships was not only to make use of the sailors as troops, but also to prevent dissidents of the Velázquez faction from reaching Cuba as Cortés makes clear.[1] Notice that Cortés's first letter is written in the third person in order to present a sense of objectivity despite the fact that his reports were, in fact, personal justifications.[2]

[1] These events are admirably discussed in J. H. Elliott, "Cortés, Velázquez, and Charles V," which appears as the introduction to *Hernan Cortes: Letters from Mexico,* trans. and ed. A. R. Pagden (New York, Orion Press, 1971), xi–xxxvii.

[2] Cortés's letters have been analyzed by many scholars. A recent examination of the letters from a literary and historical perspective is Beatriz Pastor Bodmer, *The Armature of Conquest: Spanish Accounts of the Discovery of America, 1492–1589,* trans. Lydia Longstreth Hunt (Stanford: Stanford University Press, 1992), 50–100.

BERNAL DÍAZ

From *The True History of the Conquest of New Spain*

Díaz's account provides an outline of events but also considerable detail about his companions and the political and personal factions among them. The descriptions of the battles with the Maya, the story of the Spanish castaways, and that of doña Marina are highlights of the narrative.

After the return of the Captain Juan de Grijalva to Cuba, when the Governor Diego Velásquez understood how rich were these newly discovered lands, he ordered another fleet, much larger than the former one to be sent off, and he had already collected in the Port of Santiago, where he resided, ten ships, four of them were those in which we had returned with Juan de Grijalva, which had at once been careened, and the other six had been got together from other ports in the Island. He had them furnished with provisions, consisting of Cassava bread and salt pork, for at that time there were neither sheep nor cattle in the Island of Cuba, as it had been only recently settled. These provisions were only to last

Bernal Díaz del Castillo, from *The True History of the Conquest of New Spain,* ed. A. P. Maudslay (London: Hakluyt Society, 1908), 69–77, 90–103, 107–13, 118–35, 154–60.

until we arrived at Havana, for it was at that port that we were to take in our stores, as was afterwards done.

I must cease talking of this and tell about the disputes which arose over the choice of a captain for the expedition. There were many debates and much opposition, for some gentleman said that Vasco Porcallo, a near relation of the Conde de Feria, should be captain, but Diego Velásquez feared that he would rise against him with the fleet, for he was very daring; others said that Agustin Bermudez or Antonio Velásquez Borrejo, or Bernadino Velásquez, kinsman of Diego Velásquez should go in command.

Most of us soldiers who were there said that we should prefer to go again under Juan de Grijalva, for he was a good captain, and there was no fault to be found either with his person or his capacity for command.

While things were going on in the way I have related, two great favourites of Diego Velásquez named Andrés de Duero, the Governor's Secretary, and Amador de Lares, His Majesty's accountant, secretly formed a partnership with a gentleman named Hernando Cortés, a native of Medellin, who held a grant of Indians in the Island. A short while before, Cortés had married a lady named Catalina Juarez la Marcayda; this lady was sister of a certain Juan Juarez who after the conquest of New Spain was a settler at Mexico. As far as I know, and from what others say, it was a love match. On this matter of the marriage other persons who saw it have had much to say, and for that reason I will not touch any more on this delicate subject.

I will go on to tell about this partnership, it came about in this manner:— These two great favourites of Velásquez agreed that they would get him to appoint Cortés Captain General of the whole fleet, and that they would divide between the three of them, the spoil of gold, silver and jewels which might fall to Cortés' share. For secretly Diego Velásquez was sending to trade and not to form a settlement, as was apparent afterwards from the instructions given about it, although it was announced and published that the expedition was for the purpose of founding a settlement.

When this arrangement had been made, Duero and the accountant went to work in such a way with Diego Velásquez, and addressed such honied words to him, praising Cortés highly, as the very man for the position of Captain, as in addition to being energetic he knew how to command and ensure respect, and as one who would be faithful in everything entrusted to him, both in regard to the fleet and in everything else, (pointing out too, that he was his godson, for Velásquez was his sponsor when Cortés married Doña Catalina Juarez), that they persuaded him to choose Cortés as Captain General.

Andrés de Duero, the Governor's Secretary, drew up the documents in very good ink* as the proverb says, in the way Cortés wished with very ample powers.

When the appointment was made public, some persons were pleased and others annoyed.

One Sunday when Diego Velásquez went to Mass,— and as he was Governor he was accompanied by the most distinguished persons in the town,— he placed Hernando Cortés on his right hand so as to pay him honour. A buffoon, called the mad Cervantes, ran in front of Diego Velásquez, making grimaces and cracking jokes and he cried out —

The parade of my friend Diego, Diego,
Who then is this captain of your choice?
He comes from Medellin in Estremadura
A very valiant captain indeed
Have a care lest he run off with the fleet
For all judge him a man to take care of his own. . . .

Before going any further I wish to say that the valiant and energetic Hernando Cortés was a gentleman by birth (hijo-d'algo) by four lines of descent. The first through the Cortéses, for so his father Martin Cortés was named, the second through the Pizarros, the third through the Monroys and the fourth through the Altamiranos. Although he was such a valiant, energetic and daring captain, I will not from now on, call him by any of these epithets of valiant, or energetic, nor will I speak of him as Marqués del Valle, but simply as Hernando Cortés. For the name Cortés alone was held in as high respect throughout the Indies as well as in Spain, as was the name of Alexander in Macedonia, and those of Julius Caesar and Pompey and Scipio among the Romans, and Hannibal among the Carthaginians, or in our own Castille the name of Gonzalo Hernández, the Great Captain. And the valiant Cortés himself was better pleased not to be called by lofty titles but simply by his name, and so I will call him for the future. . . .

As soon as Hernando Cortés had been appointed General in the way I have related, he began to search for all sorts of arms, guns, powder and crossbows and every kind of warlike stores which he could get together,

---

* De muy buena tinta: most efficiently.

and all sorts of articles to be used for barter, and other things necessary for the expedition.

Moreover he began to adorn himself and be more careful of his appearance than before, and he wore a plume of feathers with a medal, and a gold chain, and a velvet cloak trimmed with knots of gold, in fact he looked like a gallant and courageous Captain. However, he had no money to defray the expenses I have spoken about, for at that time he was very poor and much in debt, although he had a good *encomienda* of Indians who were getting him a return from his gold mines, but he spent all of it on his person and on finery for his wife whom he had recently married, and on entertaining some guests who had come to visit him. For he was affable in his manner and a good talker, and he had twice been chosen *Alcalde** of the town of Santiago Baracoa where he had settled, and in that country it is esteemed a great honour to be chosen as *Alcalde*.

When some merchant friends of his named Jaime Tria, Jerónimo Tria and Pedro de Jerez saw that he had obtained this command as Captain General, they lent him four thousand gold dollars in coin and gave him merchandise worth another four thousand dollars secured on his Indians and estates. Then he ordered two standards and banners to be made, worked in gold with the royal arms and a cross on each side with a legend which said, "Comrades, let us follow the sign of the holy Cross with true faith, and through it we shall conquer." And he ordered a proclamation to be made with the sound of drums and trumpets in the name of His Majesty and by Diego Velásquez in the King's name, and in his own as Captain General, to the effect that whatsoever person might wish to go in his company to the newly discovered lands to conquer them and to settle there, should receive his share of the gold, silver and riches which might be gained and an *encomienda* of Indians after the country had been pacified, and that to do these things Diego Velásquez held authority from His Majesty.

Although he put in the proclamation this about the authority of Our Lord the King, the Chaplain, Benito Martínez, had not yet arrived from Spain with the Commission which Diego Velásquez had sent him to obtain. . . .

We assembled at Santiago de Cuba, whence we set out with the fleet more than three hundred and fifty soldiers in number. From the house of Velásquez there came Diego de Ordás, the chief Mayordomo, whom

---

*Alcalde: Mayor.

Velásquez himself sent with orders to keep his eyes open and see that no plots were hatched in the fleet, for he was always distrustful of Cortés although he concealed his fears. There came also Francisco de Morla and an Escobar, whom we called The Page, and a Heredia, and Juan Ruano and Pedro Escudero, and Martin Ramos de Lares, and many others who were friends and followers of Diego Velásquez; and I place myself last on the list for I also came from the house of Diego Velásquez, for he was my kinsman. . . .

Cortés worked hard to get his fleet under way and hastened on his preparations, for already envy and malice had taken possession of the relations of Diego Velásquez who were affronted because their kinsman neither trusted them nor took any notice of them and because he had given charge and command to Cortés, knowing that he had looked upon him as a great enemy only a short time before, on account of his marriage, already mentioned by me; so they went about grumbling at their kinsman Diego Velásquez and at Cortés, and by every means in their power they worked on Diego Velásquez to induce him to revoke the commission.

Now Cortés was advised of all this, and for that reason never left the Governor's side, and always showed himself to be his zealous servant, and kept on telling him that, God willing, he was going to make him a very illustrious and wealthy gentleman in a very short time. Moreover Andrés de Duero was always advising Cortés to hasten the embarkation of himself and his soldiers, for Diego Velásquez was already changing his mind owing to the importunity of his family.

When Cortés knew this he sent orders to his wife that all provisions of food which he wished to take and any other gifts (such as women usually give to their husbands when starting on such an expedition) should be sent at once and placed on board ship.

He had already had a proclamation made that on that day by nightfall all ships, Captains, pilots and soldiers should be on board and no one should remain on shore. When Cortés had seen all his company embarked he went to take leave of Diego Velásquez, accompanied by his great friends and many other gentlemen, and all the most distinguished citizens of that town.

After many demonstrations and embraces of Cortés by the Governor, and of the Governor by Cortés, he took his leave. The next day very early after having heard Mass we went to our ships, and Diego Velásquez himself accompanied us, and again they embraced with many fair speeches one to the other until we set sail.

A few days later, in fine weather, we reached the Port of Trinidad where we brought up in the harbour and went ashore, and nearly all the citizens of that town came out to meet us; and entertained us well. . . .

There was to be no parade of the forces until we arrived at Cozumel. Cortés ordered the horses to be taken on board ship, and he directed Pedro de Alvarado to go along the North coast in a good ship named the *San Sebastian,* and he told the pilot who was in charge to wait for him at Cape San Antonio as all the ships would meet there and go in company to Cozumel. He also sent a messenger to Diego de Ordás, who had gone along the North Coast to collect supplies of food with orders to do the same and await his coming.

On the 10th February 1519, after hearing Mass, they set sail along the south coast with nine ships and the company of gentlemen and soldiers whom I have mentioned, so that with the two ships absent on the north coast there were eleven ships in all, including that which carried Pedro de Alvarado with seventy soldiers and I travelled in his company.

The Pilot named Camacho who was in charge of our ship paid no attention to the orders of Cortés and went his own way and we arrived at Cozumel two days before Cortés and anchored in the port. . . .

Cortés had not yet arrived, being delayed by the ship commanded by Francisco de Morla having lost her rudder in bad weather, however she was supplied with another rudder by one of the ships of the fleet, and all then came on in company.

To go back to Pedro de Alvarado. As soon as we arrived in port we went on shore with all the soldiers to the town of Cozumel, but we found no Indians there as they had all fled. So we were ordered to go on to another town about a league distant, and there also the natives had fled and taken to the bush, but they could not carry off their property and left behind their poultry and other things and Pedro de Alvarado ordered forty of the fowls to be taken. In an Idol house there were some altar ornaments made of old cloths and some little chests containing diadems, Idols, beads and pendants of gold of poor quality, and here we captured two Indians and an Indian woman, and we returned to the town where we had disembarked.

While we were there Cortés arrived with all the fleet, and after taking up his lodging the first thing he did was to order the pilot Camacho to be put in irons for not having waited for him at sea as he had been ordered to do. When he saw the town without any people in it, and heard that Pedro de Alvarado had gone to the other town and had taken fowls and cloths and other things of small value from the Idols, and some gold which was half copper, he showed that he was very angry both at that

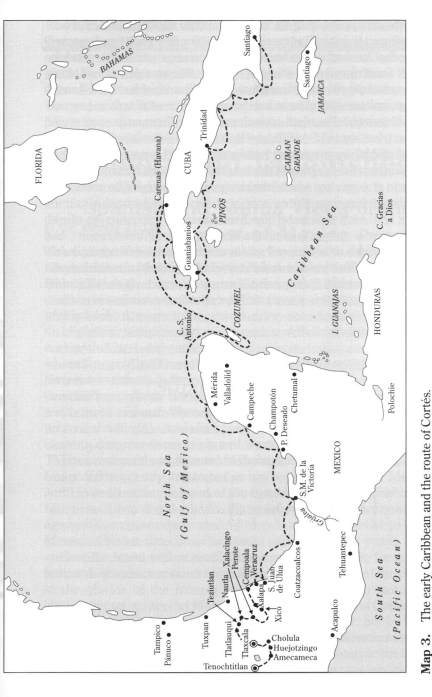

Map 3. The early Caribbean and the route of Cortés.

Source: Adapted from Itinerario de Hernán Cortés from inside cover of *Hernán Cortés: Letters from Mexico* by Anthony Pagden. Copyright © 1986, 1992 by Yale University Press. Reprinted by permission.

and at the pilot not having waited for him, and he reprimanded Pedro de Alvarado severely, and told him that we should never pacify the country in that way by robbing the natives of their property, and he sent for the two Indians and the woman whom we had captured, and through Melchorejo, (Julianillo his companion was dead) the man we had brought from Cape Catoche who understood the language well, he spoke to them telling them to go and summon the Caciques and Indians of their town, and he told them not to be afraid, and he ordered the gold and the cloths and all the rest to be given back to them, and for the fowls (which had already been eaten) he ordered them to be given beads and little bells, and in addition he gave to each Indian a Spanish shirt. So they went off to summon the lord of the town, and the next day the Cacique and all his people arrived, women and children and all the inhabitants of the town, and they went about among us as though they had been used to us all their lives, and Cortés ordered us not to annoy them in any way. Here in this Island Cortés began to rule energetically, and Our Lord so favoured him that whatever he put his hand to it turned out well for him, especially in pacifying the people and towns of these lands, as we shall see further on.

When we had been in Cozumel three days Cortés ordered a muster of his forces so as to see how many of us there were, and he found that we numbered five hundred and eight, not counting the shipmasters, pilots and sailors, who numbered about one hundred. There were sixteen horses and mares all fit to be used for sport or as chargers.

There were eleven ships both great and small, and one a sort of launch which a certain Gines Nortes brought laden with supplies.

There were thirty two crossbowmen and thirteen musketeers;— *escopeteros,* as they were then called and brass guns, and four falconets, and much powder and ball. About the number of cross bowmen my memory does not serve me very well, but it is not material to my story. . . .

As Cortés was most diligent in all matters, he sent for me and a Biscayan named Martin Ramos, and asked us what we thought about those words which the Indians of Campeche had used when we went there with Francisco Hernández de Córdova, when they cried out "Castilan, Castilan." . . . We again related to Cortés all that we had seen and heard about the matter, and he said that he also had often thought about it, and that perhaps there might be some Spaniards living in the country, and added "It seems to me that it would be well to ask these Caciques of Cozumel if they know anything about them." So through Melchorejo, the man from Cape Catoche, who already understood a little Spanish and knew the language of Cozumel very well, all the chiefs were questioned, and every one of them said that they had known of certain Spaniards and gave descriptions of them, and said that some Caciques, who lived about two days' journey inland, kept them as slaves, and that here in Cozumel were some Indian traders who spoke to them only a few days ago. We were all delighted at this news, and Cortés told the Caciques that they must go at once and summon the Spaniards, taking with them letters, (which in the Indian language they call *amales*) and he gave shirts to the Caciques and Indians who went with the letters and spoke reassuringly to them, and told them that when they returned he would give them some more beads. The Cacique advised Cortés to send a ransom to the owners who held these men as slaves, so that they should be allowed to come, and Cortés did so, and gave to the messengers all manner of beads. Then he ordered the two smallest vessels to be got ready (one of them was little larger than a launch) and twenty men with guns and crossbows, under the command of Diego de Ordás, and he sent them off to the coast near Cape Catoche where the larger vessel was to wait for eight days while the smaller vessel should go backwards and forwards and bring news of what was being done, for the land of Cape Catoche was only four leagues distant, and the one country could be seen from the other.

In the letter Cortés said:—"Gentlemen and brothers, here in Cozumel I have learnt that you are captives in the hands of a Cacique, and I pray you that you come here to Cozumel at once, and for this purpose I have sent a ship with soldiers, in case you have need of them, and a ransom to be paid to those Indians with whom you are living. The ship will wait eight days for you. Come in all haste, and you will be welcomed and protected. I am here at this Island with five hundred soldiers and eleven ships, in which I go on, please God, to a town called Tabasco or Potonchan."

The two vessels were soon dispatched with the two Indian traders from Cozumel who carried the letters, and they crossed the strait in three hours and the messengers with the letters and ransom were landed. In two days the letters were delivered to a Spaniard named Jerónimo de Aguilar, for that we found to be his name, and so I shall call him in future. When he had read the letter and received the ransom of beads which we had sent to him he was delighted, and carried the ransom to the Cacique his master, and begged leave to depart, and the Cacique at once gave him leave to go wherever he pleased. Aguilar set out for the place, five leagues distant, where his companion Gonzalo Guerrero was living, but when he read the letter to him he answered, "Brother Aguilar, I am married and have three children and the Indians look on me as a Cacique and captain in wartime,—You go and God be with you, but I have my face tattooed and my ears pierced, what would the Spaniards say should they see me in this guise? and look how handsome these boys of mine are, for God's sake give me those green beads you have brought and I will give the beads to them and say that my brothers have sent them from my own country." And the Indian wife of Gonzalo spoke to Aguilar in her own tongue very angrily and said to him, "What is this slave coming here for talking to my husband,— go off with you, and don't trouble us with any more words."

Then Aguilar reminded Gonzalo that he was a Christian and said that he should not imperil his soul for the sake of an Indian woman, and as for his wife and children he could take them with him if he did not wish to desert them. But by no words or admonishments could he be persuaded to come. It appears that Gonzalo Guerrero was a sailor and a native of Palos.

When Jerónimo de Aguilar saw that Gonzalo would not accompany him he went at once, with the two Indian messengers, to the place where the ship had been awaiting his coming, but when he arrived he saw no ship for she had already departed. The eight days during which Ordás had been ordered to await and one day more had already expired, and seeing that Aguilar had not arrived Ordás returned to Cozumel without bringing any news about that for which he had come.

When Aguilar saw that there was no ship there he became very sad, and returned to his master and to the town where he usually lived.

Now I will leave this and say that when Cortés saw Ordás return without success or any news of the Spaniards or Indian messengers he was very angry, and said haughtily to Ordás that he thought that he would have done better than to return without the Spaniards or any news of them, for it was quite clear that they were prisoners in that country. . . .

. . . [M]any Indians both the natives of the towns near Cape Catoche and those from other parts of Yucatan came on pilgrimages to the Island of Cozumel, for it appeared that there were some very hideous idols kept in a certain oratory on Cozumel to which it was the custom of the people of the land to offer sacrifices at that season. One morning the courtyard of the oratory where the Idols were kept was crowded with Indians, and many of them both men and women were burning a resin like our incense. As this was a new sight to us we stood round watching it with attention, and presently an old Indian with a long cloak, who was the priest of the Idols (and I have already said that the priests in New Spain are called *Papas*) went up on the top of the oratory and began to preach to the people. Cortés and all of us were wondering what would be the result of that black sermon. Cortés asked Melchorejo, who understood the language well, what the old Indian was saying, for he was informed that he was preaching evil things, and he sent for the Cacique and all the principal chiefs and the priest himself, and, as well as he could through the aid of our interpreter, he told them that if we were to be brothers they must cast those most evil Idols out of their temple, for they were not gods at all but very evil things which led them astray and could lead their souls to hell. Then he spoke to them about good and holy things, and told them to set up in the place of their Idols an image of Our Lady which he gave them, and a cross, which would always aid them and bring good harvests and would save their souls, and he told them in a very excellent way other things about our holy faith.

The Priest and the Caciques answered that their forefathers had worshipped those Idols because they were good, and that they did not dare to do otherwise, and that if we cast out their Idols we would see how much harm it would do us, for we should be lost at sea. Then Cortés ordered us to break the Idols to pieces and roll them down the steps, and this we did; then he ordered lime to be brought, of which there was a good store in the town, and Indian masons, and he set up a very fair altar on which we placed the figure of Our Lady; and he ordered two of our party named Alonzo Yáñez and Álvaro López who were carpenters and joiners to make a cross of some rough timber which was there, and it was placed in a small chapel near the altar and the priest named Juan Díaz said mass there, and the Cacique and the heathen priest and all the Indians stood watching us with attention. . . .

When the Spaniard who was a prisoner among the Indians, knew for certain that we had returned to Cozumel with the ships, he was very joyful and gave thanks to God, and he came in all haste with the two Indians who had carried the letters and ransom, and embarked in a canoe, and as he was able to pay well with the green beads we had sent him, he soon hired a canoe and six Indian rowers, and they rowed so fast that, meeting no head wind, in a very short time they crossed the strait between the two shores, which is a distance of about four leagues.

When they arrived on the coast of Cozumel and were disembarking, some soldiers who had gone out hunting (for there were wild pigs on the island) told Cortés that a large canoe, which had come from the direction of Cape Catoche, had arrived near the town. Cortés sent Andrés de Tápia and two other soldiers to go and see, for it was a new thing for Indians to come fearlessly in large canoes into our neighbourhood. So they set out, and as soon as the Indians who came in the canoe which Aguilar had hired caught sight of the Spaniards, they were frightened and wished to get back into the canoe and flee away. Aguilar told them in their own language not to be afraid, that these men were his brothers. When Andrés de Tápia saw that they were only Indians (for Aguilar looked neither more nor less than an Indian), he at once sent word to Cortés by a Spaniard that they were Cozumel Indians who had come in the canoe. As soon as the men had landed, the Spaniard in words badly articulated and worse pronounced, cried *Dios y Santa Maria de Sevilla,* and Tápia went at once to embrace him. The other soldier who had accompanied Tápia when he saw what had happened, promptly ran to Cortés to beg a reward for the good news, for it was a Spaniard who had come in the canoe, and we were all delighted when we heard it.

Tápia soon brought the Spaniard to Cortés, but before he arrived where Cortés was standing, several Spaniards asked Tápia where the Spaniard was? although he was walking by his side, for they could not distinguish him from an Indian as he was naturally brown and he had his hair shorn like an Indian slave, and carried a paddle on his shoulder, he was shod with one old sandal and the other was tied to his belt, he had on a ragged old cloak, and a worse loin cloth with which he covered his nakedness, and he had tied up, in a bundle in his cloak, a Book of Hours, old and worn. When Cortés saw him in this state, he too was deceived like the other soldiers, and asked Tápia "Where is the Spaniard?" On hearing this, the Spaniard squatted down on his haunches as the Indians do and said "I am he." Cortés at once ordered him to be given a shirt and doublet and drawers and a cape and sandals, for he had no other clothes, and asked him about himself and what his name was and when he came to this country. The man replied, pronouncing with difficulty, that he was called Jerónimo de Aguilar, a native of Ecija, and that he had taken holy orders, that eight years had passed since he and fifteen other men and two women left Darien[1] for the Island of Santo Domingo, where he had some disputes and a law-suit with a certain Enciso y Valdívia, and he said that they were carrying ten thousand gold dollars and the legal documents of the case, and that the ship in which they sailed, struck on the *Alacranes* so that she could not be floated, and that he and his companions and the two women got into the ship's boat, thinking to reach the Island of Cuba or Jamaica, but that the currents were very strong and carried them to this land, and that the Calachiones of that district had divided them among themselves, and that many of his companions had been sacrificed to the Idols, and that others had died of disease, and the

[1] Panama.

women had died of overwork only a short time before, for they had been made to grind corn; that the Indians had intended him for a sacrifice, but that one night he escaped and fled to the Cacique with whom since then he had been living (I don't remember the name that he gave) and that none were left of all his party except himself and a certain Gonzalo Guerrero, whom he had gone to summon, but he would not come.

When Cortés heard all this, he gave thanks to God, and said that he would have him well looked after and rewarded. He questioned Aguilar about the country and the towns, but Aguilar replied that having been a slave, he knew only about hewing wood and drawing water and digging in the fields, that he had only once travelled as far as four leagues from home when he was sent with a load, but, as it was heavier than he could carry, he fell ill, but that he understood that there were very many towns. When questioned about Gonzalo Guerrero, he said that he was married and had three sons, and that his face was tattooed and his ears and lower lip were pierced, that he was a seaman and a native of Palos, and that the Indians considered him to be very valiant; that when a little more than a year ago a captain and three vessels arrived at Cape Catoche, (it seems probable that this was when we came with Francisco Hernández de Córdova) it was at the suggestion of Guerrero that the Indians attacked them, and that he was there himself in the company of the Cacique of the large town, whom I have spoken about when describing the expedition of Francisco Hernández de Córdova. When Cortés heard this he exclaimed "I wish I had him in my hands for it will never do to leave him here."

When the Caciques of Cozumel found out that Aguilar could speak their language, they gave him to eat of their best, and Aguilar advised them always to respect and revere the holy image of Our Lady and the Cross, for they would find that it would benefit them greatly.

On the advice of Aguilar the Caciques asked Cortés to give them a letter of recommendation, so that if any other Spaniards came to that port they would treat the Indians well and do them no harm, and this letter was given to them. After bidding the people good-bye with many caresses and promises we set sail for the Rio de Grijalva.

This is the true story of Aguilar, and not the other which the historian Gómara has written; however, I am not surprised that what he says is news to me. Now I must go on with my story.

On the 12th March, 1519, we arrived with all the fleet at the Rio de Grijalva, which is also called Tabasco, and as we already knew from our experience with Grijalva that vessels of large size could not enter into the river, the larger vessels were anchored out at sea, and from the smaller vessels and boats all the soldiers were landed at the Cape of the Palms (as they were in Grijalva's time) which was about half a league distant from the town of Tabasco. The river, the river banks and the mangrove thickets were swarming with Indians, at which those of us who had not been here in Grijalva's time were much astonished.

In addition to this there were assembled in the town more than twelve thousand warriors all prepared to make war on us, for at this time the town was of considerable importance and other large towns were subject to it and they had all made preparation for war and were well supplied with the arms which they are accustomed to use.

The reason for this was that the people of Potonchan and Lázaro and the other towns in that neighbourhood had looked upon the people of Tabasco as cowards, and had told them so to their faces, because they had given Grijalva the gold jewels which I have spoken about in an earlier chapter, and they said that they were too faint hearted to attack us although they had more towns and more warriors than the people of Potonchan and Lázaro. This they said to annoy them and added that they in their towns had attacked us and killed fifty six of us. So on account of these taunts which had been uttered, the people of Tabasco had determined to take up arms.

When Cortés saw them drawn up ready for war he told Aguilar the interpreter, who spoke the language of Tabasco well,* to ask the Indians who passed near us, in a large canoe and who looked like chiefs, what they were so much disturbed about, and to tell them that we had not come to do them any harm, but were willing to give them some of the things we had brought with us and to treat them like brothers, and we prayed them not to begin a war as they would regret it, and much else was said to them about keeping the peace. However, the more Aguilar talked to them the more violent they became, and they said that they would kill us all if we entered their town, and that it was fortified all round with fences and barricades of large trunks of trees.

Aguilar spoke to them again and asked them to keep the peace, and allow us to take water and barter our goods with them for food, and permit us to tell the Calachones things which would be to their advantage and to the service of God our Lord, but they still persisted in saying that if we advanced beyond the palm trees they would kill us.

When Cortés saw the state of affairs he ordered the boats and small vessels to be got ready and ordered three cannon to be placed in each

---

*These people were Tzendals, a branch of the Maya stock, and Aguilar, who spoke Maya, could understand and speak to them.

boat and divided the crossbowmen and musketeers among the boats. We remembered that when we were here with Grijalva we had found a narrow path which ran across some streams from the palm grove to the town, and Cortés ordered three soldiers to find out in the night if that path ran right up to the houses, and not to delay in bringing the news, and these men found out that it did lead there. After making a thorough examination of our surroundings the rest of the day was spent in arranging how and in what order we were to go in the boats.

The next morning we had our arms in readiness and after hearing mass Cortés ordered the Captain Alonzo de Avila and a hundred soldiers among whom were ten crossbowmen, to go by the little path which led to the town, and, as soon as he heard the guns fired, to attack the town on one side while he attacked it on the other. Cortés himself and all the other Captains and soldiers went in the boats and light draft vessels up the river. When the Indian warriors who were on the banks and among the mangroves saw that we were really on the move, they came after us with a great many canoes with intent to prevent our going ashore at the landing place, and the whole river bank appeared to be covered with Indian warriors carrying all the different arms which they use, and blowing trumpets and shells and sounding drums. When Cortés saw how matters stood he ordered us to wait a little and not to fire any shots from guns or crossbows or cannon, for as he wished to be justified in all that he might do he made another appeal to the Indians through the interpreter Aguilar, in the presence of the King's Notary, Diego de Godoy, asking the Indians to allow us to land and take water and speak to them about God and about His Majesty, and adding that should they make war on us, that if in defending ourselves some should be killed and others hurt, theirs would be the fault and the burden and it would not lie with us, but they went on threatening that if we landed they would kill us.

Then they boldly began to let fly arrows at us, and made signals with their drums, and like valiant men they surrounded us with their canoes, and they all attacked us with such a shower of arrows that they kept us in the water in some parts up to our waists. As there was much mud and swamp at that place we could not easily get clear of it, and so many Indians fell on us, that what with some hurling their lances with all their might and others shooting arrows at us, we could not reach the land as soon as we wished.

While Cortés was fighting he lost a shoe in the mud and could not find it again, and he got on shore with one foot bare. Presently someone picked the shoe out of the mud and he put it on again.

While this was happening to Cortés, all of us Captains as well as soldiers, with the cry of "Santiago," * fell upon the Indians and forced them to retreat, but they did not fall back far, as they sheltered themselves behind great barriers and stockades formed of thick logs until we pulled them apart and got to one of the small gateways of the town. There we attacked them again, and we pushed them along through a street to where other defences had been erected, and there they turned on us and met us face to face and fought most valiantly, making the greatest efforts, shouting and whistling and crying out "al calacheoni," "al calacheoni," which in their language meant an order to kill or capture our Captain. While we were thus surrounded by them Alonzo de Ávila and his soldiers came up.

As I have already said they came from the Palm grove by land and could not arrive sooner on account of the swamps and creeks. Their delay was really unavoidable, just as we also had been delayed over the summons of the Indians to surrender, and in breaking openings in the barricades, so as to enable us to attack them. Now we all joined together to drive the enemy out of their strongholds, and we compelled them to retreat, but like brave warriors they kept on shooting showers of arrows and fire-hardened darts, and never turned their backs on us until [we gained] a great court with chambers and large halls, and three Idol houses, where they had already carried all the goods they possessed. Cortés then ordered us to halt, and not to follow on and overtake the enemy in their flight.

There and then Cortés took possession of that land for His Majesty, performing the act in His Majesty's name. It was done in this way; he drew his sword and as a sign of possession he made three cuts in a huge tree called a *Ceiba,* which stood in the court of that great square, and cried that if any person should raise objection, that he would defend the right with the sword and shield which he held in his hands.

All of us soldiers who were present when this happened cried out that he did right in taking possession of the land in His Majesty's name, and that we would aid him should any person say otherwise. This act was done in the presence of the Royal Notary. The partizans of Diego Velásquez chose to grumble at this act of taking possession.

I call to mind that in that hard fought attack which the Indians made on us, they wounded fourteen soldiers, and they gave me an arrow wound in the thigh, but it was only a slight wound; and we found eighteen Indians dead in the water where we disembarked.

---

* Santiago or St. James was the patron saint of Spain.

We slept there [in the great square] that night with guards and sentinels on the alert. I will stop here and go on to tell what more happened. . . .

I have already said how we were marching along when we met all the forces of the enemy which were moving in search of us, and all the men wore great feather crests and they carried drums and trumpets, and their faces were coloured black and white, and they were armed with large bows and arrows, lances and shields and swords shaped like our two-handed swords, and many slings and stones and fire-hardened javelins, and all wore quilted cotton armour. As they approached us their squadrons were so numerous that they covered the whole plain, and they rushed on us like mad dogs completely surrounding us, and they let fly such a cloud of arrows, javelins and stones that on the first assault they wounded over seventy of us, and fighting hand to hand they did us great damage with their lances, and one soldier fell dead at once from an arrow wound in the ear, and they kept on shooting and wounding us. With our muskets and crossbows and with good sword play we did not fail as stout fighters, and when they came to feel the edge of our swords little by little they fell back, but it was only so as to shoot at us in greater safety. Mesa, our artilleryman, killed many of them with his cannon, for they were formed in great squadrons and they did not open out so that he could fire at them as he pleased, but with all the hurts and wounds which we gave them, we could not drive them off. I said to Diego de Ordás "it seems to me that we ought to close up and charge them," for in truth they suffered greatly from the strokes and thrusts of our swords, and that was why they fell away from us, both from fear of these swords, and the better to shoot their arrows and hurl their javelins and the hail of stones. Ordás replied that it was not good advice, for there were three hundred Indians to every one of us, and that we could not hold out against such a multitude,—so there we stood enduring their attack. However, we did agree to get as near as we could to them, as I had advised Ordás, so as to give them a bad time with our swordsmanship, and they suffered so much from it that they retreated towards a swamp.

During all this time Cortés and his horsemen failed to appear, although we greatly longed for him, and we feared that by chance some disaster had befallen him.

I remember that when we fired shots the Indians gave great shouts and whistles and threw dust and rubbish into the air so that we should not see the damage done to them, and they sounded their trumpets and drums and shouted and whistled and cried " Alala! alala!"

Just at this time we caught sight of our horsemen, and as the great Indian host was crazed with its attack on us, it did not at once perceive them coming up behind their backs, and as the plain was level ground and the horsemen were good riders, and many of the horses were very handy and fine gallopers, they came quickly on the enemy and speared them as they chose. As soon as we saw the horsemen we fell on the Indians with such energy that with us attacking on one side and the horsemen on the other, they soon turned tail. The Indians thought that the horse and its rider was all one animal, for they had never seen horses up to this time.

The savannas and fields were crowded with Indians running to take refuge in the thick woods near by.

After we had defeated the enemy Cortés told us that he had not been able to come to us sooner as there was a swamp in the way, and he had to fight his way through another force of warriors before he could reach us, and three horsemen and five horses had been wounded.

As soon as the horsemen had dismounted under some trees and houses, we returned thanks to God for giving us so complete a victory.

As it was Lady day we gave to the town which was afterwards founded here the name of Santa Maria de la Victoria, on account of this great victory being won on Our Lady's day. This was the first battle that we fought under Cortés in New Spain.

After this we bound up the hurts of the wounded with cloths, for we had nothing else, and we doctored the horses by searing their wounds with the fat from the body of a dead Indian which we cut up to get out the fat, and we went to look at the dead lying on the plain and there were more than eight hundred of them, the greater number killed by thrusts, the others by the cannon, muskets and crossbows, and many were stretched on the ground half dead. Where the horsemen had passed, numbers of them lay dead or groaning from their wounds. The battle lasted over an hour, and the Indians fought all the time like brave warriors, until the horsemen came up.

We took five prisoners, two of them Captains. As it was late and we had had enough of fighting, and we had not eaten anything, we returned to our camp. Then we buried the two soldiers who had been killed, one by a wound in the ear, and the other by a wound in the throat, and we seared the wounds of the others and of the horses with the fat of the Indian, and after posting sentinels and guards, we had supper and rested.

It is on this occasion that Francisco López de Gomara says that Francisco de Morla set out on a dapple gray horse before Cortés and the other horsemen arrived, and that the sainted apostles Señor Santiago and Señor San Pedro appeared. I say that all our doings and our victories are at the hands of our Lord Jesus Christ, and that in this battle there were so many Indians to every one of us that they could have blinded us with the dust they raised but for the pity of God who always helped us. It may be that as Gomara says the Glorious Apostles Señor Santiago and Señor San Pedro came to our aid and that I, being a sinner was not worthy to behold them. What I saw was Francisco de Morla, on a chestnut horse, who came up at the same time as Cortés, and it seems to me that now as I write I can see again with these sinful eyes all that battle in the very way that it took place, and although I am a poor sinner and not worthy to see either of those glorious apostles, there were there in our company over four hundred soldiers and Cortés himself and many other gentlemen, and it would have been talked about, and evidence would have been taken, and a church would have been built when the town was founded, and the town would have been named Santiago de la Victoria, or San Pedro de la Victoria instead of Santa Maria de la Victoria. If it was as Gomara says we must have all been very bad Christians, when our Lord God sent his holy Apostle to us, not to recognise the great favour that he was showing to us, and not daily to have venerated that church. I wish to God it were as the historian Gomara says, but, until I read his history, one never heard about it among the conquistadors who were there at the time. . . .

I have already said that we captured five Indians during the battle of whom two were captains. When Aguilar spoke to these men he found out from what they said that they were fit persons to be sent as messengers, and he advised Cortés to free them, so that they might go and talk to the Caciques of the town and any others they might see. These two messengers were given green and blue beads, and Aguilar spoke many pleasant and flattering words to them, telling them that they had nothing to fear as we wished to treat them like brothers, that it was their own fault that they had made war on us, and that now they had better collect together all the Caciques of the different towns as we wished to talk to them, and he gave them much other advice in a gentle way so as to gain their good will. The messengers went off willingly and spoke to the Caciques and chief men, and told them all we wished them to know about our desire for peace.

When our envoys had been listened to, it was settled among them that fifteen Indian slaves, all with stained faces and ragged cloaks and loin cloths, should at once be sent to us with fowls and baked fish and maize cakes. When these men came before Cortés he received them graciously, but Aguilar the interpreter asked them rather angrily why they had come with their faces in that state, that it looked more as though they came to fight than to treat for peace; and he told them to go back to the Caciques and inform them, that if they wished for peace in the way we offered it, chieftains should come and treat for it, as was always the custom, and that they should not send slaves. But even these painted faced slaves were treated with consideration by us and blue beads were sent by them in sign of peace, and to soothe their feelings.

The next day thirty Indian Chieftains, clad in good cloaks, came to visit us and brought fowls, fish, fruit and maize cakes, and asked leave from Cortés to burn and bury the bodies of the dead who had fallen in the recent battles, so that they should not smell badly or be eaten by lions and tigers. Permission was at once given them and they hastened to bring many people to bury and burn the bodies according to their customs.

Cortés learnt from the Caciques that over eight hundred men were missing, not counting those who had been carried off wounded.

They said that they could not tarry with us either to discuss the matter or make peace, for on the morrow the chieftains and leaders of all the towns would have assembled, and that then they would agree about a peace.

As Cortés was very sagacious about everything, he said, laughing, to us soldiers who happened to be in his company, "Do you know, gentlemen, that it seems to me that the Indians are terrified at the horses and may think that they and the cannon alone make war on them. I have thought of something which will confirm this belief, and that is to bring the mare belonging to Juan Sedeño, which foaled the other day on board ship, and tie her up where I am now standing and also to bring the stallion of Ortiz the musician, which is very excitable, near enough to scent the mare, and when he has scented her to lead each of them off separately so that the Caciques who are coming shall not hear the horse neighing as they approach, not until they are standing before me and are talking to me." We did just as Cortés ordered and brought the horse and mare, and the horse soon detected the scent of her in Cortés's quarters. In addition to this Cortés ordered the largest cannon that we possessed to be loaded with a large ball and a good charge of powder.

About mid-day forty Indians arrived, all of them Caciques of good bearing, wearing rich mantles such as are used by them. They saluted Cortés and all of us, and brought incense and fumigated all of us who were present, and they asked pardon for their past behaviour, and said that henceforth they would be friendly.

Cortés, through Aguilar the Interpreter, answered them in a rather grave manner, as though he were angry, that they well knew how many times he had asked them to maintain peace, that the fault was theirs, and that now they deserved to be put to death, they and all the people of their towns, but that as we were the vassals of a great King and Lord named the Emperor Don Carlos, who had sent us to these countries, and ordered us to help and favour those who would enter his royal service, that if they were now as well disposed as they said they were, that we would take this course, but that if they were not, some of those *Tepustles* would jump out and kill them (they call iron *Tepustle* in their language) for some of the *Tepustles* were still angry because they had made war on us. At this moment the order was secretly given to put a match to the cannon which had been loaded, and it went off with such a thunderclap as was wanted, and the ball went buzzing over the hills, and as it was midday and very still it made a great noise, and the Caciques were terrified on hearing it. As they had never seen anything like it they believed what Cortés had told them was true. Then Cortés told them, through Aguilar, not to be afraid for he had given orders that no harm should be done to them.

Just then the horse that had scented the mare was brought and tied up not far distant from where Cortés was talking to the Caciques, and, as the mare had been tied up at the place where Cortés and the Indians were talking, the horse began to paw the ground and neigh and become wild with excitement, looking all the time towards the Indians and the place whence the scent of the mare had reached him, and the Caciques thought that he was roaring at them and they were terrified. When Cortés observed their state of mind, he rose from his seat and went to the horse and told two orderlies to lead it far away, and said to the Indians that he had told the horse not to be angry as they were friendly and wished to make peace.

While this was going on there arrived more than thirty Indian carriers, whom the natives call *Tamenes,* who brought a meal of fowls and fish and fruits and other food, and it appears that they had lagged behind and could not reach us at the same time as the Caciques.

Cortés had a long conversation with these chieftains and Caciques and they told him that they would all come on the next day and would bring a present and would discuss other matters, and then they went away quite contented.

And there I will leave them until the next day.

Early the next morning, the 15th March, 1519,* many Caciques and chiefs of Tabasco and the neighbouring towns arrived and paid great

---

*This is evidently an error, as Bernal Díaz has already stated that the Battle of Cintla was fought on Lady day, the 25th March.

Figure 5.   Malintzin, or doña Marina, became Cortés's interpreter and a major figure in the conquest. Later indigenous pictorial descriptions of these events usually emphasize her role.
Source: Lienzo de Tlaxcala, taken from C. A. Burland, *Montezuma: Lord of the Aztecs* (New York: G. P. Putnam's Sons, 1973), 194.

respect to us all, and they brought a present of gold, consisting of four diadems and some gold lizards, and two [ornaments] like little dogs, and earrings, and five ducks, and two masks with Indian faces, and two gold soles for sandals, and some other things of little value. I do not remember how much the things were worth; and they brought cloth, such as they make and wear, which was quilted stuff. My readers will have heard from those who know that province that there is nothing of much value in it.

This present, however, was worth nothing in comparison with the twenty women that were given us, among them one very excellent woman called Doña Marina, for so she was named when she became a Christian. I will leave off talking about her and the other women who were brought to us, and will tell how Cortés received this present with pleasure and went aside with all the Caciques, and with Aguilar, the interpreter, to hold converse, and he told them that he gave them thanks for what they had brought with them, but there was one thing that he must ask of them, namely, that they should re-occupy the town with all their people, women and children, and he wished to see it repeopled within two days, for he would recognize that as a sign of true peace. The Caciques sent at once to summon all the inhabitants with their women and children and within two days they were again settled in the town.

One other thing Cortés asked of the chiefs and that was to give up their idols and sacrifices, and this they said they would do, and, through Aguilar, Cortés told them as well as he was able about matters concerning our holy faith, how we were Christians and worshipped one true and only God, and he showed them an image of Our Lady with her precious Son in her arms and explained to them that we paid the greatest reverence to it as it was the image of the Mother of our Lord God who was in heaven. The Caciques replied that they liked the look of the great Teleciguata (for in their language great ladies are called Teleciguatas) and [begged] that she might be given them to keep in their town, and Cortés said that the image should be given to them and ordered them to make a well-constructed altar, and this they did at once.

The next morning, Cortés ordered two of our carpenters, named Alonzo Yañez and Alvaro López, to make a very tall cross.

When all this had been settled Cortés asked the Caciques what was their reason for attacking us three times when we had asked them to keep the peace; the chief replied that he had already asked pardon for their acts and had been forgiven, that the Cacique of Chanpoton, his brother, had advised it, and that he feared to be accused of cowardice, for he had already been reproached and dishonoured for not having attacked the other captain who had come with four ships, (he must have meant Juan de Grijalva) and he also said that the Indian whom we had brought as an Interpreter, who escaped in the night, had advised them to attack us both by day and night.

Cortés then ordered this man to be brought before him without fail, but they replied that when he saw that the battle was going against them, he had taken to flight, and they knew not where he was although search had been made for him; but we came to know that they had offered him as a sacrifice because his counsel had cost them so dear.

Cortés also asked them where they procured their gold and jewels, and they replied, from the direction of the setting sun, and said "Culua" and "Mexico," and as we did not know what Mexico and Culua meant we paid little attention to it.

Then we brought another interpreter named Francisco, whom we had captured during Grijalva's expedition, who has already been mentioned by me, but he understood nothing of the Tabasco language only that of

Culua which is the Mexican tongue. By means of signs he told Cortés that Culua was far ahead, and he repeated "Mexico" which we did not understand.

So the talk ceased until the next day when the sacred image of Our Lady and the Cross were set up on the altar and we all paid reverence to them, and Padre Fray Bartolomé de Olmedo said mass and all the Caciques and chiefs were present and we gave the name of Santa Maria de la Victoria to the town, and by this name the town of Tabasco is now called. The same friar, with Aguilar as interpreter, preached many good things about our holy faith to the twenty Indian women who had been given us, telling them not to believe in the Idols which they had been wont to trust in, for they were evil things and not gods, and that they should offer no more sacrifices to them for they would lead them astray, but that they should worship our Lord Jesus Christ, and immediately afterwards they were baptized. One Indian lady who was given to us here was christened Doña Marina, and she was truly a great chieftainess and the daughter of great Caciques and the mistress of vassals, and this her appearance clearly showed. Later on I will relate why it was and in what manner she was brought here.

I do not clearly remember the names of all the other women, and it is not worth while to name any of them; however, they were the first women to become Christians in New Spain.

Cortés allotted one of them to each of his captains and Doña Marina, as she was good looking and intelligent and without embarrassment, he gave to Alonzo Hernández Puertocarrero, who I have already said was a distinguished gentleman, and cousin of the Count of Medellin. When Puertocarrero went to Spain, Doña Marina lived with Cortés, and bore him a son named Don Martin Cortés.

We remained five days in this town, to look after the wounded and those who were suffering from pain in the loins, from which they all recovered. Furthermore, Cortés drew the Caciques to him by kindly converse, and told them how our master the Emperor, whose vassals we were, had under his orders many great lords, and that it would be well for them also to render him obedience, and that then, whatever they might be in need of, whether it was our protection or any other necessity, if they would make it known to him, no matter where he might be, he would come to their assistance.

The Caciques all thanked him for this, and thereupon all declared themselves the vassals of our great Emperor. These were the first vassals to render submission to His Majesty in New Spain.

Cortés then ordered the Caciques to come with their women and children early the next day, which was Palm Sunday, to the altar, to pay homage to the holy image of Our Lady and to the Cross, and at the same time Cortés ordered them to send six Indian carpenters to accompany our carpenters to the town of Cintla where our Lord God was pleased to give us victory in the battle which I have described, there to cut a cross on a great tree called a Ceiba which grew there, and they did it so that it might last a long time, for as the bark is renewed the cross will show there for ever. When this was done he ordered the Indians to get ready all the canoes that they owned to help us to embark, for we wished to set sail on that holy day because the pilots had come to tell Cortés that the ships ran a great risk from a *Norther* which is a dangerous gale.

The next day, early in the morning, all the Caciques and chiefs came in their canoes with all their women and children and stood in the court where we had placed the church and cross, and many branches of trees had already been cut ready to be carried in the procession. Then the Caciques beheld us all, Cortés, as well as the captains, and every one of us marching together with the greatest reverence in a devout procession, and the Padre de la Merced and the priest, Juan Diaz, clad in their vestments, said mass, and we paid reverence to and kissed the Holy Cross, while the Caciques and Indians stood looking on at us.

When our solemn festival was over the chiefs approached and offered Cortés ten fowls, and baked fish and vegetables, and we took leave of them, and Cortés again commended to their care the Holy image and the sacred crosses and told them always to keep the place clean and well swept and to deck the cross with garlands and to reverence it, and then they would enjoy good health and bountiful harvests.

It was growing late when we got on board ship and the next day, Monday, we set sail in the morning and with a fair wind laid our course for San Juan de Ulúa, keeping close in shore all the time. . . .

Before telling about the great Montezuma and his famous City of Mexico and the Mexicans, I wish to give some account of Doña Marina, who from her childhood had been the mistress and Cacica* of towns and vassals. It happened in this way:

Her father and mother were chiefs and Caciques of a town called Paynala, which had other towns subject to it, and stood about eight leagues from the town of Coatzacoalcos. Her father died while she was still a

---

* Feminine form of cacique.

little child, and her mother married another Cacique, a young man, and bore him a son. It seems that the father and mother had a great affection for this son and it was agreed between them that he should succeed to their honours when their days were done. So that there should be no impediment to this, they gave the little girl, Doña Marina, to some Indians from Xicalango * and this they did by night so as to escape observation, and they then spread the report that she had died, and as it happened at this time that a child of one of their Indian slaves died they gave out that it was their daughter and the heiress who was dead.

The Indians of Xicalango gave the child to the people of Tabasco, and the Tabasco people gave her to Cortés. I myself knew her mother, and the old woman's son and her half-brother, when he was already grown up and ruled the town jointly with his mother, for the second husband of the old lady was dead. When they became Christians, the old lady was called Marta and the son Lázaro. I knew all this very well because in the year 1523 after the conquest of Mexico and the other provinces, when Cristóval de Olid revolted in Honduras, and Cortés was on his way there, he passed through Coatzacoalcos and I and the greater number of the settlers of that town accompanied him on that expedition as I shall relate in the proper time and place. As Doña Marina proved herself such an excellent woman and good interpreter throughout the wars in New Spain, Tlascala and Mexico (as I shall show later on) Cortés always took her with him, and during that expedition she was married to a gentleman named Juan Jaramillo at the town of Orizaba, before certain witnesses, one of whom was named Aranda, a settler in Tabasco and this man told [me] about the marriage (not in the way the historian Gomara relates it).

Doña Marina was a person of the greatest importance and was obeyed without question by the Indians throughout New Spain.

When Cortés was in the town of Coatzacoalcos he sent to summon to his presence all the Caciques of that province in order to make them a speech about our holy religion, and about their good treatment, and among the Caciques who assembled was the mother of Doña Marina and her half-brother, Lázaro.

Some time before this Doña Marina had told me that she belonged to that province and that she was the mistress of vassals, and Cortés also knew it well, as did Aguilar, the interpreter. In such a manner it was that mother, daughter and son came together, and it was easy enough to see

---

*Xicalango, on the southern side of the Laguna de Términos, was an outlying stronghold of the Aztec Empire.

that she was the daughter from the strong likeness she bore to her mother.

These relations were in great fear of Doña Marina, for they thought that she had sent for them to put them to death, and they were weeping.

When Doña Marina saw them in tears, she consoled them and told them to have no fear, that when they had given her over to the men from Xicalango, they knew not what they were doing, and she forgave them for doing it, and she gave them many jewels of gold, and raiment, and told them to return to their town, and said that God had been very gracious to her in freeing her from the worship of idols and making her a Christian, and letting her bear a son to her lord and master Cortés and in marrying her to such a gentleman as Juan Jaramillo, who was now her husband. That she would rather serve her husband and Cortés than anything else in the world, and would not exchange her place to be Cacica of all the provinces in New Spain.

All this which I have repeated here I know for certain (and I swear to it).

This seems to me very much like what took place between Joseph and his brethren in Egypt when they came into his power over the matter of the wheat. It is what actually happened and not the story which was told to Gomara, who also says other things which I will leave unnoticed.

To go back to my subject: Doña Marina knew the language of Coatzacoalcos, which is that common to Mexico, and she knew the language of Tabasco, as did also Jerónimo de Aguilar, who spoke the language of Yucatan and Tabasco, which is one and the same. So that these two could understand one another clearly, and Aguilar translated into Castilian for Cortés.

This was the great beginning of our conquests and thus, thanks be to God, things prospered with us. I have made a point of explaining this matter, because without the help of Doña Marina we could not have understood the language of New Spain and Mexico.

Here I will leave off, and go on later to tell how we disembarked in the Port of San Juan de Ulúa.

I have already said that the relations and friends of Diego Velásquez were going about the camp raising objections to our going on any further and insisting that we should return at once from San Juan de Ulúa to the Island of Cuba. It appears that Cortés had already talked the matter over with Alonza Hernández Puertocarrero, and Pedro de Alvarado and his four brothers, Jorge, Gonzalo, Gómez and Juan, and with

Cristóbal de Olid, Alonzo de Ávila, Juan de Escalante, Francisco de Lugo, and with me and other gentlemen and captains, and suggested that we should beg of him to be our captain. Francisco de Montejo understood what was going on and was on the watch. One night, after midnight, Alonzo Hernández Puertocarrero, Juan de Escalante and Francisco de Lugo, came to my hut. Francisco de Lugo and I came from the same country and were distant kinsmen. They said to me: "Señor Bernal Díaz, come out with your arms and go the rounds; we will accompany Cortés who is just now going the rounds." When I was a little distance from the hut they said to me: "Look to it, sir, that you keep secret for a time what we wish to tell you, for it is a matter of importance, and see that your companions in your hut know nothing about it, for they are of the party of Diego Velásquez." What they said to me was: "Sir, does it seem to you to be right that Hernando Cortés should have deceived us all in bringing us here, he having proclaimed in Cuba that he was coming to settle, and now we find out that he has no power to do so, but only to trade, and they want us to return to Santiago de Cuba with all the gold that has been collected, and we shall lose our all, for will not Diego Velásquez take all the gold as he did before? Look, sir, counting this present expedition, you have already come to this country three times, spending your own property and contracting debts and risking your life many times with the wounds you have received. Many of us gentlemen who know that we are your honour's friends wish you to understand that this must not go on; that this land must be settled in the name of His Majesty, and by Hernando Cortés in His Majesty's name, while we await the opportunity to make it known to our lord the King in Spain. Be sure, sir, to cast your vote so that all of us unanimously and willingly choose him captain, for it will be a service to God and our lord the King." I replied that it was not a wise decision to return to Cuba and that it would be a good thing for the country to be settled and that we should choose Cortés as General and Chief Justice until his Majesty should order otherwise. This agreement passed from soldier to soldier and the friends and relations of Diego Velásquez, who were more numerous than we were, got to know of it, and with overbold words asked Cortés why he was craftily arranging to remain in this country instead of returning to render an account of his doings to the man who had sent him as captain, and they told him that Diego Velásquez would not approve of it, and that the sooner we embarked the better; that there was no use in his subterfuges and secret meetings with the soldiers, for we had neither supplies nor men, nor any possibility of founding a settlement. Cortés answered without a sign of anger, and said that he agreed with them; that he would not go against the instructions and notes which he had received from Diego Velásquez, and he issued an order for us all to embark on the following day, each one in the ship in which he had come. We who had made the agreement answered that it was not fair to deceive us so, that in Cuba he had proclaimed that he was coming to make a settlement, whereas he had only come to trade; and we demanded on behalf of our Lord God and of His Majesty that he should at once form a settlement and give up any other plan, because that would be of the greatest benefit and service to God and the King; and they placed many other well-reasoned arguments before him saying that the natives would never let us land again as they had done this time, and that as soon as a settlement was made in the country soldiers would gather in from all the islands to give us help and that Velásquez had ruined us all by stating publicly that he had received a decree from His Majesty to form a settlement, the contrary being the case; that we wished to form a settlement, and to let those depart who desired to return to Cuba. So Cortés agreed to it, although he pretended to need much begging, as the saying goes: "You are very pressing, and I want to do it,"—and he stipulated that we should make him Chief Justice and Captain General, and the worst of all that we conceded was that we should give him a fifth of all the gold which should be obtained, after the royal fifth had been deducted, and then we gave him the very fullest powers in the presence of the King's Notary, Diego de Godoy, embracing all that I have here stated. We at once set to work to found and settle a town, which was called the "Villa rica de la Vera Cruz" because we arrived on Thursday of the (last) supper and landed on "Holy Friday of the Cross" and "rich" because of what that gentleman said, as I have related in a former chapter who approached Cortés and said to him: "Behold rich lands! May you know how to govern them well!" and what he wanted to say was—"May you remain as their Captain General." That gentleman was Alonzo Hernández Puertocarrero.

To go back to my story: as soon as the town was founded we appointed alcaldes and regidores; the former were Alonzo Hernández Puertocarrero and Francisco Montejo. In the case of Montejo, it was because he was not on very good terms with Cortés that Cortés ordered him to be named as Alcalde, so as to place him in the highest position. I need not give the names of the Regidores, for it is no use naming only a few of them; but I must mention the fact that a pillory was placed in the Plaza and a gallows set up outside the town. We chose Pedro de Alvarado as captain of expeditions and Cristóbal de Olid as Maestro de Campo.* Juan de Escalante was chosen chief Alguacil;† Gonzalo Mejia, treasurer, and Alonzo de Ávila accountant. A certain Corral was named as Ensign, because Villaroel who had been Ensign was dismissed from the post on account of some offence (I do not exactly know what) he had given Cortés about an Indian woman from Cuba. Ochoa, a Biscayan, and Alonzo Romero were appointed Alguaciles of the Camp.‡

It will be said that I have made no mention of the Captain Gonzalo de Sandoval, he of whom our lord the Emperor has heard such reports, who was such a renowned captain that he ranked next to Cortés in our estimation. I say this was because at that time he was a youth, and we did not take such count of him and of other valiant captains until we saw him grow in worth in such a way that Cortés and all the soldiers held him in the same esteem as Cortés himself, as I shall tell later on.

I must leave my story here and say that the historian, Gomara, states that he was told all that which he has written down. But I assert that these things happened as I have related them. Gomara is wrong in other things that he wrote because his informants did not give him a true account. However good the style may be in which he tells the story, so that all may appear to be true, I assert that all he says about this matter is wrong.

I will drop the subject now and go on to tell how the party of Diego Velásquez tried to stop the election of Cortés as captain, and to insist on our returning to the Island of Cuba.

When the partisans of Diego Velásquez realized the fact that we had chosen Cortés for our Captain and Chief Justice, and had founded a town and chosen the Alcaldes and Regidores, and appointed Pedro de Alvarado as captain [of expeditions] and named the Alguacil Mayor and Maestro de Campo and had done all that I have narrated, they were angry and furious and they began to excite factions and meetings and to use abusive language about Cortés and those of us who had elected him, saying that it was not right to do these things unless all the captains and soldiers who had come on the expedition had been parties to it; that Diego Velásquez had given Cortés no such powers, only authority to trade, and that we partisans of Cortés should take care that our insolence did not so increase as to bring us to blows. Then Cortés secretly told

* Maestro de Campo: Quartermaster.
† Alguacil Mayor: High Constable.
‡ Alguacil del Real: Constables and storekeepers.

Juan de Escalante that we should make him produce the instructions given him by Diego Velásquez. Upon this Cortés drew them from his bosom and gave them to the King's scribe to read aloud. In these instructions were the words: "As soon as you have gained all you can by trading, you will return," and the document was signed by Diego Velásquez and countersigned by his Secretary, Andrés de Duero. We begged Cortés to cause this document to be attached to the deed recording the power we had given him, as well as the proclamation which he issued in the Island of Cuba. And this was done so that his Majesty in Spain should know that all that we did was done in his royal service, and that they should not bring against us anything but the truth; and it was a good precaution, seeing how we were treated in Spain by Don Juan Rodriguez de Fonseca, Bishop of Burgos and Archbishop of Rosano (for such were his titles) who, we knew for certain, took steps to destroy us as I shall tell later on.

After this was done, these same friends and dependents of Diego Velásquez returned to Cortés to say that it was not right that he should have been chosen Captain without their consent and that they did not wish to remain under his command, but to return at once to the Island of Cuba. Cortés replied that he would detain no one by force, and that to anyone who came to ask leave to return, he would willingly grant it, even although he were left alone. With this some of them were quieted, but not Juan Velásquez de Leon who was a relation of Diego Velásquez, and Diego de Ordás, and Escobar, whom we called the Page, for he had been brought up by Diego Velásquez, and Pedro Escudero and other friends of Diego Velásquez; and it came to this, that they refused all obedience to Cortés. With our assistance, Cortés determined to make prisoners of Juan Velásquez de Leon, and Diego de Ordás, and Escobar the Page, and Pedro Escudero and others whose names I do not remember, and we took care that the others should create no disturbance. These men remained prisoners for some days, in chains and under guard. . . .

When all that I have related had been settled and done with, it was arranged that Pedro de Alvarado should go inland to some towns which we had been told were near by and see what the country was like and bring back maize and some sort of supplies, for there was a great want of food in camp. Alvarado took one hundred soldiers with him, among them fifteen crossbowmen and six musketeers. More than half his soldiers were partisans of Diego Velásquez. All Cortés's party remained with him for fear there should be any further disturbance or tricks played or any rising against him, until things became more settled.

Alvarado went first to some small towns subject to another town called Cotastan,* where the language of Culua was spoken. This name, Culua, in this country means the common language of the partisans of Mexico and Montezuma; so that in all that country when Culua is mentioned, it means people vassal and subject to Mexico, and must be thus understood, just as we should speak of the Romans and their allies.

When Pedro de Alvarado reached these towns he found that they had all been deserted that same day, and he found in the *cues*[2] bodies of men and boys who had been sacrificed, and the walls and altars stained with blood and the hearts placed as offerings before the Idols. He also found the stones on which the sacrifices were made and the stone knives with which to open the chest so as to take out the heart.

Pedro de Alvarado said that he found most of the bodies without arms or legs, and that he was told by some Indians that they had been carried off to be eaten, and our soldiers were astounded at such great cruelty. I will not say any more of the number of sacrifices, although we found the same thing in every town we afterwards entered, and I will go back to Pedro de Alvarado and say that he found the towns well provisioned but deserted that very day by their inhabitants, so that he could not find more than two Indians to carry maize, and each soldier had to load himself with poultry and vegetables, and he returned to camp without doing any other damage (although he had good opportunity for doing it) because Cortés had given orders to that effect, so that there should be no repetition of what happened at Cozumel.

We were pleased enough in camp even with the little food that had been brought, for all evils and hardships disappear when there is plenty to eat.

Here it is that the historian, Gomara, says that Cortés went inland with four hundred soldiers. He was misinformed, for the first to go was [Alvarado] as I have stated here, and no other. . . .

* Cotaxtla.
[2] *Cues:* Temples.

HERNÁN CORTÉS

Letters to Charles V

After disregarding Governor Velázquez's instructions and feeling threatened by those still faithful to him, Cortés needed to justify his actions. Cortés's first report to the king, written while still in Yucatan, has never been found. In this short extract from his first surviving letter, the so-called Letter from Vera Cruz, Cortés provides an account in which, for the greater service of God and the king, the men prevail on Cortés to take the actions he did. Written in the third person as though by a disinterested observer, the letter also reports the sending of treasure to the king, certainly done in hopes of gaining royal support for Cortés's actions. Those hopes also seem to lay behind the first enthusiastic reports Cortés gives of the land itself, a land seeming to promise further riches (see page 78). The tension between Cortés's supporters and the followers of Velázquez did not abate and the final excerpt from Cortés's second letter explains the reason for his grounding of the ships.

Letter I

. . . Now as many of us who ventured in this fleet were persons of rank, knights and gentlemen, eager to serve our Lord and your Majesties, and desirous alike of extending the power of their royal crown and increasing their dominions and revenue, we joined ourselves together at this time and conferred with the Captain Hernando Cortés, pointing out that this land was fruitful, rich in gold, so far as could be judged from the samples which the chief had brought us, and that the chief and all the natives seemed to bear us very good will; on which account it seemed to us profitable to the service of your Majesties that the instructions given by Diego Velázquez to the Captain Hernando Cortés should not be carried out in that land, to wit that as much gold as possible should be obtained by barter from the natives, and once obtained an immediate return made to Cuba, by which the said Diego Velázquez and our Captain would alone reap the fruits of the expedition: but to all of us it seemed better that a

Hernando Cortés: Five Letters, 1519–1526, ed. J. Bayard Morris (New York: Norton, 1991), 16–20, 33–34.

town should be founded there in the name of your Majesties with a justiciary and council, so that in this land your Majesties might possess overlordship as in their other kingdoms and domains; for, the land once settled with Spaniards, in addition to the royal dominions and revenues being increased, your Majesties might be graciously pleased to grant favours both to us and to settlers who should come from further lands.

And thus agreed we joined ourselves together, no man being dissentient, but with one mind and purpose we made a demand of the said Captain in which we declared: That since he must perceive how agreeable it was both to the service of God and your Majesties that this land should be settled, giving him the reasons which have been set forth above to your Majesties, we therefore required him to cease forthwith from such barter with the natives as he had come to do, since by such means the land would be truly destroyed and your Majesties done no small disservice: likewise we asked and required him to appoint *alcaldes* and *regidores* for the town which was to be founded by us, all this with certain protestations if so be he should not carry out what we demanded. On our presenting this request the Captain replied that he would give his answer on the following day, and considering how agreeable our request was to the service of your Majesties, he accordingly replied, saying that he was desirous above all things of doing some service to your Majesties, and hence unmindful of the profit which would accrue to him should he continue bartering as had been his intention (by which he might reimburse himself for the great expenses incurred with the aforesaid Diego Velázquez in the fitting out of the fleet) but rather putting all this aside, he was well pleased and content to do what we demanded, since it was agreeable to the service of your Majesties. And upon this he began immediately with great diligence to settle and found a town to which he gave the name of the Rica Villa of Vera Cruz, and appointed those whose names appear at the foot of this letter as *alcaldes* and *regidores* of the town, duly receiving from us the solemn oath as is wont and customary on such occasions.

This done, on the following day we entered into our office and charges, and being thus met together we sent to the Captain Hernando Cortés asking him in the name of your Majesties to show us the powers and instructions which the aforementioned Diego Velázquez had given to him on coming to these parts. He lost no time in sending for them, and having seen, read and carefully examined them we found that to the best of our understanding the Captain no longer held any authority according to the documents before mentioned, and such authority having expired he could no longer execute justice or act as Captain. But it appeared to us well, most excellent Princes, that for the sake of peace, quietness and good government amongst us, there should be one person elected in your Majesties' name to act in this town and district in the service of your Majesties as Chief Justice and Captain General of the forces, to whom we should all pay respect until such time as your Majesties having received our report should provide other means by which your Majesties might best be served. Now there was no person better fitted for such a charge than Hernando Cortés, for in addition to being just such a man as is fitting for an office of this kind, he is very greatly desirous of serving your Majesties, and not only has he wide experience of the islands and mainland of these parts, by reason of which he has always given a good account of himself, but he spent freely what he had in order to accompany this fleet in the service of your Majesties, and moreover held of small account (as we have already related) all that he might gain should he continue bartering with the natives as was his first intent, and accordingly we appointed him in your Majesties' name Chief Justice and *alcalde mayor,* and received from him the oath which is necessary in such case. This done, as was agreeable to the royal service of your Majesties, we received him in his official capacity in our public assembly as Chief Justice and Captain of your Majesties' royal armies, and thus he will remain until such time as your Majesties may provide what is more agreeable to their royal service. We desire to give an account of all this to your Majesties so that they may know what has been done here and the state and manner in which we now remain.

This matter concluded, being united in public assembly we agreed to write to your Majesties sending them all the gold, silver and jewels which we have obtained in this country over and above the fifth part which belonged to them by right, and it was agreed that by giving the whole of the first fruits, not keeping so much as a single thing for ourselves, we should be doing some service to your Majesties and show plainly the very great zeal that we have in their service, as we have already displayed in adventuring our lives and fortunes. This being agreed upon, we elected as our messengers Alonso Fernández Portocarrero and Francisco de Montejo, whom we send to your Majesties with all the aforementioned treasure, that they may on our behalf kiss their royal hands and in our name and the name of this town and council beg your Majesties to favour us with certain things necessary to the service of God and your Majesties and the common weal of this town, as is more minutely set out in the special instructions which we have given them. Which requests with all due respect we humbly beg your Majesties to grant, and to concede all those privileges which in the name of this council and of ourselves they may beg, for in addition to your Majesties doing great service to our Lord in this matter, they will be conferring a very signal favour on this town and council such as we daily hope may be the pleasure of your Majesties. . . .

Letter II

. . . Now, as I believe I wrote to your Majesty, certain of those in my company who were friends and servants of Diego Velázquez were vexed at what I did in your Majesty's service, and indeed certain of them were desirous of leaving me and quitting the land, in particular four Spaniards, by name, Juán Escudero, Diego Cermeño, Gonzalo de Ungría, pilots, and Alonso Peñate. These men, as they afterwards confessed, had decided to seize a brig which was in the port together with a certain amount of provisions in the way of bread and salt pork, kill the captain and set sail for Cuba to inform Diego Velázquez of the vessel which I was sending to your Majesty, what it contained and the route which it was to take, so that Velázquez might send out ships to intercept it, which indeed on getting to hear by other means of its departure he did: for, as I have been informed, he dispatched a light caravel after my vessel which would have captured it had it not already passed the strait of the Bahamas. These men confessed moreover that there were others who had the same design of informing Diego Velázquez of the treasure ship's departure. In view of their confessions I punished them according to the law and (as it seemed to me) the exigencies of the moment and the furtherance of your Majesty's interests. Further, in addition to those who desired to quit the land because they were friends or servants of Diego Velázquez there were others who seeing the great extent of the land, its natives, their manners and numbers, so large in comparison with so few Spaniards, were of the same mind. Accordingly, thinking that if I left the ships there they would make off with them and leave me practically alone, by which had been prevented the great service which has been done to God and to your Majesty in this land, I found a means under the pretence that the ships were no longer navigable to pile them up on the shore. On this all abandoned any hope of leaving the land and I set out relieved from the suspicion that once my back was turned I should be deserted by the men whom I had left behind in the town. . . .

3

Encounters

The Spaniards and the Mexica had contrasting ways in how they viewed and tried to make sense of each other. The Nahua seemed to be ambivalent, alternating between a view that the Spaniards were strange but understandable simply as a new kind of foreigner and an alternative vision of them as supernatural beings. The Spaniards looked to earlier encounters with other Native Americans and to their older traditions of diplomacy and contact with other non-Europeans. The Europeans were already creating a kind of ethnography about the peoples of the new conquest.

In the first document in this chapter, Cortés in his earliest surviving letter to the king includes a description of the land and the people. In it, he frequently compares Muslim (Moorish) customs to native customs to make sense of indigenous ways. He also concentrates on the practice of human sacrifice as a singularly reprehensible custom and one which helped to further justify the spreading of Catholicism by the extension of the king's control. This union of observation with self-serving emphases was typical of many European descriptions of the peoples of the Americas.

Bernal Díaz's account (see pp. 85–91) takes note of the exchange of gifts and of Cortés's strategies to learn about the politics and wealth of the region. His report is also sensitive to native ways of doing things. For example, he remarks on the importance of pictographic representation for the Mexica and how those images were used to communicate information.

The Nahua account (see pp. 91–99) presented here is more problematic. It is drawn from Lockhart's translation of the Nahuatl relations gathered by the Franciscan Bernardino de Sahagún about thirty years after the conquest. While its attention to certain details — the style of the capes offered as gifts, the costumes of the gods — seems authentic, the emphasis on Moctezuma's weakness and on the possible supernatural nature of the strangers indicates a "shading" of the account made by those interviewed in order to please the Spanish authorities of the time or to criticize the failed Mexica leadership. The tendency to identify the Spaniards with a returning deity come to reclaim his kingdom — in some accounts Huitzilopoctli, patron of the Mexica, himself, in others, Quetzalcoatl, the ancient god of the Toltecs — became a standard aspect of the indigenous accounts, and later by the Spanish chroniclers and the mestizo historians. As discussed in the introduction, there were many aspects of the story that made this identification plausible. The year one-Reed in the Mexica calendar was a year associated with Quetzalcoatl; the Spanish had come from his direction, the east, and Cortés's anger when offered sacrifice seemed to reinforce the association with Quetzalcoatl who supposedly had opposed such offerings. Finally, we must recall that for the Nahua, myth, history, and propaganda were not discrete categories and none was more "true" than the others. Traditionally, for peoples of Mesoamerica, history's main function was not so much to describe events as they "really" happened, but rather to fit them into a specific vision of the past and the future. How much of this ancient vision of history influenced Sahagún's informants is open to debate.

HERNÁN CORTÉS

Letter to Charles V

The letters of Cortés were really reports that mixed self-explanations and justifications with more general information of the kind to interest a king. Religion, politics, and ethnography are combined here along with observation and assessment. How much the observations are shaped by preconceptions and previous experiences is a matter of considerable dispute among historians. It also has been suggested that Cortés sometimes "invented" facts to fit his purposes.

. . . In a former paragraph of this letter we said that we are sending an account of this land that your Majesties may be better informed of its peculiarities, its riches, the people who possess it and the beliefs, rites and

Hernando Cortés: Five Letters, 1519–1526, ed. J. Bayard Morris (New York: Norton, 1991), 20–25.

ceremonies which they hold. The land which in the name of your Majesties we now occupy stretches for some fifty leagues on either side of this town; the coast is entirely flat and on the sea shore there are sandy beaches stretching for miles and more. Inland, behind the sand dunes, the land is also flat, comprising very fine meadow lands and river banks, such as cannot be bettered in all Spain, as pleasing to the eye moreover as they are fertile in producing all manner of crops, and very well looked after and of easy access, all kinds of herds being found there both grazing and for use as beasts of burden.

All kinds of hunting is to be met with in this land and both birds and beasts similar to those we have in Spain, such as deer, both red and fallow, wolves, foxes, partridges, pigeons, turtle doves of several kinds, quails, hares and rabbits: so that in the matter of birds and beasts there is no great difference between this land and Spain, but there are in addition lions and tigers about five miles inland, of which more are to be found in some districts than in others. There is a great range of very fine mountains, some very high and one in particular overtopping all the rest, from which one can discern a great expanse of the sea and land; indeed it is so high that if the day be not very clear its summit cannot be seen at all since the top half of it is entirely covered with clouds, and on other occasions when the weather is very fine one can see its summit rising above the clouds so white that we judge it to be snow: this the natives also confirm, but since we have not seen it very clearly although approaching quite near to it, and considering that this region is exceptionally hot we cannot affirm it to be so for certain. We shall endeavour to find out by personal observation about this and other matters of which we have heard reports in order to send your Majesties a true account of it, as well as of the riches of the country in gold, silver and precious stones, of all of which your Majesties may form some idea from the samples which we are sending them. To our mind it is probable that this land contains as many riches as that from which Solomon is said to have obtained the gold for the temple: but so little time has passed since our landing that we have been unable to explore the country further than some five leagues inland and some ten or a dozen leagues along the coast on either side of the place where we first landed; from the sea much more may be seen and more we certainly saw while skirting the coast in our ships.

The natives who inhabit the island of Cozumel and the land of Yucatan from its northern point to where we are now settled, are of middle height, and well-proportioned, except that in our district they disfigure their faces in various ways, some piercing the ears and introducing large and extremely ugly ornaments, others the lower part of the nose and upper lip in which they insert large circular stones having the appearance of mirrors, others still piercing the thick underlip right through to the teeth and hanging therefrom round stones or pieces of gold so heavy that they drag the lip down, giving an extraordinarily repulsive appearance. They wear as clothes a kind of highly coloured shawl, the men wear breech clouts, and on the top half of the body cloaks finely worked and painted after the fashion of Moorish draperies. The common women wear highly coloured robes reaching from the waist to the feet and others which cover only the breast, all the rest of the body being uncovered; but the women of high rank wear bodices of fine cotton, very loose fitting, cut and embroidered after the fashion of the vestment worn by our bishops and abbots. Their food is composed of maize and such cereals as are to be found on the other Islands, *potuoyuca* * almost exactly similar to that eaten in Cuba, except that they roast it instead of making it into bread; in addition they have whatever they can obtain by fishing or hunting; and they also breed large numbers of hens similar to those of the mainland which are as big as peacocks. There are a few large towns very passably laid out. The houses in those parts which can obtain stone are of rough masonry and mortar, the rooms being low and small, very much after the Moorish fashion. Where no stone can be got they build their houses of baked bricks, covering them over with plaster and the roofs with a rough kind of thatch. Certain houses belonging to chiefs are quite airy and have a considerable number of rooms; we have seen as many as five inner corridors or *patios* in a single house and its rooms very well laid out around them, each person of importance having his own private servants to wait upon him. The wells and tanks of water are also contained inside, together with rooms for the servants and underservants of which there are many. Each one of the chief men has in front of the entrance of his house a large patio, and some as many as two, three or four, sometimes raised a considerable way off the ground with steps leading up to them, and very well built. In addition they have their mosques, temples and walks, all of very fair size, and in them are the idols which they worship whether of stone, clay or wood, the which they honour and obey in such a manner and with such ceremonies that many sheets of paper would not suffice to give your Majesties a minute and true account of them. These private mosques where they exist are the largest, finest and most elaborately built buildings of any that there are in the town, and as such they keep them very much bedecked with

*Yuca or manioc.

strings of feathers, gaily painted cloths and all manner of finery. And always on the day before they are to begin some important enterprise they burn incense in these temples, and sometimes even sacrifice their own persons, some cutting out their tongues, others their ears, still others slicing their bodies with knives in order to offer to their idols the blood which flows from their wounds; sometimes sprinkling the whole of the temple with blood and throwing it up in the air, and many other fashions of sacrifice they use, so that no important task is undertaken without previous sacrifice having been made. One very horrible and abominable custom they have which should certainly be punished and which we have seen in no other part, and that is that whenever they wish to beg anything of their idols, in order that their petition may find more acceptance, they take large numbers of boys and girls and even of grown men and women and tear out their heart and bowels while still alive, burning them in the presence of those idols, and offering the smoke of such burning as a pleasant sacrifice. Some of us have actually seen this done and they say that it is the most terrible and frightful thing that they have ever seen. Yet the Indians perform this ceremony so frequently that, as we are informed and have in part seen from our own scanty experience since we have been in this land, there is no year passes in which they do not thus kill and sacrifice fifty souls in every such temple, and the practice is general from the island of Cozumel to the region in which we have now settled. Your Majesties can therefore be certain that since the land is large and they seem to have a large number of temples there can be no year (so far as we have been able up to the present to ascertain) in which they have not sacrificed in this manner some three or four thousand souls. Your Majesties may therefore perceive whether it is not their duty to prevent such loss and evil, and certainly it will be pleasing to God if by means of and under the protection of your royal Majesties these peoples are introduced into and instructed in the holy Catholic Faith, and the devotion, trust and hope which they now have in their idols turned so as to repose in the divine power of the true God; for it is certain that if they should serve God with that same faith, fervour and diligence they would work many miracles. And we believe that not without cause has God been pleased to allow this land to be discovered in the name of your royal Majesties, that your Majesties may reap great merit and reward from Him in sending the Gospel to these barbarian people who thus by your Majesties' hands will be received into the true faith; for from what we know of them we believe that by the aid of interpreters who should plainly declare to them the truths of the Holy Faith and the error in which they are, many, perhaps all of them, would very quickly depart from their evil ways and would come to true knowledge, for they live more equably and reasonably than any other of the tribes which we have hitherto come across.

To give your Majesties full and detailed account of this land and people would probably be only to include many errors, for there are many particulars which we have not seen for ourselves but only heard from the natives, and consequently we are only venturing to report those things which can definitely be vouched for as truth. Your Majesties may well command full investigation to be made, and that done, if it so please your Majesties, a true account may be made to our holy Father, that all diligence and good order may be applied to the work of converting these people, since from such conversion so much good fruit may be expected: his Holiness may thus see fit to permit evil and rebellious people having first been warned to be proceeded against and punished as enemies to our holy Catholic Faith, such punishment serving as a further occasion of warning and dread to those who still rebel, and thus bringing them to a knowledge of the truth, and rescuing them from such great evils as are those which they work in the service of the devil: for in addition to those which we have already reported to your Majesties, in which children and men and women are killed and offered in sacrifice, we know and have been informed without room for doubt that all practice the abominable sin of sodomy. In all of which we beg your Majesties to provide as may seem to them most fitting to the service of God and of your royal Majesties and that we who remain here in your service may constantly enjoy your Majesties' favour and protection. . . .

BERNAL DÍAZ

From *The True History of the Conquest of New Spain*

Bernal Díaz provides an interesting view of the first encounter with the Mexica representatives of Moctezuma who begin to appear in this account as individuals. Díaz's attention to the actions of the ambassadors, to the de-

Bernal Díaz, from *The True History of the Conquest of New Spain,* ed. A. P. Maudslay (London: Hakluyt Society, 1908), 136–44.

tails of the gifts exchanged, and to Cortés's manipulation of the horses and artillery as a way of impressing the Mexica give a sense of the Spanish reaction to the meeting and of their desire to push forward toward Moctezuma's capital.

On Holy Thursday, the anniversary of the Last Supper of Our Lord, in the year 1519, we arrived with all the fleet at the Port of San Juan de Ulúa, and as the Pilot Alaminos knew the place well from having come there with Juan de Grijalva he at once ordered the vessels to drop anchor where they would be safe from the northerly gales. The flagship hoisted her royal standards and pennants, and within half an hour of anchoring, two large canoes (which in those parts are called piraguas) came out to us, full of Mexican Indians. Seeing the big ship with the standards flying they knew that it was there they must go to speak with the captain; so they went direct to the flagship and going on board asked who was the Tatuan* which in their language means the chief. Doña Marina who understood the language well, pointed him out. Then the Indians paid many márks of respect to Cortés, according to their usage, and bade him welcome, and said that their lord, a servant of the great Montezuma, had sent them to ask what kind of men we were and of what we were in search, and added that if we were in need of anything for ourselves or the ships, that we should tell them and they would supply it. Our Cortés thanked them through the two interpreters, Aguilar and Doña Marina, and ordered food and wine to be given them and some blue beads, and after they had drunk he told them that we came to see them and to trade with them and that our arrival in their country should cause them no uneasiness but be looked on by them as fortunate. The messengers returned on shore well content, and the next day, which was Good Friday, we disembarked with the horses and guns, on some sand hills which rise to a considerable height, for there was no level land, nothing but sand dunes; and the artilleryman Mesa placed the guns in position to the best of his judgment. Then we set up an altar where mass was said and we made huts and shelters for Cortés and the captains, and three hundred of the soldiers brought wood and made huts for themselves and we placed the horses where they would be safe and in this way was Good Friday passed.

*Tlatoan.

The next day, Saturday, Easter Eve, many Indians arrived sent by a chief who was a governor under Montezuma, named Pitalpitoque* (whom we afterwards called Ovandillo), and they brought axes and dressed wood for the huts of the captain Cortés and the other ranchos near to it, and covered them with large cloths on account of the strength of the sun, for as it was in Lent the heat was very great — and they brought fowls and maize cakes and plums, which were then in season, and I think that they brought some gold jewels, and they presented all these things to Cortés; and said that the next day a governor would come and would bring more food. Cortés thanked them heartily and ordered them to be given certain articles in exchange with which they went away well content. The next day, Easter Sunday, the governor whom they spoke of arrived. His name was Tendile, a man of affairs, and he brought with him Pitalpitoque who was also a man of importance amongst the natives and there followed them many Indians with presents of fowls and vegetables. Tendile ordered these people to stand aside on a hillock and with much humility he made three obeisances to Cortés according to their custom, and then to all the soldiers who were standing around. Cortés bade them welcome through our interpreters and embraced them and asked them to wait, as he wished presently to speak to them. Meanwhile he ordered an altar to be made as well as it could be done in the time, and Fray Bartolomé de Olmedo, who was a fine singer, chanted Mass, and Padre Juan Diaz assisted, and the two governors and the other chiefs who were with them looked on. When Mass was over, Cortés and some of our captains and the two Indian officers of the great Montezuma dined together. When the tables had been cleared away — Cortés went aside with the two Caciques and our two interpreters and explained to them that we were Christians and vassals of the greatest lord on earth, called the Emperor Don Carlos, who had many great princes as his vassals and servants, and that it was at his orders that we had come to this country, because for many years he had heard rumours about the country and the great prince who ruled it. That he wished to be friends with this prince and to tell him many things in the name of the Emperor which things, when he knew and understood them, would please him greatly. Moreover he wished to trade with their prince and his Indians in good friendship, and he wanted to know where this prince would wish that they should meet so that they might confer together. Tendile replied somewhat proudly, and said — "You have only just now arrived and you already ask to speak with our prince; accept now this present which we give you in his name, and afterwards you will tell me

---

* Cuitlalpitoc, who had been sent as an ambassador to meet Grijalva.

what you think fitting." With that he took out a *petaca*—which is a sort of chest, many articles of gold beautifully and richly worked and ordered ten loads of white cloth made of cotton and feathers to be brought, wonderful things to see, and there were other things which I do not remember, besides quantities of food consisting of fowls of the country, fruit and baked fish. Cortés received it all with smiles in a gracious manner and gave in return, beads or twisted glass and other small beads from Spain, and he begged them to send to their towns to ask the people to come and trade with us as he had brought many beads to exchange for gold, and they replied that they would do as he asked. As we afterwards found out, these two men, Tendile and Pitalpitoque, were the governors of the provinces named Cotustan, Tustepeque,* Guazpaltepeque and Tatalteco, and of some other townships lately conquered. Cortés then ordered his servants to bring an arm-chair, richly carved and inlaid and some *margaritas,* stones with many [intricate] designs in them, and a string of twisted glass beads packed in cotton scented with musk and a crimson cap with a golden medal engraved with a figure of St. George on horseback, lance in hand, slaying the dragon, and he told Tendile that he should send the chair to his prince Montezuma (for we already knew that he was so called) so that he could be seated in it when he, Cortés, came to see and speak with him, and that he should place the cap on his head, and that the stones and all the other things were presents from our lord the King, as a sign of his friendship, for he was aware that Montezuma was a great prince, and Cortés asked that a day and a place might be named where he could go to see Montezuma. Tendile received the present and said that his lord Montezuma was such a great prince that it would please him to know our great King and that he would carry the present to him at once and bring back a reply.

It appears that Tendile brought with him some clever painters such as they had in Mexico and ordered them to make pictures true to nature of the face and body of Cortés and all his captains, and of the soldiers, ships, sails and horses, and of Doña Marina and Aguilar, even of the two greyhounds, and the cannon and cannon balls, and all of the army we had brought with us, and he carried the pictures to his master. Cortés ordered our gunners to load the lombards with a great charge of powder so that they should make a great noise when they were fired off, and he told Pedro de Alvarado that he and all the horsemen should get ready so that these servants of Montezuma might see them gallop and told them to attach little bells to the horses' breastplates. Cortés also mounted his horse and said—"It would be well if we could gallop on these sand

---

* Cotaxtl, Tuxtepec.

dunes but they will observe that even when on foot we get stuck in the
sand — let us go out to the beach when the tide is low and gallop two and
two;" — and to Pedro de Alvarado whose sorrel coloured mare was a
great galloper, and very handy, he gave charge of all the horsemen.

All this was carried out in the presence of the two ambassadors, and
so that they should see the cannon fired, Cortés made as though he
wished again to speak to them and a number of other chieftains, and the
lombards were fired off, and as it was quite still at that moment, the
stones went flying through the forest resounding with a great din, and
the two governors and all the other Indians were frightened by things so
new to them, and ordered the painters to record them so that Montezuma might see. It happened that one of the soldiers had a helmet half
gilt but somewhat rusty and this Tendile noticed, for he was the more forward of the two ambassadors, and said that he wished to see it as it was
like one that they possessed which had been left to them by their ancestors of the race from which they had sprung, and that it had been
placed on the head of their god — Huichilobos,* and that their prince
Montezuma would like to see this helmet. So it was given to him, and
Cortés said to them that as he wished to know whether the gold of this
country was the same as that we find in our rivers, they could return the
helmet filled with grains of gold so that he could send it to our great Emperor. After this, Tendile bade farewell to Cortés and to all of us and after many expressions of regard from Cortés he took leave of him and
said that he would return with a reply without delay. After Tendile had
departed we found out that besides being an Indian employed in matters
of great importance, Tendile was the most active of the servants whom
his master, Montezuma, had in his employ, and he went with all haste
and narrated everything to his prince, and showed him the pictures
which had been painted and the present which Cortés had sent. When
the great Montezuma gazed on it he was struck with admiration and received it on his part with satisfaction. When he examined the helmet and
that which was on his Huichilobos, he felt convinced that we belonged
to the race which, as his forefathers had foretold would come to rule over
that land. It is here that the historian Gomara relates many things which
were not told to him correctly.

I will leave off here, and then go on to say what else happened.

When Tendile departed with the present which the Captain Cortés gave
him for his prince Montezuma, the other governor, Pitalpitoque, stayed

* Huitzilopochtli.

in our camp and occupied some huts a little distance from ours, and they brought Indian women there to make maize bread, and brought fowls and fruit and fish, and supplied Cortés and the captains who fed with him. As for us soldiers, if we did not hunt for shell fish on the beach, or go out fishing, we did not get anything.

About that time, many Indians came from the towns already mentioned by me over which these two servants of Montezuma were governors, and some of them brought gold and jewels of little value, and fowls to exchange with us for our goods, which consisted of green beads and clear glass beads and other articles, and with this we managed to supply ourselves with food. Almost all the soldiers had brought things for barter, as we learnt in Grijalva's time that it was a good thing to bring beads — and in this manner six or seven days passed by.

Then one morning, Tendile arrived with more than one hundred laden Indians, accompanied by a great Mexican Cacique, who in his face, features and appearance bore a strong likeness to our Captain Cortés and the great Montezuma had sent him purposely, for it is said that when Tendile brought the portrait of Cortés all the chiefs who were in Montezuma's company said that a great chief named Quintalbor looked exactly like Cortés and that was the name of the Cacique who now arrived with Tendile; and as he was so like Cortés we called them in camp "our Cortés" and "the other Cortés." To go back to my story, when these people arrived and came before our Captain they first of all kissed the earth and then fumigated him and all the soldiers who were standing around him, with incense which they brought in brasiers of pottery. Cortés received them affectionately and seated them near himself, and that chief who came with the present (who I have already said was named Quintalbor) had been appointed spokesman together with Tendile. After welcoming us to the country and after many courteous speeches had passed he ordered the presents which he had brought to be displayed, and they were placed on mats which they call petates over which were spread cotton cloths. The first article presented was a wheel like a sun, as big as a cartwheel, with many sorts of pictures on it, the whole of fine gold, and a wonderful thing to behold, which those who afterwards weighed it said was worth more than ten thousand dollars. Then another wheel was presented of greater size made of silver of great brilliancy in imitation of the moon with other figures shown on it, and this was of great value as it was very heavy — and the chief brought back the helmet full of fine grains of gold, just as they are got out of the mines, and this was worth three thousand dollars. This gold in the helmet was worth more to us than if it had contained $20,000, because it showed us that there were good mines there. Then were brought twenty golden ducks, beautifully worked and very natural looking, and some [ornaments] like dogs, of the kind they keep, and many articles of gold worked in the shape of tigers and lions and monkeys, and ten collars beautifully worked and other necklaces; and twelve arrows and a bow with its string, and two rods like staffs of justice, five palms long, all in beautiful hollow work of fine gold. Then there were presented crests of gold and plumes of rich green feathers, and others of silver, and fans of the same materials, and deer copied in hollow gold and many other things that I cannot remember for it all happened so many years ago. And then over thirty loads of beautiful cotton cloth were brought worked with many patterns and decorated with many coloured feathers, and so many other things were there that it is useless my trying to describe them for I know not how to do it. When all these things had been presented, this great Cacique Quintalbor and Tendile asked Cortés to accept this present with the same willingness with which his prince had sent it, and divide it among the *teules** and men who accompanied him. Cortés received the present with delight and then the ambassadors told Cortés that they wished to repeat what their prince, Montezuma, had sent them to say. First of all they told him that he was pleased that such valiant men, as he had heard that we were, should come to his country, for he knew all about what we had done at Tabasco, and that he would much like to see our great emperor who was such a mighty prince and whose fame was spread over so many lands, and that he would send him a present of precious stones; and that meanwhile we should stay in that port; that if he could assist us in any way he would do so with the greatest pleasure; but as to the interview, they should not worry about it; that there was no need for it and they (the ambassadors) urged many objections. Cortés kept a good countenance, and returned his thanks to them, and with many flattering expressions gave each of the ambassadors two holland shirts and some blue glass beads and other things, and begged them to go back as his ambassadors to Mexico and to tell their prince, the great Montezuma, that as we had come across so many seas, and had journeyed from such distant lands solely to see and speak with him in person, that if we should return thus, that our great king and lord would not receive us well, and that wherever their prince Montezuma might be we wished to go and see him and do what he might order us to do. The ambassadors replied that they would go back and give this message to their prince, but as to the question of the desired interview — they con-

---

* *Teules,* "for so they call the Idols which they worship."

sidered it superfluous. By these ambassadors Cortés sent what our poverty could afford as a gift to Montezuma: a glass cup of Florentine ware, engraved with trees and hunting scenes and gilt, and three holland shirts and other things, and he charged the messengers to bring a reply. The two governors set out and Pitalpitoque remained in camp; for it seems that the other servants of Montezuma had given him orders to see that food was brought to us from the neighbouring towns. Here I will leave off, and then go on to tell what happened in our camp.

FRAY BERNARDINO DE SAHAGÚN

From the *Florentine Codex*

The Nahua account contained in the Florentine Codex *provides considerable detail of this same meeting described by Díaz: the nobles involved, the exchange of gifts, and of the way in which the encounter was reported to Moctezuma. Here the attention to detail is comparable to Díaz's account except that the focus is on different items, in this case, the costumes of the gods, reflecting the different values and goals of Nahuas and Spaniards. The descriptions of the Spaniards, their weapons, and animals have a sense of immediacy, but whether the reports of these first meetings filled Moctezuma and the people with forebodings of catastrophe at that moment is difficult to know since these accounts were collected at least twenty years after the events described.*

. . . When those who came to the seashore were seen, they were going along by boat. Then Pinotl of Cuetlaxtlan, a high steward, went in person, taking other stewards with him: [second], Yaotzin, the steward of Mictlanquauhtla; third, the steward of Teocinyocan, named Teocinyocatl; fourth, Cuitlalpitoc, who was only a dependent, a subordinate leader; and fifth, Tentlil, also a subordinate leader.

These were the only ones who first went to see [the Spaniards]. They

James Lockhart, *We People Here: Nahuatl Accounts of the Conquest of Mexico,* Repertorium Columbianum, UCLA Center for Medieval and Renaissance Studies (Los Angeles: University of California Press, 1993), 56–86, even pages only.

went as if to sell them things, so that they could spy on them and contemplate them. They gave them precious cloaks, precious goods, the very cloaks pertaining to Moteucçoma which no one else could don, which were assigned to him alone.

It was by boat that they went to see them. As they were doing it, Pinotzin said, "Let us not lie to the lord Moteucçoma, for you would live no longer. Let's just go, lest we die, so that he can hear the real truth." (Moteucçoma was his personal name, and Tlacateucth was his title as ruler.)

Then they embarked, launched off, and went out on the water; the water folk paddled for them. When they approached the Spaniards, they made the earth-eating gesture at the prow of the boat(s). They thought that it was Quetzalcoatl Topiltzin who had arrived.

The Spaniards called to them, saying to them, "Who are you? Where have you come from? Where is your homeland?"

Immediately they said, "It is from Mexico that we have come."

They answered them back, "If you are really Mexica, what is the name of the ruler of Mexico?"

They told them, "O our lords, Moteucçoma is his name."

Then they gave them all the different kinds of precious cloaks they carried, to wit, like those mentioned here: the sun-covered style, the blue-knotted style, the style covered with jars, the one with painted eagles, the style with serpent faces, the style with wind jewels, the style with (turkey blood), or with whirlpools, the style with smoking mirrors.

For all these things that they gave them, [the Spaniards] gave them things in return; they gave them green and yellow strings of beads, which one might imagine to be amber. And when they had taken them and looked at them, greatly did they marvel.

And [the Spaniards] took leave of them, saying to them, "Go off, while we go to Spain; we will not be long in getting to Mexico."

Thereupon they went, and [the local people] also came away, coming back. And when they came out on dry land, they came straight to Mexico, moving along in this direction day and night to come inform Moteucçoma, to tell him and report to him the truth [. . .]. They took the goods they had received.

Then they spoke to him: "O our lord, o master, destroy us [if you will, but] here is what we have seen and done at the place where your subordinates stand guard for you beside the ocean. For we went to see our lords the gods out on the water; we gave them all your cloaks, and here are the fine things belonging to them that they gave us. They said, 'If you have really come from Mexico, here is what you are to give the ruler

Moteucçoma, whereby he will recognize us.'" They told him everything [the Spaniards] had told them out on the water.

And Moteucçoma said to them, "You are doubly welcome; take your rest. What I have seen is a secret. No one is to say anything, to let it escape from his lips, to let a word slip out, to open his mouth, to mention it, but it is to stay inside you."

Third chapter, where it is said what Moteucçoma ordered when he heard the statement of those who saw the first boat that came.

Thereupon Moteucçoma gave instructions to the man from Cuetlaxtlan and the rest, telling them, "Give orders that watch be kept everywhere along the coast, at [the places] called Nauhtlan, Toztlan, and Mictlanquauhtla, wherever they will come to land." Then the stewards left and gave orders for watch to be kept.

And Moteucçoma assembled his lords, the Cihuacoatl Tlilpotonqui, the Tlacochcalcatl Quappiaztzin, the Ticocyahuacatl Quetzalaztatzin, and the Huitznahuatlailotlac Ecatenpatiltzin. He reported the account to them, and showed them, put before them, the beads they had brought.

He said to them, "We have beheld the fine blue turquoise; it is to be guarded well, the custodians are to take good care of it; if they let one piece get away from them, [their] homes, children, and women with child will be ours."

Then the year changed to the one following, Thirteen Rabbit, and when it was nearly over, at the end of the year Thirteen Rabbit, [the Spaniards] made an appearance and were seen once again. Then the stewards quickly came to tell Moteucçoma.

When he heard it, he quickly sent out a party. He thought and believed that it was Topiltzin Quetzalcoatl who had landed. For they were of the opinion that he would return, that he would appear, that he would come back to his seat of authority, because he had gone in that direction [eastward] when he left. And [Moteucçoma] sent five [people] to go to meet him and give him things. The leader had the official title of Teohua [custodian of the god] and the personal name of Yohualli ichan. The second was Tepoztecatl, the third Tiçahua, the fourth Huehuetecatl, and the fifth Hueicamecatl eca.

Fourth chapter, where it is said what orders Moteucçoma gave when he found out that the Spaniards had returned. The second time they came it was [with] don Hernando Cortés.

He said to them, "Come, o men of unique valor, do come. It is said that our lord has appeared at last. Do go to meet him; listen well, make good use of your ears, bring back in your ears a good record of what he says. Here is what you will take to our lord."

[First] were the appurtenances of Quetzalcoatl: a serpent mask, made of turquoise; a quetzal-feather head fan; a plaited neckband of green-stone beads, with a golden disk in the middle of it; and a shield with gold [strips] crossing each other, or with gold and seashells crossing, with quetzal feathers spread about the edge and with a quetzal-feather banner; and a mirror with quetzal feathers to be tied on his back; and this mirror for the back seemed to have a turquoise shield, with turquoise glued on it, and there were green-stone neck bands with golden shells on them; then there was the turquoise spear thrower, entirely of turquoise, with a kind of serpent head; and there were obsidian sandals.

The second set of things they went to give him were the appurtenances of Tezcatlipoca: a feather headpiece, covered with golden stars, and his golden bell earplugs; and a seashell necklace; the chest ornament, decorated with many small seashells, with its fringe made of them; and a sleeveless jacket, painted all over, with eyes on its border and teased feathers at the fringe; and a cloak with blue-green knots, called a *tzitzilli,* tied on the back by taking its corners, also with a mirror for the back over it; and another item, golden bells tied to the calves of the legs; and another item, white sandals. [A third and fourth god's costume was also sent.] . . .

These then were the things, called gods' appurtenances, that the messengers carried with them, and they took many other things by way of greeting: a shell-shaped gold headpiece with yellow parrot feathers hanging from it, a golden miter, etc.

Then baskets were filled and carrying frames were adjusted. And then Moteuccoma gave orders to the aforementioned five [emissaries], saying to them, "Now go, don't tarry anywhere, and address yourselves to our lord the god. Tell him, 'Your agent Moteuccoma has sent us; here is what he is giving you. You have arrived in Mexico, your home.'"

And when they reached the coast, they were taken across [a river or inlet] by boat at Xicalanco. There again they left by boat, taken by the water folk. Everything went into the boats; the goods were placed in boats. And when the boats were full, they left. They cast off and reached [the Spaniards'] boat[s], bringing their own boat close.

Then [the Spaniards] said to them, "Who are you? Where have you come from?"

Then [the emissaries] answered them, "Why, we have come from Mexico."

Again [the Spaniards] replied to them, "Perhaps not. Perhaps you are just claiming to be from there, perhaps you are making it up, perhaps you are deceiving us."

But when they were convinced and satisfied, they hooked the prow of the boat with an iron staff and hauled them in; then they also put down a ladder.

Fifth chapter, where it is said what happened when Moteucçoma's messengers went into don Hernando Cortés's boat.

Then they climbed up, carrying in their arms the goods. When they had gotten up into the boat, each of them made the earth-eating gesture before the Captain. Then they addressed him, saying,

"May the god attend: his agent Moteucçoma who is in charge in Mexico for him addresses him and says, 'The god is doubly welcome.'"

Then they dressed up the Captain. They put on him the turquoise serpent mask attached to the quetzal-feather head fan, to which were fixed, from which hung the green-stone serpent earplugs. And they put the sleeveless jacket on him, and around his neck they put the plaited green-stone neckband with the golden disk in the middle. On his lower back they tied the back mirror, and also they tied behind him the cloak called a *tzitzilli*. And on his legs they placed the green-stone bands with the golden bells. And they gave him, placing it on his arm, the shield with gold and shells crossing, on whose edge were spread quetzal feathers, with a quetzal banner. And they laid the obsidian sandals before him.

And the other three outfits, the gods' appurtenances, they only arranged in rows before him.

When this had been done, the Captain said to them, "Is this everything you have by way of greeting and rapprochement?"

They answered, "That is all with which we have come, o our lord."

Then the Captain ordered that they be tied up: they put irons on their feet and necks. When this had been done they shot off the cannon. And at this point the messengers truly fainted and swooned; one after another they swayed and fell, losing consciousness. And the Spaniards lifted them into a sitting position and gave them wine to drink. Then they gave them food, fed them, with which they regained strength and got their breath back.

When this had been done the Captain said to them, "Do listen, I have found out and heard that by what they say these Mexica are very strong, great warriors, able to throw others down. Where there is one of them he can chase, push aside, overcome, and turn back his enemies, even though there should be ten or twenty. Now I wish to be satisfied, I want to see you, I want to try out how strong and manly you are." Then he gave them leather shields, iron swords, and iron lances. [He said,]

"Well now, very early in the morning, as dawn is about to come, we will struggle against each other, we will challenge each other, we will find out by comparison who will fall down first."

They answered the Captain, saying, "May the lord pay heed, this is not at all what his agent Moteucçoma ordered us. All we came to do was to greet and salute you. We were not charged with what the lord wishes. If we should do that, won't Moteucçoma be very angry with us because of it, won't he destroy us for it?"

Then the Captain said, "No indeed; it is simply to be done. I want to see and behold it, for word has gone to Spain that you are very strong, great warriors. Eat while it is still before dawn, and I will eat then too. Outfit yourselves well."

Sixth chapter, where it is said how Moteucçoma's messengers came back here to Mexico to tell Moteucçoma what they had seen.

Then [Cortés] let them go. [The Spaniards] lowered them into their boat, and when they had descended into the boat, they paddled hard; each one paddled as hard as he could, and some used their hands to paddle. They fled with all possible speed, saying to one another as they came, "O warriors, exert all your strength, paddle hard! Let's not do something [wrong] here, lest something happen to us!"

By water they quickly reached the place called Xicalanco, where they did nothing but catch their breath, then again came running along as fast as possible. Then they reached Tecpantlayacac, whereupon they again left and came fleeing. They quickly got to Cuetlaxtlan, where they caught their breath and also quickly came away.

And the (ruler or steward) of Cuetlaxtlan said to them, "First take your rest for a day or so, until you recover your strength."

But they said to him, "No, rather we are going hurrying to talk to the lord ruler Moteucçoma, to tell him what we saw, these very terrifying things the like of which have never been seen. Should you be the very first to hear them?"

Then they quickly got on their way and soon reached Mexico. It was night when they got there; they came in by night.

During this time Moteucçoma neither slept nor touched food. Whatever he did, he was abstracted; it seemed as though he was ill at ease, frequently sighing. He tired and felt weak. He no longer found anything tasteful, enjoyable, or amusing.

Therefore he said, "What is to come of us? Who in the world must endure it? Will it not be me [as ruler]? My heart is tormented, as though chile water were poured on it; it greatly burns and smarts. Where in the world [are we to turn], o our lord?"

Then [the messengers] notified those who guarded [Moteucçoma], who kept watch at the head of his bed, saying to them, "Even if he is asleep, tell him. 'Those whom you sent out on the sea have come back.'"

But when they went to tell him, he replied, "I will not hear it here. I will hear it at the Coacalco; let them go there." And he gave orders, saying, "Let some captives be covered with chalk [for sacrifice]."

Then the messengers went to the Coacalco, and so did Moteucçoma. Thereupon the captives died in their presence; they cut open their chests and sprinkled their blood on the messengers. (The reason they did it was that they had gone to very dangerous places and had seen, gazed on the countenances of, and spoken to the gods.)

Seventh chapter, where is told the account that the messengers who went to see the boat gave to Moteucçoma.

When this was done, they talked to Moteucçoma, telling him what they had beheld, and they showed him what [the Spaniards'] food was like.

And when he heard what the messengers reported, he was greatly afraid and taken aback, and he was amazed at their food. It especially made him faint when he heard how the guns went off at [the Spaniards'] command, sounding like thunder, causing people actually to swoon, blocking the ears. And when it went off, something like a ball came out from inside, and fire went showering and spitting out. And the smoke that came from it had a very foul stench, striking one in the face. And if they shot at a hill, it seemed to crumble and come apart. And it turned a tree to dust; it seemed to make it vanish, as though someone had conjured it away. Their war gear was all iron. They clothed their bodies in iron, they put iron on their heads, their swords were iron, their bows were iron, and their shields and lances were iron.

And their deer that carried them were as tall as the roof. And they wrapped their bodies all over; only their faces could be seen, very white. Their faces were the color of limestone and their hair yellow-reddish, though some had black hair. They had long beards, also yellow-reddish. [The hair of some] was tightly curled. And their food was like fasting food, very large, white, not heavy, like chaff, like dried maize stalks, as tasty as maize stalk flour, a bit sweet or honeyed, honeyed and sweet to eat.

And their dogs were huge creatures, with their ears folded over and their jowls dragging. They had burning eyes, eyes like coals, yellow and fiery. They had thin, gaunt flanks with the rib lines showing; they were very tall. They did not keep quiet, they went about panting, with their tongues hanging down. They had spots like a jaguar's, they were varicolored.

When Moteucçoma heard it, he was greatly afraid; he seemed to faint away, he grew concerned and disturbed.

Eighth chapter, where it is said how Moteucçoma sent witches, wizards, and sorcerers to do something to the Spaniards.

Then at that time Moteucçoma sent out emissaries. Those whom he sent were all bad people, soothsayers and witches. He also sent elders, strong warriors, to see to all [the Spaniards] needed as to food: turkey hens, eggs, white tortillas, and whatever they might request, and to look after them well so that they would be satisfied in every way. He sent captives in case [the Spaniards] should drink their blood. And the emissaries did as indicated.

But when [the Spaniards] saw it, they were made sick to their stomachs, spitting, rubbing their eyelids, blinking, shaking their heads. And [the emissaries] sprinkled blood in the food, they bloodied it, which made their stomachs turn and disgusted them, because of the great stench of the blood.

Moteucçoma did this because he took them for gods, considered them gods, worshiped them as gods. They were called and given the name of gods who have come from heaven, and the blacks were called soiled gods.

After that they ate white tortillas, grains of maize, turkey eggs, turkeys, and all the fruits: custard apple, mammee, yellow sapote, black sapote, sweet potato, manioc, white sweet potato, yellow sweet potato, colored sweet potato, jicama, plum, jobo, guava, *cuajilote,* avocado, acacia [bean], *tejocote,* American cherry, tuna cactus fruit, mulberry, white cactus fruit, yellow cactus fruit, whitish-red cactus fruit, pitahaya, water pitahaya. And the food for the deer was *pipillo* and *tlachicaztli.*

They say that Moteucçoma sent the witches, the rainmakers, to see what [the Spaniards] were like and perhaps be able to enchant them, cast spells on them, to use conjury or the evil eye on them or hurl something else at them, perhaps addressing some words of wizardry to them so that they would take sick, die, or turn back. But when they performed the assignment they had been given concerning the Spaniards, they could do nothing; they had no power at all. Then they quickly returned to tell Moteucçoma what they were like, how strong they were, [saying,] "We are not their match; we are as nothing."

Then Moteucçoma gave strict orders; he scolded and charged the stewards and all the lords and elders, under pain of death, that they see to and take care of everything [the Spaniards] might need. And when [the Spaniards] came onto dry land and finally started moving in this direction and coming along the road toward here, they were well cared for and made much of. They were always in the hands of someone as they came progressing; they were very well attended to.

Ninth chapter, where it is said how Moteucçoma wept, and the Mexica wept, when they found out that the Spaniards were very strong.

And Moteucçoma lamented his troubles at length; he was afraid and shocked. He told the troubles of the altepetl. And everyone was very afraid. Fear reigned, and shock, laments, and expressions of distress. People talked, assembled, gathered, wept for themselves and for others. Heads hung, there were tearful greetings, words of encouragement, and stroking of hair. Little children's heads were stroked. Fathers would say, "Alas, my children, how is it with you, that what is about to happen has happened to you?" And mothers said, "O my children, how is it with you who are to behold what is about to happen to us?"

And it was told, presented, made known, announced, and reported to Moteucçoma, and brought to his attention that a woman, one of us people here, came accompanying them as interpreter. Her name was Marina and her homeland was Tepeticpac, on the coast, where they first took her. . . .

4

The March Inland: Tlaxcala and Cholula

From the town of Vera Cruz Cortés entered into peaceful relations with the coastal peoples, especially in the major city of the region, Cempoala. According to his report, the Cempoalans only recently had been brought under Mexica domination and were restive under their overlords. Thus, they easily changed their support to the Spaniards. Once Cortés decided to strike inland, he left a garrison of about 150 men in Vera Cruz and with his remaining 350 Spaniards, now aided by large numbers of Cempoalan *tememes* or bearers, he began to trek westward, climbing through the mountains that lay just beyond the coast. The expedition passed through a number of small towns and at various points they received "ambassadors," forward observers sent from Tenochtitlan by Moctezuma to gather information about the strangers. Cortés used a combination of diplomacy, bravado, guile, and terror to impress these representatives as well as to awe the towns and villages through which the Spaniards passed. Cortés, by now well informed about local and regional politics, chose to lead his force through Tlaxcala, an *altepetl* whose people were linguistically and culturally akin to the Mexica, but who were also their traditional political enemies.

Despite Cortés's diplomacy, the Tlaxcalans received the expedition with suspicion and hostility. Under the leadership of a young and intransigent captain, Xicotencatl the Younger, some of the Tlaxcalans and their Otomí allies carried out an active resistance. The Tlaxcalan state itself was composed of four major political divisions, and its leadership was not united on the course of action to take against the invaders.

Figure 6. (*opposite*) The Lords of Tlaxcala. The present-day town hall of Tlaxcala has been decorated with murals of the region's history by the local artist, Desiderio Hernández Xochitiotzin. In this section of the mural the glories of the ancient city and the marketplace are represented.
Source: From *Historia de una Pueblo: Tlaxcala,* by Citlalli Xochitiotzin Ortega (Mexico City: Gobierno del Estado de Tlaxcala, 1994).

This indecision certainly helped the Spaniards defeat the Tlaxcalans in a number of open battles which Bernal Díaz recounts in detail. Eventually, the factions in favor of an alliance with the Spaniards won out and the strangers were welcomed into the city with the usual presentations of food, supplies, and women. Some Tlaxcalans viewed the Spaniards as potential allies. Caciques or leaders like Mase Escasi and Xicotencatl the Elder, father of the hostile captain, gave Cortés much information about Tenochtitlan and Moctezuma. With the alliance with Tlaxcala, Cortés now had a firm logistical base for further operations.

Cortés's victories over Tlaxcala impressed Moctezuma's representatives, and they realized that the strangers had gained a valuable, if for the Mexica, dangerous ally. Cortés's decision to march from Tlaxcala to the nearby city and religious center of Cholula, a firm supporter of Tenochtitlan and a traditional enemy of Tlaxcala, may have been due to the urgings of the Tlaxcalans who hoped to take advantage of the new alliance to settle traditional grudges. In any case, although the Spaniards were welcomed at first, fighting erupted in Cholula and resulted in a bloody massacre of the inhabitants, which was perhaps intended to terrorize the Mexica.

The whole story of the defeat of and then alliance with Tlaxcala is central to the course of subsequent events. Without Tlaxcalan help, the trajectory of the conquest might have been very different. Tlaxcala became a privileged province after the conquest. Tlaxcalans always pointed to their vital role as a justification for honors, rewards, and exemptions during the colonial era. Twentieth-century critics have sometimes described the Tlaxcalans as traitors to a "native" cause, but such labels make little sense in the context of the ethnic rivalries and politics of central Mexico at the time of the conquest.

The selections on the campaign against Tlaxcala included here are excerpts from Bernal Díaz's account of events, the description provided by another conquistador Andrés de Tapia, the Mexica views collected by Sahagún, and a sixteenth-century Tlaxcalan pictorial account, the so-called *Lienzo de Tlaxcala,* that combines indigenous elements and European artistic influences.

BERNAL DÍAZ

From *The True History of the Conquest of New Spain*

In an extensive excerpt, Bernal Díaz provides the feel of battle and a view of Spanish tactics in the fighting against Tlaxcala. Despite his descriptions of the ferocity of battle, the low casualty rate of the Spaniards underlines the technological disparity between the opponents. Díaz also presents a view in which the soldiers like himself influenced Cortés rather than vice versa. His displeasure with Gómara's history is apparent in a number of passages. In Díaz's account of the events at Cholula, he emphasizes the treachery of the Cholulans and the role of doña Marina in revealing their intentions.

... In such order we arrived at a little town of Xalacingo, where they gave us a golden necklace and some cloth and two Indian women, and from that town we sent two Cempoalan chieftains as messengers to Tlaxcala, with a letter, and a fluffy red Flemish hat, such as was then worn. We well knew that the Tlaxcalans could not read the letter, but we thought that when they saw paper different from their own, they would understand that it contained a message; and what we sent to tell them was that we were coming to their town, and hoped they would receive us well, as we came, not to do them harm, but to make them our friends. We did this because in this little town they assured us that the whole of Tlaxcala was up in arms against us, for it appears that they had already received news of our approach and that we were accompanied by many friends, both from Cempoala and Zocotlan, and other towns through which we had passed. As all these towns usually paid tribute to Montezuma, the Tlaxcalans took it for granted that we were coming to attack Tlaxcala, as their country had often been entered by craft and cunning and then laid to waste, and they thought that this was another attempt to do so. So as soon as our two messengers arrived with the letter and the hat and began to deliver their message, they were seized as prisoners before their story was finished, and we waited all that day and the next for an answer and none arrived.

Bernal Díaz, from *The True History of the Conquest of New Spain,* ed. A. P. Maudslay (London: Hakluyt Society, 1908), 225–30, 237–40, 243–45, 264–70.

Then Cortés addressed the chiefs of the town [where we had halted] and repeated all he was accustomed to tell the Indians about our holy religion and how we were vassals of our Lord and King who had sent us to these parts to put an end to human sacrifices, and the eating of human flesh, and the other evils which they were used to practise, and he told them many other things which we usually repeated in most of the towns we passed through, and after making them many promises of assistance, he asked for twenty Indian warriors of quality to accompany us on our march, and they were given us most willingly.

After commending ourselves to God, with a happy confidence we set out on the following day for Tlaxcala, and as we were marching along, we met our two messengers who had been taken prisoners. It seems that the Indians who guarded them were perplexed by the warlike preparations and had been careless of their charge, and in fact, had let them out of prison. They arrived in such a state of terror at what they had seen and heard that they could hardly succeed in expressing themselves.

According to their account, when they were prisoners the Tlaxcalans had threatened them, saying: "Now we are going to kill those whom you call Teules, and eat their flesh, and we will see whether they are as valiant as you announce; and we shall eat your flesh too, you who come here with treasons and lies from that traitor Montezuma!" and for all that the messengers could say, that we were against the Mexicans, and wished to be brothers to the Tlaxcalans, they could not persuade them of its truth.

When Cortés and all of us heard those haughty words, and learned how they were prepared for war, although it gave us matter for serious thought, we all cried — "If this is so, forward — and good luck to us!" We commended ourselves to God and marched on, the Alferez, Corral, unfurling our banner and carrying it before us, for the people of the little town where we had slept, as well as the Cempoalans assured us that the Tlaxcalans would come out to meet us and resist our entry into their country.

Marching along as I have described, we discussed how the horsemen — in parties of three so as to help one another — should charge and return at a hard gallop with their lances held rather short, and when they broke through the hostile ranks should hold their lances before their faces and not stop to give thrusts, so that the Indians should not be able to seize hold of their lances; and if by chance a lance were seized, the horseman should use all his strength and put spurs to his horse, so that helped by the leverage of the lance held beneath his arm, the furious rush of the horse might enable him to wrench it from the grasp of the Indian, or should drag him along with it. It will be said to-day — what was the use of all this preparation when there were no hostile warriors in sight to attack us? I answer this by repeating the words of Cortés:— "Gentlemen and comrades, seeing how few of us there are, it behoves us to be always as well prepared and as much on the alert as though we saw the enemy approaching to attack us, and not only saw them approaching, but we should behave as though we were already fighting them; and, as it often happens that they seize the lances with their hands, we have to be prepared for such an emergency as well as for anything else that may happen to a soldier. I have fully understood that, when fighting, there should be no need of directions, for I know, and am very willing to acknowledge it, that you behave much more courageously [without them]."

In this way we marched about two leagues, when we came upon a fortress strongly built of stone and lime and some other cement, so strong that with iron pickaxes it was difficult to demolish it and it was constructed in such a way both for offence and defence, that it would be very difficult to capture. We halted to examine it, and Cortés asked the Indians from Zocotlan for what purpose the fortress had been built in such a way. They replied that, as war was always going on between the people of Tlaxcala and their lord, Montezuma, the Tlaxcalans had built this fort so strong the better to defend their towns, for we were already in their territory. We rested awhile and this, our entry into the land of Tlaxcala and the fortress, gave us plenty to think about. Cortés said: "Sirs, let us follow our banner which bears the sign of the holy cross, and through it we shall conquer!" Then one and all we answered him: "May good fortune attend our advance, for in God lies the true strength." So we began our march again in the order I have already noted.

We had not gone far when our scouts observed about thirty Indians who were spying. These carried two-handed swords, shields, lances and plumes of feathers. The swords are made with stones which cut worse than knives, so cleverly arranged, that one can neither break nor pull out the blades; they are as long as broadswords; and as I have already said, these spies wore devices and feather headdresses, and when our scouts observed them they came back to give us notice. Cortés then ordered the same scouts to follow the spies, and to try and capture one of them without hurting them; and then he sent five more mounted men as a support, in case there should be an ambush. Then all our army hastened on in good order and with quick step, for our Indian friends who were with us said that there was sure to be a large body of warriors waiting in ambush.

When the thirty Indian spies saw the horsemen coming towards them, and beckoning to them with their hands, they would not wait for them to come up and capture one of them; furthermore, they defended themselves so well, that with their swords and lances they wounded some of the horses.

When our men saw how fiercely the Indians fought and that their horses were wounded, they were obliged to kill five of the Indians. As soon as this happened, a squadron of Tlaxcalans,* more than three thousand strong, which was lying in ambush, fell on them all of a sudden, with great fury and began to shower arrows on our horsemen who were now all together; and they made a good fight with their arrows and fire-hardened darts, and did wonders with their two-handed swords. At this moment we came up with our artillery, muskets and crossbows, and little by little the Indians gave way, but they had kept their ranks and fought well for a considerable time.

In this encounter they wounded four of our men and I think that one of them died of his wounds a few days later.

As it was now late the Tlaxcalans beat a retreat and we did not pursue them; they left about seventeen dead on the field, not counting many wounded. Where these skirmishes took place the ground was level and there were many houses and plantations of maize and magueys, which is the plant from which they make their wine.

We slept near a stream, and with the grease from a fat Indian whom we had killed and cut open, we dressed our wounds, for we had no oil, and we supped very well on some dogs which the Indians breed [for food] for all the houses were abandoned and the provisions carried off, and they had even taken the dogs with them, but these came back to their homes in the night, and there we captured them, and they proved good enough food.

All night we were on the alert with watches and patrols and scouts, and the horses bitted and saddled, in fear lest the Indians would attack us. . . .

The next morning, the 5th of September, 1519, we mustered the horses. There was not one of the wounded men who did not come forward to join the ranks and give as much help as he could. The crossbowmen were warned to use the store of darts very cautiously, some of them loading while the others were shooting, and the musketeers were to act in the same way, and the men with sword and shield were instructed to aim their cuts and thrusts at the bowels [of their enemies] so that they would not dare to come as close to us as they did before. The

---

*Probably Otomís from the Otomí town of Tecoac. Cortés says the chiefs of Tlaxcala sent messengers to say that the attack was made by communities (of Otomís?) without their knowledge.

artillery was all ready for action, and the horsemen had already been instructed to aid one another and to hold their lances short, and not to stop to spear anyone except in the face and eyes — charging and returning at a hard gallop and no soldier was on any account to break away from the ranks. With our banner unfurled, and four of our comrades guarding the standard-bearer, Corral, we set out from our camp. We had not marched half a quarter of a league before we began to see the fields crowded with warriors with great feather crests and distinguishing devices, and to hear the blare of horns and trumpets.

Here would be a great opportunity to write down in proper order what happened to us in this most perilous and doubtful battle, for so many warriors surrounded us on all sides that [the situation] might be compared to a great plain, two leagues long and about the same breadth, and in its midst, four hundred men. Thus all the plain was swarming with warriors and we stood four hundred men in number, and of those many sick and wounded. And we knew for certain that this time our foe came with the determination to leave none of us alive excepting those who would be sacrificed to their idols.

To go back to our battle: How they began to charge on us! What a hail of stones sped from their slings! As for their bowmen, the javelins lay like corn on the threshing floor; all of them barbed and fire-hardened, which would pierce any armour and would reach the vitals where there is no protection; the men with swords and shields and other arms larger than swords, such as broadswords, and lances, how they pressed on us and with what valour and what mighty shouts and yells they charged upon us! The steady bearing of our artillery, musketeers and crossbowmen, was indeed a help to us, and we did the enemy much damage, and those of them who came close to us with their swords and broadswords met with such sword play from us that they were forced back and they did not close in on us so often as in the last battle. The horsemen were so skilful and bore themselves so valiantly that, after God who protected us, they were our bulwark. However, I saw that our troops were in considerable confusion, so that neither the shouts of Cortés nor the other captains availed to make them close up their ranks, and so many Indians charged down on us that it was only by a miracle of sword play that we could make them give way so that our ranks could be reformed. One thing only saved our lives, and that was that the enemy were so numerous and so crowded one on another that the shots wrought havoc among them, and in addition to this they were not well commanded, for all the captains with their forces could not come into action, and from what we knew, since the last battle had been fought, there had been disputes and quarrels between the Captain Xicotenga and another captain the son of Chichimecatecle, over what the one had said to the other, that he had not fought well in the previous battle; to this the son of Chichimecatecle replied that he had fought better [/] than Xicotenga and was ready to prove it by personal combat. So in this battle Chichimecatecle and his men would not help Xicotenga, and we knew for a certainty that he had also called on the company of Huexotzinco to abstain from fighting. Besides this, ever since the last battle they were afraid of the horses and the musketry, and the swords and crossbows, and our hard fighting; above all was the mercy of God which gave us strength to endure. So Xicotenga was not obeyed by two of the commanders, and we were doing great damage to his men, for we were killing many of them, and this they tried to conceal; for as they were so numerous, whenever one of their men was wounded, they immediately bound him up and carried him off on their shoulders, so that in this battle, as in the last, we never saw a dead man.

The enemy were already losing heart, and knowing that the followers of the other two captains whom I have already named, would not come to their assistance, they began to give way. It seems that in that battle we had killed one very important captain, not to mention others, and the enemy began to retreat in good order, our horsemen following them at a hard gallop for a short distance, for they could not sit their horses for fatigue, and when we found ourselves free from that multitude of warriors, we gave thanks to God.

In this engagement, one soldier was killed, and sixty were wounded, and all the horses were wounded as well. They gave me two wounds, one in the head with a stone, and one in the thigh with an arrow; but this did not prevent me from fighting, and keeping watch, and helping our soldiers, and all the soldiers who were wounded did the same; for if the wounds were not very dangerous, we had to fight and keep guard, wounded as we were, for few of us remained unwounded.

Then we returned to our camp, well contented, and giving thanks to God. We buried the dead in one of those houses which the Indians had built underground, so that the enemy should not see that we were mortals, but should believe that, as they said, we were Teules. We threw much earth over the top of the house, so that they should not smell the bodies, then we doctored all the wounded with the fat of the Indian, as I have related before. It was cold comfort to be even without salt or oil with which to cure the wounded. There was another want from which we suffered, and it was a severe one — and that was clothes with which to cover ourselves, for such a cold wind came from the snow mountains, that it made us shiver, for our lances and muskets and crossbows made a poor covering. That night we slept with more tranquility than on the night before, when we had so much duty to do, with scouting, spies, watchmen and patrols.

I will leave off here and relate what we did on the next day. In this battle we captured three Indian chieftains.

. . . When we awoke and saw how all of us were wounded, even with two or three wounds, and how weary we were and how others were sick and clothed in rags, and knew that Xicotenga was always after us, and already over forty-five of our soldiers had been killed in battle, or succumbed to disease and chills, and another dozen of them were ill, and our Captain Cortés himself was suffering from fever as well as the Padre de la Merced, and what with our labours and the weight of our arms which we always carried on our backs, and other hardships from chills and the want of salt, for we could never find any to eat, we began to wonder what would be the outcome of all this fighting, and what we should do and where we should go when it was finished. To march into Mexico we thought too arduous an undertaking because of its great armies, and we said to one another that if those Tlaxcalans, which our Cempoalan friends had led us to believe were peacefully disposed, could reduce us to these straits, what would happen when we found ourselves at war with the great forces of Montezuma? In addition to this we had heard nothing from the Spaniards whom we had left settled in Villa Rica, nor they of us. As there were among us very excellent gentlemen and soldiers, steady and valiant men of good counsel, Cortés never said or did anything [important] without first asking well considered advice, and acting in concert with us. Although the historian Gomara says Cortés did this and that, and came here and went there, and says many other things without reason, even if Cortés were made of iron, as Gomara in his history says he was, he could not be everywhere at once. Suffice it to say that he bore himself like a good commander. This I say, for after all the great mercies which our Lord granted us in all our doings, and in the late victories, and in everything else, it seems that God gave us soldiers grace and good counsel to advise Cortés how to do all things in the right way.

Let us cease praising and cease speaking of past praises, for they do not add much to our history, and let me relate how one and all we put heart into Cortés, and told him that he must get well again and reckon upon us, and that as with the help of God we had escaped from such perilous battles, our Lord Jesus Christ must have preserved us for some good end; that he [Cortés] should at once set our prisoners free and send them to the head Caciques already named by me, so as to bring them to peace, when all that had taken place would be pardoned, including the death of the mare.

Let us leave this and say how Doña Marina who, although a native woman, possessed such manly valour that, although she had heard every day how the Indians were going to kill us and eat our flesh with chili, and had seen us surrounded in the late battles, and knew that all of us were wounded and sick, yet never allowed us to see any sign of fear in her, only a courage passing that of woman. So Doña Marina and Jerónimo de Aguilar spoke to the messengers whom we were now sending and told them that they must come and make peace at once, and that if it was not concluded within two days we should go and kill them all and destroy their country and would come to seek them in their city, and with these brave words they were dispatched to the capital where Xicotenga the elder and Mase Escasi were [residing].

Let us leave this, and I will mention another thing that I have noticed, that the historian Gomara does not mention or make any record in his history of the fact that any of us were killed or wounded, or underwent any hardships, or suffered, but writes about it all as though we were going to a wedding, and it is thus that we find it recorded. Oh! — how badly those men advised him when they told him to put such things in his history! It has made all of us conquerors reflect upon what he wrote down, which not being true, he ought to have remembered, that as soon as we saw his history we must out with the truth! . . .

As our Lord God, through his great loving kindness, was pleased to give us victory in those battles in Tlaxcala, our fame spread throughout the surrounding country, and reached the ears of the great Montezuma in the great City of Mexico; and if hitherto they took us for Teules, which is the same as their idols, from now on they held us in even greater respect as valiant warriors, and terror fell on the whole country at learning how, being so few in number and the Tlaxcalans in such great force, we had conquered them and that they had sued us for peace. So that now Montezuma, the great Prince of Mexico, powerful as he was, was in fear of our going to his city, and sent five chieftains, men of much importance, to our camp at Tlaxcala to bid us welcome, and say that he was rejoiced at our great victory against so many squadrons of warriors, and he sent a present, a matter of a thousand dollars worth of gold, in very rich jewelled ornaments, worked in various shapes, and twenty loads of fine cotton cloth, and he sent word that he wished to become the vassal of our great Emperor, and that he was pleased that we were already near his city, on account of the good will that he bore Cortés and all his brothers, the Teules, who were with him (for so they called us) and that he

[Cortés] should decide how much tribute he wished for every year for our great Emperor, and that he [Montezuma] would give it in gold and silver, cloth and chalchihuites, provided we would not come to Mexico. This was not because he would not receive us with the greatest willingness, but because the land was rough and sterile, and he would regret to see us undergo such hardships which perchance he might not be able to alleviate as well as he could wish. Cortés answered by saying that he highly appreciated the good will shown us, and the present which had been sent, and the offer to pay tribute to his Majesty, and he begged the messengers not to depart until he went to the capital of Tlaxcala, as he would despatch them from that place, for they could then see how that war ended, and he did not wish to give them his reply at once, because he had purged himself the day before with some camomiles such as are found in the Island of Cuba, and are very good for one who knows how to take them. I will leave this subject and tell what else happened in our camp.

Cortés was talking to the ambassadors of Montezuma, as I have already said, and wanted to take some rest, for he was ill with fever and had purged himself the day before, when they came to tell him that the Captain Xicotenga was arriving with many other Caciques and Captains, all clothed in white and red cloaks, half of the cloak was white and the other half red, for this was the device and livery of Xicotenga, [who was approaching] in a very peaceful manner, and was bringing with him in his company about fifty chieftains.

When Xicotenga reached Cortés's quarters he paid him the greatest respect by his obeisance, and ordered much copal to be burned. Cortés, with the greatest show of affection, seated him by his side and Xicotenga said that he came on behalf of his father and of Mase Escasi and all the Caciques, and Commonwealth of Tlaxcala to pray Cortés to admit them to our friendship, and that he came to render obedience to our King and Lord, and to ask pardon for having taken up arms and made war upon us. That this had been done because they did not know who we were, and they had taken it for certain that we had come on behalf of their enemy Montezuma, and as it frequently happened that craft and cunning was used to gain entrance to their country so as to rob and pillage it, they had believed that this was now the case, and for that reason had endeavoured to defend themselves and their country, and were obliged to show fight. He said that they were a very poor people who possessed neither gold, nor silver, nor precious stones, nor cotton cloth, nor even salt to eat, because Montezuma gave them no opportunity to go out and search for it, and that although their ancestors possessed some gold and precious stones, they had been given to Montezuma on former occasions when, to save themselves from destruction, they had made peace or a truce, and this had been in times long past; so that if they had nothing to give now, we must pardon them for it, for poverty and not the want of good will was the cause of it. He made many complaints of Montezuma and his allies who were all hostile to them and made war on them, but they had defended themselves very well. Now they had thought to do the same against us, but they could not do it although they had gathered against us three times with all their warriors, and we must be invincible, and when they found this out about our persons they wished to become friends with us and the vassals of the great prince the Emperor Don Carlos, for they felt sure that in our company they and their women and children would be guarded and protected, and would not live in dread of the Mexican traitors, and he said many other words placing themselves and their city at our disposal.

Xicotenga was tall, broad shouldered and well made; his face was long, pockmarked and coarse, he was about thirty-five years old and of a dignified deportment.

Cortés thanked him very courteously, in a most flattering manner, and said that he would accept them as vassals of our King and Lord, and as our own friends. Then Xicotenga begged us to come to his city, for all the Caciques, elders and priests were waiting to receive us with great rejoicing. Cortés replied that he would go there promptly, and would start at once, were it not for some negotiations which he was carrying on with the great Montezuma, and that he would come after he had despatched the messengers. Then Cortés spoke somewhat more sharply and severely about the attacks they had made on us both by day and night, adding that as it could not now be mended he would pardon it. Let them see to it that the peace we now were granting them was an enduring one, without any change, for otherwise he would kill them and destroy their city and that he [Xicotenga] should not expect further talk about peace, but only of war.

When Xicotenga and all the chieftains who had come with him heard these words they answered one and all, that the peace would be firm and true, and that to prove it they would all remain with us as hostages.

There was further conversation between Cortés and Xicotenga and most of his chiefs, and they were given blue and green beads for Xicotenga's father, for himself, and for the other Caciques, and were told to report that Cortés would soon set out for their city.

The Mexican Ambassadors were present during all these discussions and heard all the promises that were made, and the conclusion of peace weighed on them heavily, for they fully understood that it boded them no good. And when Xicotenga had taken his leave these Ambassadors of Montezuma half laughingly asked Cortés whether he believed any of those promises which were made on behalf of all Tlaxcala, [alleging] that it was all a trick which deserved no credence, and the words were those of traitors and deceivers; that their object was to attack and kill us as soon they had us within their city in a place where they could do so in safety; that we should bear in mind how often they had put forth all their strength to destroy us and had failed to do so, and had lost many killed and wounded, and that now they offered a sham peace so as to avenge themselves. Cortés answered them, with a brave face, that their alleged belief that such was the case did not trouble him, for even if it were true he would be glad of it so as to punish them [the Tlaxcalans] by taking their lives, that it did not matter to him whether they attacked him by day or by night, in the city or in the open, he did not mind one way or the other, and it was for the purpose of seeing whether they were telling the truth that he was determined to go to their city.

The Ambassadors seeing that he had made up his mind begged him to wait six days in our camp as they wished to send two of their companions with a message to their Lord Montezuma, and said that they would return with a reply within six days. To this Cortés agreed, on the one hand because, as I have said he was suffering from fever, and on the other because, although when the Ambassadors had made these statements he had appeared to attach no importance to them, he thought that there was a chance of their being true, and that until there was greater certainty of peace, they were of a nature requiring much consideration.

As at the time that this peace was made the towns all along the road that we had traversed from our Villa Rica de Vera Cruz were allied to us and friendly, Cortés wrote to Juan de Escalante who, as I have said, remained in the town to finish building the fort, and had under his command the sixty old or sick soldiers who had been left behind. In these letters he told them of the great mercies which our Lord Jesus Christ had vouchsafed to us in the victories which we had gained in our battles and encounters since we had entered the province of Tlaxcala, which had now sued for peace with us, and asked that all of them would give thanks to God for it. He also told them to see to it that they always kept on good terms with our friends in the towns of the Totonacs, and he told him to send at once two jars of wine which had been left behind, buried in a certain marked place in his lodgings, and some sacred wafers for the Mass, which had been brought from the Island of Cuba, for those which we had brought on this expedition were already finished.

These letters were most welcome, and Escalante wrote in reply to say what had happened in the town, and all that was asked for arrived very quickly.

About this time we set up a tall and sumptuous cross in our camp, and Cortés ordered the Indians of Tzumpantzingo and those who dwelt in the houses near our camp to whitewash it, and it was beautifully finished.

I must cease writing about this and return to our new friends the Caciques of Tlaxcala, who when they saw that we did not go to their city, came themselves to our camp and brought poultry and tunas,* which were then in season, each one brought some of the food which he had in his house and gave it to us with the greatest good will without asking anything in return, and they always begged Cortés to come with them soon to their city. As we had promised to wait six days for the return of the Mexicans, Cortés put off the Tlaxcalans with fair speeches. When the time expired, according to their word, six chieftains, men of great importance, arrived from Mexico, and brought a rich present from the great Montezuma consisting of valuable gold jewels wrought in various shapes worth three thousand pesos in gold, and two hundred pieces of cloth, richly worked with feathers and other patterns. When they offered this present the Chieftains said to Cortés that their Lord Montezuma was delighted to hear of our success, but that he prayed him most earnestly on no account to go with the people of Tlaxcala to their town, nor to place any confidence in them, that they wished to get him there to rob him of his gold and cloth, for they were very poor, and did not possess a decent cotton cloak among them, and that the knowledge that Montezuma looked on us as friends, and was sending us gold and jewels and cloth, would still more induce the Tlaxcalans to rob us.

Cortés received the present with delight, and said that he thanked them for it and would repay their Lord Montezuma with good works, and if he should perceive that the Tlaxcalans had that in mind against which Montezuma had sent them to warn him, they would pay for it by having all their lives taken, but he felt sure they would be guilty of no such villainy, and he still meant to go and see what they would do.

While this discussion was proceeding, many other messengers from Tlaxcala came to tell Cortés that all the old Caciques from the Capital and from the whole province had arrived at our ranchos and huts, in order to see Cortés and all of us, and to take us to their city. When Cortés

---

*Tuna: The prickly pear, the fruit of the Nopal Cactus (Opuntia).

heard this he begged the Mexican Ambassadors to wait for three days for the reply to their prince, as he had at present to deliberate and decide about the past hostilities and the peace which was now offered, and the Ambassadors said that they would wait. . . .

ANDRÉS DE TAPIA
Another Spanish View of the Cholula Massacre

Cortés's own report of the events in Cholula gave little detail of his bloody actions, but another Spanish observer, the captain Andrés de Tapia, provides a succinct and frank record of the destruction of that city. Tapia was one of Cortés's captains and a man of great courage. In his mid-twenties during the conquest, he was often mentioned in Bernal Díaz's book as an able commander and companion. "Well-made and with a scanty beard," is the way Díaz remembered him. In the 1540s, Tapia was asked to give a deposition in an investigation of Cortés's actions. This deposition served as the basis for his "Relation of some things that happened to the Very Illustrious Don Hernando Cortés, Marqués del Valle. . . ." A concise account by another eyewitness of the conquest, Tapia's brutally frank description of the two days of destruction wrought by the Spaniards and Tlaxcalans at Cholula was not published until the nineteenth century.

. . . The marqués left Tlaxcala after gathering as much information as he could of the territory ahead, and the Indians said they would go with him to show the way as far as they knew it. They also said that about four leagues from here was an enemy city called Cholula which was a state in itself and a friend and ally of Moctezuma. And so the Spaniards set out for this city accompanied by forty thousand warriors who by order of the marqués marched at a distance from us.

The morning of the day we arrived at the city of Cholula, ten or twelve thousand men in squadrons came out to meet us, bringing maize bread and turkeys. Each squadron advanced toward the marqués to bid him

The Conquistadores: First-Person Accounts of the Conquest of Mexico, ed. Patricia de Fuentes (Norman: University of Oklahoma Press, 1993), 33–36.

welcome and then withdrew. The Cholulans earnestly begged the marqués not to allow the Tlaxcalans to enter their territory, so the marqués ordered them to go back, but the Tlaxcalans said: "Beware of the people of this city, who are traders and not men of war, and who have one heart and show another, resorting to trickery and lies. We dislike having to leave you, for we gave ourselves as your friends." In spite of this the marqués ordered that all their men were to go back, but that if some of the notables wished to stay they could be quartered outside the city with a few men to serve them, and that is the way it was done.

As we entered the city the rest of the men came out in their squadrons, greeting the Spaniards they met, who were marching in formation. After the squadrons came all the ministers who served the idols. They were dressed in sleeveless robes, some of which were closed in front like surplices, with heavy cotton fringe at the edges, and other kinds of dress. Many of them were playing flutes and trumpets, and carrying certain idols that were covered, and many incense burners. They approached the marqués first and then the other men, perfuming them with a resin they burned in the censers.

In this city they had a principal god who at one time had been a man. They called him Quetzalcoatl. He is said to have founded this city, and to have commanded them not to kill men, but instead to build edifices to the creator of the sun and the heavens, in which to offer him quail and other things of the hunt. They were to wish no harm and do no harm to one another. Quetzalcoatl is supposed to have worn a white vesture like a monk's tunic, and over it a mantle covered with red crosses. They had certain green stones there, one of them a monkey's head, which they said had belonged to this man, and they regarded them as relics.

The marqués and his men stayed here several days, and he sent certain men as volunteers to explore a volcano we could see on a high ridge five leagues away, and which gave out much smoke. They were to look out from there in all directions and bring back news of the disposition of the land.

Certain persons of rank came to this city as messengers of Moctezuma and made their speeches over and over again. Sometimes they said there was no reason for us to go on, and where would we go anyway, since they had no provisions for us to eat where they lived. At other times they told us Moctezuma said that if we went to see him he would die of fright. Also they said there was no road by which to go. When they saw that the marqués was undisturbed by all this, they made the people of the city tell us that where Moctezuma lived there were great numbers of lions and tigers and other wild beasts that he let loose any time he wanted to, and that they were enough to tear us to pieces and eat us.

When they saw that none of this served to deter us, Moctezuma's messengers plotted with the people of the city to kill us. The way they proposed to do it was to take us to the left of the road leading to Mexico, where there were dangerous crossings formed by the waters flowing from the ridge where the volcano was. Since the earth there is soft and sandy, a little water can make a big ravine, and some of them are more than a hundred *estados* deep. They are also so narrow that there is timber tall enough to make bridges across the ravines, and these exist, because we later saw them.

As we were preparing to leave, an Indian woman of this city of Cholula, the wife of one of the notables, told the woman who was our interpreter along with the Christian, that she would like her to stay there because she was very fond of her and would be grieved to see her killed. Then she told her what they were plotting and thus the marqués learned of it and delayed his departure two days. He repeatedly told the Cholulans that it caused him no surprise or anger when men fought, even if they fought against him; but that he would be greatly displeased if they told him lies, so he warned them not to lie in their dealings with him, nor to resort to treachery. They assured him they were his friends and always would be, and that they would never lie to him. Then they asked him when he wished to leave, and he said that on the following day. They said they wanted to assemble many men to send with him, but the marqués said he wanted only slaves to carry the Spaniards' baggage. They still insisted on giving him warriors, and he refused, repeating that he wanted only enough men to carry the baggage.

Next day there came unbidden many men with weapons of the kind they use, saying they were slaves and bearers, though it later turned out that they were among the bravest of their warriors. The marqués said he wished to take his leave of all the lords, and asked that they be summoned. There was no one lord of this city, but only captains of the republic, since it was in the nature of a dominion and they governed themselves in that way. The dignitaries then arrived, and the marqués took about thirty of them, those who looked most important, into a courtyard of the house where he was lodged, and he said to them: "In everything have I spoken the truth to you, and I have given orders to all the Christians of my company to do you no harm, and no harm has been done you, yet with evil intention you asked that the Tlaxcalans be kept from entering your territory. And although you have not given me to eat as you should, I have not allowed so much as a chicken to be taken from you. Also I have asked you not to lie to me. But in payment for these good deeds you have conspired to kill me and my companions, bringing men to fight me as soon as we have reached the bad terrain over which you plan to lead us. For this wickedness you shall all die, and as a sign that you are traitors I shall destroy your city so that no edifice remains. It is needless for you to deny this, for I know it as well as I am saying it to you."

They were astonished, and kept looking at one another. There were guards to keep them from escaping and there were also men guarding the people that would carry our baggage, who were outside in the large courtyards of the idols. The marqués then said to these dignitaries: "I wish to have you tell me the truth, though I already know it, so that these messengers and all the rest hear it from your mouths and not think that I have accused you falsely."

Five or six were taken aside, and each confessed separately, without torture of any kind, that it was as the marqués had said. When he saw that they were in agreement with one another he brought everyone together again and they all confessed that it was so, and said among themselves: "He is like our gods, who know all; there is no use in denying it to him."

The marqués had Moctezuma's messengers brought, and said to them: "These people wanted to kill me, and they say that Moctezuma was behind it, but I do not believe it because I hold him as friend and know that he is a great lord, and a lord does not lie. I believe they wanted to do me this injury by treachery, as scoundrels that they are, and people who have no lord; and for this they shall die. But you have nothing to fear, for besides being messengers you are the envoys of that lord I regard as friend, who I have reason to believe is very good, and nothing will I hear to the contrary."

Then he ordered most of those lords killed, leaving a few of them fettered, and ordered the signal given the Spaniards to attack the men in the courtyards and kill them all, and so it was done. They defended themselves the best they could, and tried to take the offensive, but since they were walled inside the courtyards with the entrances guarded, most of them died anyway.

This done, the Spaniards and Indians in our company went out in squads to different parts of the city, killing warriors and burning houses. In a short time a number of the Tlaxcalans arrived, and they looted the city and destroyed everything possible, making off with a great amount of plunder.

Certain priests of the devil climbed to the top of the principal idol's tower and would not give themselves up but stayed there to be burned, lamenting and complaining to their idol how wrong of him it was to forsake them. So everything possible was done to destroy this city, but the marqués ordered us to refrain from killing women and children. The destruction took two days, during which many of the inhabitants went to hide in the hills and fields, and others took refuge in surrounding enemy country.

At the end of two days the marqués ordered the destruction ceased, and within another two or three days, it later appeared, many of the natives of the city must have gathered together, for they sent word to the marqués begging for pardon and for permission to reoccupy the city, offering themselves protectorate of the Tlaxcalans.

FRAY BERNARDINO DE SAHAGÚN

From the *Florentine Codex*

The Nahua accounts collected by Sahagún emphasize the progress of the Spaniards toward Tenochtitlan and the treachery of the Tlaxcalans. Here the Cholula massacre is presented as an unprovoked act of violence. Once again we turn to the modern translations from the Nahuatl in Lockhart's We People Here.

Tenth chapter, where it is said how the Spaniards landed uncontested and came on their way in this direction, and how Moteucçoma left the great palace and went to his personal home.

Then Moteucçoma abandoned his patrimonial home, the great palace, and came back to his personal home.

When at last [the Spaniards] came, when they were coming along and moving this way, a certain person from Cempoallan, whose name was Tlacochcalcatl, whom they had taken when they first came to see the land and the various altepetl, also came interpreting for them, planning

James Lockhart, *We People Here: Nahuatl Accounts of the Conquest of Mexico,* Repertorium Columbianum, UCLA Center for Medieval and Renaissance Studies (Los Angeles: University of California Press, 1993), 90–96, 106, even pages only.

their route, conducting them, showing them the way, leading and guiding them.

And when they reached Tecoac, which is in the land of the Tlaxcalans, where their Otomis lived, the Otomis met them with hostilities and war. But they annihilated the Otomis of Tecoac, who were destroyed completely. They lanced and stabbed them, they shot them with guns, iron bolts, crossbows. Not just a few but a huge number of them were destroyed.

After the great defeat at Tecoac, when the Tlaxcalans heard it and found out about it and it was reported to them, they became limp with fear, they were made faint; fear took hold of them. Then they assembled, and all of them, including the lords and rulers, took counsel among themselves, considering the reports.

They said, "How is it to be with us? Should we face them? For the Otomis are great and valiant warriors, yet they thought nothing of them, they regarded them as nothing; in a very short time, in the blink of an eyelid, they destroyed the people. Now let us just submit to them, let us make friends with them, let us be friends, for something must be done about the common people."

Thereupon the Tlaxcalan rulers went to meet them, taking along food: turkey hens, eggs, white tortillas, fine tortillas. They said to them, "Welcome, our lords."

[The Spaniards] answered them back, "Where is your homeland? Where have you come from?"

They said, "We are Tlaxcalans. Welcome, you have arrived, you have reached the land of Tlaxcala, which is your home."

(But in olden times it was called Texcallan and the people Texcalans.)

Eleventh chapter, where it is said how the Spaniards reached Tlaxcala, [also] called Texcallan.

[The Tlaxcalans] guided, accompanied, and led them until they brought them to their palace(s) and placed them there. They showed them great honors, they gave them what they needed and attended to them, and then they gave them their daughters.

Then [the Spaniards] asked them, "Where is Mexico? What kind of a place is it? Is it still far?"

They answered them, "It's not far now. Perhaps one can get there in three days. It is a very favored place, and [the Mexica] are very strong, great warriors, conquerors, who go about conquering everywhere."

Now before this there had been friction between the Tlaxcalans and the Cholulans. They viewed each other with anger, fury, hate, and disgust; they could come together on nothing. Because of this they put [the Spaniards] up to killing them treacherously.

They said to them, "The Cholulans are very evil; they are our enemies. They are as strong as the Mexica, and they are the Mexica's friends."

When the Spaniards heard this, they went to Cholula. The Tlaxcalans and Cempoalans went with them, outfitted for war. When they arrived, there was a general summons and cry that all the noblemen, rulers, subordinate leaders, warriors, and commoners should come, and everyone assembled in the temple courtyard. When they had all come together, [the Spaniards and their friends] blocked the entrances, all of the places where one entered. Thereupon people were stabbed, struck, and killed. No such thing was in the minds of the Cholulans; they did not meet the Spaniards with weapons of war. It just seemed that they were stealthily and treacherously killed, because the Tlaxcalans persuaded [the Spaniards] to do it.

And a report of everything that was happening was given and relayed to Moteucçoma. Some of the messengers would be arriving as others were leaving; they just turned around and ran back. There was no time when they weren't listening, when reports weren't being given. And all the common people went about in a state of excitement; there were frequent disturbances, as if the earth moved and (quaked), as if everything were spinning before one's eyes. People took fright.

And after the dying in Cholula, [the Spaniards] set off on their way to Mexico, coming gathered and bunched, raising dust. Their iron lances and halberds seemed to sparkle, and their iron swords were curved like a stream of water. Their cuirasses and iron helmets seemed to make a clattering sound. Some of them came wearing iron all over, turned into iron beings, gleaming, so that they aroused great fear and were generally seen with fear and dread. Their dogs came in front, coming ahead of them, keeping to the front, panting, with their spittle hanging down.

Twelfth chapter, where it is said how Moteucçoma sent a great nobleman along with many other noblemen to go to meet the Spaniards, and what their gifts of greeting were when they greeted the Captain between Iztactepetl and Popocatepetl.

Thereupon Moteucçoma named and sent the noblemen and a great many other agents of his, with Tzihuacpopocatzin as their leader, to go meet [Cortés] between Popocatepetl and Iztactepetl, at Quauhtechcac. They gave [the Spaniards] golden banners, banners of precious feathers, and golden necklaces.

And when they had given the things to them, they seemed to smile, to rejoice and be very happy. Like monkeys they grabbed the gold. It was as though their hearts were put to rest, brightened, freshened. For gold was what they greatly thirsted for; they were gluttonous for it, starved for it, piggishly wanting it. They came lifting up the golden banners, waving them from side to side, showing them to each other. They seemed to babble; what they said to each other was in a babbling tongue.

And when they saw Tzihuacpopocatzin, they said, "Is this one then Moteucçoma?" They said it to the Tlaxcalans and Cempoalans, their lookouts, who came among them, questioning them secretly. They said, "It is not that one, o our lords. This is Tzihuacpopocatzin, who is representing Moteucçoma."

[The Spaniards] said to him, "Are you then Moteucçoma?" He said, "I am your agent Moteucçoma."

Then they told him, "Go on with you! Why do you lie to us? What do you take us for? You can't lie to us, you can't fool us, (turn our heads), flatter us, (make faces at us), trick us, confuse our vision, distort things for us, blind us, dazzle us, throw mud in our eyes, put muddy hands on our faces. It is not you. Moteucçoma exists; he will not be able to hide from us, he will not be able to find refuge. Where will he go? Is he a bird, will he fly? Or will he take an underground route, will he go somewhere into a mountain that is hollow inside? We will see him, we will not fail to gaze on his face and hear his words from his lips."

. . . They spent the night at Amaquemecan, then came straight on along the road and reached Cuitlahuac, where they also spent the night. They assembled the rulers from each of the kingdoms among the chinampa people: Xochimilco, Cuitlahuac, Mizquic. They told them what they had told the rulers of Chalco. And the rulers of the chinampa people also submitted to them.

And when the Spaniards were satisfied, they moved on this way and made a halt in Itztapalapan. Then they summoned, had summoned the rulers there as well, called the Four Lords, of Itztapalapan, Mexicatzinco, Colhuacan, and Huitzilopochco. They talked with them in the same way they had spoken to [the chinampa people] (as was said). And they too peacefully submitted to the Spaniards.

Moteucçoma did not give orders for anyone to make war against them or for anyone to meet them in battle. No one was to meet them in battle. He just ordered that they be strictly obeyed and very well attended to.

And at this time there was silence here in Mexico. No one went out any more; mothers no longer let [their children] go out. The roads were as if swept clean, wide open, as if at dawn, with no one crossing. People assembled in the houses and did nothing but grieve. The people said, "Let it be that way; curses on it. What more can you do? For we are about to die and perish, we are awaiting our deaths."

From the *Lienzo de Tlaxcala*

The Lienzo de Tlaxcala *contains a series of paintings on cloth done in the sixteenth century to celebrate the alliance with the Spaniards (see Figures 7–10). It was apparently prepared for the Viceroy Luis de Velasco to inform him of Tlaxcala's contribution to the Spanish conquest. The* Lienzo *underlines the importance of visual images to the indigenous people of Mexico as a way of recording the past. The Tlaxcalan artists by this time, however, were influenced by European artistic styles. This can be seen in the composition and manner of drawing the figures, although traditional iconographic conventions such as burning temples signifying defeat or the stylized presentation of native warriors point to a continuing indigenous artistic and representational tradition.*

The content of the Lienzo, *like the history written by the Tlaxcalan native son Juan Muñoz Camargo in the sixteenth century, demonstrates how history can be manipulated.[1] The early battles between the Spaniards and Tlaxcalans described by Bernal Díaz were carefully omitted from the Tlaxcalan record which preferred to concentrate on later cooperation and alliance. In the* Lienzo *doña Marina or Malintzin plays a central role and is shown as a major figure next to Cortés in many of the illustrations.*

Three copies of the Lienzo *were originally prepared but were lost by the mid-nineteenth century. What survives is a copy that dates from that time.*

---

[1] Juan Muñoz Camargo, *Historia de Tlaxcala,* ed. Alfredo Chavero (Mexico City: Secretaria de Fomento, 1892), also avoids discussing the first battles between Tlaxcala and the Spaniards.

From Prospero Cahuzortzi, ed., *Lienzo de Tlaxcala* (Mexico City: Libreria Antiquaria G. M. Echaniz, 1939).

Figure 7. (*opposite, top*) Cortés embraces the Tlaxcalan leaders before the symbol of the cross while Malintzin looks on.

Figure 8. (*opposite, bottom*) The baptism of the governors of Tlaxcala with Cortés aided by Malintzin as witness. Here the Tlaxcalans emphasize their conversion and loyalty to Spanish aims.

Figure 9. (*page 126, top*) Tlaxcalans and Spaniards occupy Cholula. The burning temple was the usual sign of conquest in indigenous painted manuscripts. Notice once again Malintzin figures prominently in the scene. Notice also the lack of perspective in the presentation of the Cholulans in a building at the top of the scene.

Figure 10. (*page 126, bottom*) Cortés aided by doña Marina meets Moctezuma. The game and fowls provided to the Spaniards are portrayed above. Both leaders sit in European-style chairs which came to symbolize authority in postconquest indigenous documents.

ycinonauatecque.tlaxcallā.

ycmoquayateq̃
que tlatoque

125

Chololă.

Tenochtitlan.

5

Tenochtitlan

After the massacre at Cholula, Cortés and his companions continued toward the Mexica capital, ignoring both the attempts to have them turn back and the hardships of the march. The entry of the Spaniards into Tenochtitlan on November 8, 1519 was one of the quintessential moments of world history. It represents the encounter and clash of two worlds that until that moment had developed in ignorance of each other. From the European side it was a moment of marvel and wonder. "And some of our soldiers asked whether the things we saw were not a dream," wrote Bernal Díaz. Some Spaniards who had been to Rome or Venice could compare Tenochtitlan to those cities, but most like Bernal Díaz thought that what they were seeing could only compare to the popular books of chivalry filled with fantasies, dreams, and dangers. And on the Mexica side, the Spanish entry seemed just as wondrous. Thousands of people lined the causeways, stood on the rooftops, or took to the thousands of canoes that filled the lake to catch a glimpse of the strange "deer" and the bearded men dressed in metal. They also wondered and worried about the meaning of the thousands of Tlaxcalan and other auxiliaries, their traditional enemies who, with the Spaniards, also entered the city.

A ritualized meeting took place between Moctezuma and Cortés at the entrance to the city, which both Spanish and Nahuatl accounts recorded, and then the Spaniards were lodged in the palaces within the main temple complex at the heart of the city. Within a week, Cortés imprisoned Moctezuma in his own palaces. The seizure of the Mexica leader, even a hospitable one, was a treachery to be sure, but a tactic that had already been used effectively against other indigenous leaders in the Caribbean. During the following eight months the Spaniards resided in Tenochtitlan as guests and invaders. While the city was restive, there was no overt resistance against them in the city. It was during this period that both Spaniards and Mexica had an opportunity to observe each other closely. Bernal Díaz's account is filled with details about Moctezuma and his court. But in reality, neither the Spanish nor the Nahua accounts provide much detail of the day-to-day interactions of the two peoples. The Spanish used this time to install Catholic images in the temples and prohibit the practice of human sacrifice. They also discovered treasure in the palaces and seized it. Their delight and greed caught the notice of the Mexica.

What might have happened had this situation continued we cannot tell, but events were soon to change conditions leading to open Mexica resistance (called rebellion by Cortés).

The Nahua accounts (see pp. 130–132) gathered by Sahagún describe the Spanish entry into the city. The observations about the panting of the Spanish dogs, the sweating of the horses, and the strange weapons of the Spaniards contain both details and a sense of awe that convey the feel of eyewitness observation. The excerpts from Bernal Díaz (see pp. 133–155) are some of his most colorful writing and provide us with the sense of awe that he felt. Moreover, they are filled with ethnographic details that make his account so valuable as a limited vision of Mexica life, especially that of the palace. Included here also are Bernal Díaz's discussions of Moctezuma's reactions to the Spanish attempts at conversion as well as Díaz's description of Moctezuma's personality and the curious relationship that began to develop between the emperor and his Spanish captors.

FRAY BERNARDINO DE SAHAGÚN

From the *Florentine Codex*

The Spaniards approached Tenochtitlan from the south, crossing to the city along the causeway from Ixtapalapa (see Figure 11). The Nahua accounts concentrate on those things that were new and strange like horses and crossbows but also seek to find parallels and comparisons between their own practices and customs and the ways of the strangers. Here, for example, Cortés is compared to the tlacatecatl *or military commander. The wel-*

James Lockhart, *We People Here: Nahuatl Accounts of the Conquest of Mexico,* Repertorium Columbianum, UCLA Center for Medieval and Renaissance Studies (Los Angeles: University of California Press, 1993), 108–18.

coming "speech" of Moctezuma and his concession of authority to Cortés is particularly interesting and raises questions about the nature of "polite" political discourse among the Nahua as well as the possibility of later interpretations and explanations being placed in the historical record after the conquest.

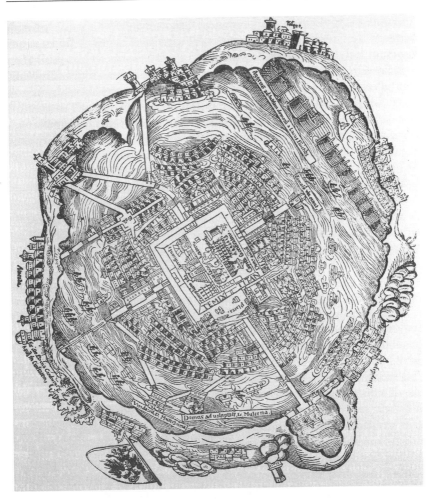

Figure 11. Tenochtitlan in the European imagination. An image of the city from the first publication of Cortés's letters.

Source: From *Praeclara Fernandi Cortesii de Nova Maris Oceani Hispana Narratio* (Nuremberg, 1524). Courtesy of the Rare Books Division, The New York Public Library, Astor, Lenox, and Tilden Foundations.

Fifteenth chapter, where it is said how the Spaniards came from Itztapalapan when they reached Mexico.

Then they set out in this direction, about to enter Mexico here. Then
they all dressed and equipped themselves for war. They girded themselves, tying their battle gear tightly on themselves and then on their
horses. Then they arranged themselves in rows, files, ranks.

Four horse[men] came ahead, going first, staying ahead, leading.
They kept turning about as they went, facing people, looking this way
and that, looking sideways, gazing everywhere between the houses, examining things, looking up at the roofs.

Also the dogs, their dogs, came ahead, sniffing at things and constantly panting.

By himself came marching ahead, all alone, the one who bore the
standard on his shoulder. He came waving it about, making it spin, toss-
ing it here and there. It came stiffening, rising up like a warrior, twisting
and turning.

Following him came those with iron swords. Their iron swords came
bare and gleaming. On their shoulders they bore their shields, of wood
or leather.

The second contingent and file were horses carrying people, each
with his cotton cuirass, his leather shield, his iron lance, and his iron
sword hanging down from the horse's neck. They came with bells on, jin-
gling or rattling. The horses, the deer, neighed, there was much neighing, and they would sweat a great deal; water seemed to fall from them.
And their flecks of foam splattered on the ground, like soapsuds splat-
ting. As they went they made a beating, throbbing, and hoof-pounding
like throwing stones. Their hooves made holes, they dug holes in the
ground wherever they placed them. Separate holes formed wherever
they went placing their hindlegs and forelegs.

The third file were those with iron crossbows, the crossbowmen. As
they came, the iron crossbows lay in their arms. They came along test-
ing them out, brandishing them, (aiming them). But some carried them
on their shoulders, came shouldering the crossbows. Their quivers went
hanging at their sides, passed under their armpits, well filled, packed
with arrows, with iron bolts. Their cotton upper armor reached to their
knees, very thick, firmly sewn, and dense, like stone. And their heads
were wrapped in the same cotton armor, and on their heads plumes
stood up, parting and spreading.

The fourth file were likewise horse[men]; their outfits were the same
as has been said.

The fifth group were those with harquebuses, the harquebusiers,
shouldering their harquebuses; some held them [level]. And when they

went into the great palace, the residence of the ruler, they repeatedly shot off their harquebuses. They exploded, sputtered, discharged, thundered, (disgorged). Smoke spread, it grew dark with smoke, everyplace filled with smoke. The fetid smell made people dizzy and faint.

And last, bringing up the rear, went the war leader, thought to be the ruler and director in battle, like [among us] a *tlacateccatl.* Gathered and massed about him, going at his side, accompanying him, enclosing him were his warriors, those with devices, his [aides], like [among us] those with scraped heads [*quaquachictin*] and the Otomi warriors, the strong and valiant ones of the altepetl, its buttress and support, its heart and foundation.

Then all those from the various altepetl on the other side of the mountains, the Tlaxcalans, the people of Tliliuhquitepec, of Huexotzinco, came following behind. They came outfitted for war with their cotton upper armor, shields, and bows, their quivers full and packed with feathered arrows, some barbed, some blunted, some with obsidian points. They went crouching, hitting their mouths with their hands and yelling, singing in Tocuillan style, whistling, shaking their heads.

Some bore burdens and provisions on their backs; some used [tump lines for] their foreheads, some [bands around] their chests, some carrying frames, some board cages, some deep baskets. Some made bundles, perhaps putting the bundles on their backs. Some dragged the large cannons, which went resting on wooden wheels, making a clamor as they came.

Sixteenth chapter, where it is said how Moteucçoma went in peace and quiet to meet the Spaniards at Xoloco, where the house of Alvarado is now, or at the place they call Huitzillan.

And when they [the Spaniards] had come as far as Xoloco, when they had stopped there, Moteucçoma dressed and prepared himself for a meeting, along with other great rulers and high nobles, his rulers and nobles. Then they went to the meeting. On gourd bases they set out different precious flowers, in the midst of the shield flowers and heart flowers stood popcorn flowers, yellow tobacco flowers, cacao flowers, [made into] wreaths for the head, wreaths to be girded around. And they carried golden necklaces, necklaces with pendants, wide necklaces.

And when Moteucçoma went out to meet them at Huitzillan, thereupon he gave various things to the war leader, the commander of the warriors; he gave him flowers, he put necklaces on him, he put flower necklaces on him, he girded him with flowers, he put flower wreaths on his head. Then he laid before him the golden necklaces, all the different things for greeting people. He ended by putting some of the necklaces on him.

Then [Cortés] said in reply to Moteucçoma, "Is it not you? Is it not you then? Moteucçoma?"

Moteucçoma said, "Yes, it is me." Thereupon he stood up straight, he stood up with their faces meeting. He bowed down deeply to him. He stretched as far as he could, standing stiffly. Addressing him, he said to him,

"O our lord, be doubly welcomed on your arrival in this land; you have come to satisfy your curiosity about your altepetl of Mexico, you have come to sit on your seat of authority, which I have kept a while for you, where I have been in charge for you, for your agents the rulers—Itzcoatzin, the elder Moteucçoma, Axayacatl, Tiçocic, and Ahuitzotl—have gone, who for a very short time came to be in charge for you, to govern the altepetl of Mexico. It is after them that your poor vassal [myself] came. Will they come back to the place of their absence? If only one of them could see and behold what has now happened in my time, what I now see after our lords are gone! For I am not just dreaming, not just sleepwalking, not just seeing it in my sleep. I am not just dreaming that I have seen you, have looked upon your face. For a time I have been concerned, looking toward the mysterious place from which you have come, among clouds and mist. It is so that the rulers on departing said that you would come in order to acquaint yourself with your altepetl and sit upon your seat of authority. And now it has come true, you have come. Be doubly welcomed, enter the land, go to enjoy your palace; rest your body. May our lords be arrived in the land."

And when the speech that Moteucçoma directed to the Marqués had concluded, Marina reported it to him, interpreting it for him. And when the Marqués had heard what Moteucçoma had said, he spoke to Marina in return, babbling back to them, replying in his babbling tongue,

"Let Moteucçoma be at ease, let him not be afraid, for we greatly esteem him. Now we are truly satisfied to see him in person and hear him, for until now we have greatly desired to see him and look upon his face. Well, now we have seen him, we have come to his homeland of Mexico. Bit by bit he will hear what we have to say."

Thereupon [the Spaniards] took [Moteucçoma] by the hand. They came along with him, stroking his hair to show their good feeling. And the Spaniards looked at him, each of them giving him a close look. They would start along walking, then mount, then dismount again in order to see him. . . .

BERNAL DÍAZ

From *The True History of the Conquest of New Spain*

Bernal Díaz provides not only a description of the Spanish entry to the city, the encounter between Cortés and Moctezuma, and the reception by the population, but also an account of the life of the Mexica tlatoani and a great deal about his personality. Díaz's description of the buildings, gardens, the zoo, the temples, and religious practices convey a combination of apprecia- tion and disgust, but his report of Moctezuma's defense of his religion and of the ruler's conver~ations with Cortés are not unsympathetic.

Early next day we left Iztapalapa with a large escort of those great Caciques whom I have already mentioned. We proceeded along the Causeway which is here eight paces in width and runs so straight to the City of Mexico that it does not seem to me to turn either much or little, but, broad as it is, it was so crowded with people that there was hardly room for them all, some of them going to and others returning from Mexico, besides those who had come out to see us, so that we were hardly able to pass by the crowds of them that came; and the towers and cues were full of people as well as the canoes from all parts of the lake. It was not to be wondered at, for they had never before seen horses or men such as we are.

Gazing on such wonderful sights, we did not know what to say, or whether what appeared before us was real, for on one side, on the land, there were great cities, and in the lake ever so many more, and the lake itself was crowded with canoes, and in the Causeway were many bridges at intervals, and in front of us stood the great City of Mexico, and we,— we did not even number four hundred soldiers! and we well remembered the words and warnings given us by the people of Huexotzingo and Tlax- cala and Tlamanalco, and the many other warnings that had been given that we should beware of entering Mexico, where they would kill us, as soon as they had us inside.

Let the curious readers consider whether there is not much to ponder over in this that I am writing. What men have there been in the world

---

Bernal Díaz, from *The True History of the Conquest of New Spain,* ed. A. P. Maudslay (Lon- don: Hakluyt Society, 1908), 39–44, 53–83.

who have shown such daring? But let us get on, and march along the Causeway. When we arrived where another small causeway branches off (leading to Coyoacan, which is another city) where there were some buildings like towers, which are their oratories, many more chieftains and Caciques approached clad in very rich mantles, the brilliant liveries of one chieftain differing from those of another, and the causeways were crowded with them. The Great Montezuma had sent these great Caciques in advance to receive us, and when they came before Cortés they bade us welcome in their language, and as a sign of peace, they touched their hands against the ground, and kissed the ground with the hand.

There we halted for a good while, and Cacamatzin, the Lord of Texcoco, and the Lord of Iztapalapa and the Lord of Tacuba and the Lord of Coyoacan went on in advance to meet the Great Montezuma, who was approaching in a rich litter accompanied by other great Lords and Caciques, who owned vassals. When we arrived near to Mexico, where there were some other small towers, the Great Montezuma got down from his litter, and those great Caciques supported him with their arms beneath a marvellously rich canopy of green coloured feathers with much gold and silver embroidery and with pearls and chalchihuites suspended from a sort of bordering, which was wonderful to look at. The Great Montezuma was richly attired according to his usage, and he was shod with sandals [*cotoras*], for so they call what they wear on their feet, the soles were of gold and the upper part adorned with precious stones. The four Chieftains who supported his arms were also richly clothed according to their usage, in garments which were apparently held ready for them on the road to enable them to accompany their prince, for they did not appear in such attire when they came to receive us. Besides these four Chieftains, there were four other great Caciques, who supported the canopy over their heads, and many other Lords who walked before the Great Montezuma, sweeping the ground where he would tread and spreading cloths on it, so that he should not tread on the earth. Not one of these chieftains dared even to think of looking him in the face, but kept their eyes lowered with great reverence, except those four relations, his nephews, who supported him with their arms.

When Cortés was told that the Great Montezuma was approaching, and he saw him coming, he dismounted from his horse, and when he was near Montezuma, they simultaneously paid great reverence to one another. Montezuma bade him welcome and our Cortés replied through Doña Marina wishing him very good health. And it seems to me that Cortés, through Doña Marina, offered him his right hand, and Montezuma did not wish to take it, but he did give his hand to Cortés and Cortés brought out a necklace which he had ready at hand, made of glass stones, which I have already said are called Margaritas, which have within them many patterns of diverse colours, these were strung on a cord of gold and with musk so that it should have a sweet scent, and he placed it round the neck of the Great Montezuma and when he had so placed it he was going to embrace him, and those great Princes who accompanied Montezuma held back Cortés by the arm so that he should not embrace him, for they considered it an indignity.

Then Cortés through the mouth of Doña Marina told him that now his heart rejoiced at having seen such a great Prince, and that he took it as a great honour that he had come in person to meet him and had frequently shown him such favour.

Then Montezuma spoke other words of politeness to him, and told two of his nephews who supported his arms, the Lord of Texcoco and the Lord of Coyoacan, to go with us and show us to our quarters, and Montezuma with his other two relations, the Lord of Cuitlahuac and the Lord of Tacuba who accompanied him, returned to the city, and all those grand companies of Caciques and chieftains who had come with him returned in his train. As they turned back after their Prince we stood watching them and observed how they all marched with their eyes fixed on the ground without looking at him, keeping close to the wall, following him with great reverence. Thus space was made for us to enter the streets of Mexico, without being so much crowded. But who could now count the multitude of men and women and boys who were in the streets and on the azoteas,[1] and in canoes on the canals, who had come out to see us. It was indeed wonderful, and, now that I am writing about it, it all comes before my eyes as though it had happened but yesterday. Coming to think it over it seems to be a great mercy that our Lord Jesus Christ was pleased to give us grace and courage to dare to enter into such a city; and for the many times He has saved me from danger of death, as will be seen later on, I give Him sincere thanks, and in that He has preserved me to write about it, although I cannot do it as fully as is fitting or the subject needs. Let us make no words about it, for deeds are the best witnesses to what I say here and elsewhere.

Let us return to our entry to Mexico. They took us to lodge in some large houses, where there were apartments for all of us, for they had belonged to the father of the Great Montezuma, who was named Axayaca, and at that time Montezuma kept there the great oratories for his idols,

[1] Rooftops.

and a secret chamber where he kept bars and jewels of gold, which was the treasure that he had inherited from his father Axayaca, and he never disturbed it. They took us to lodge in that house, because they called us Teules, and took us for such, so that we should be with the Idols or Teules which were kept there. However, for one reason or another, it was there they took us, where there were great halls and chambers canopied with the cloth of the country for our Captain, and for every one of us beds of matting with canopies above, and no better bed is given, however great the chief may be, for they are not used. And all these palaces were [coated] with shining cement and swept and garlanded.

As soon as we arrived and entered into the great court, the Great Montezuma took our Captain by the hand, for he was there awaiting him, and led him to the apartment and saloon where he was to lodge, which was very richly adorned according to their usage, and he had at hand a very rich necklace made of golden crabs, a marvelous piece of work, and Montezuma himself placed it round the neck of our Captain Cortés, and greatly astonished his [own] Captains by the great honour that he was bestowing on him. When the necklace had been fastened, Cortés thanked Montezuma through our interpreters, and Montezuma replied — "Malinche you and your brethren are in your own house, rest awhile," and then he went to his palaces which were not far away, and we divided our lodgings by companies, and placed the artillery pointing in a convenient direction, and the order which we had to keep was clearly explained to us, and that we were to be much on the alert, both the cavalry and all of us soldiers. A sumptuous dinner was provided for us according to their use and custom, and we ate it at once. So this was our lucky and daring entry into the great city of Tenochtitlan Mexico on the 8th day of November the year of our Saviour Jesus Christ 1519.

Thanks to our Lord Jesus Christ for it all. And if I have not said anything that I ought to have said, may your honours pardon me, for I do not know now even at the present time how better to express it.

Let us leave this talk and go back to our story of what else happened to us, which I will go on to relate.

When the Great Montezuma had dined and he knew that some time had passed since our Captain and all of us had done the same, he came in the greatest state to our quarters with a numerous company of chieftains, all of them his kinsmen. When Cortés was told that he was approaching he came out to the middle of the Hall to receive him, and Montezuma took him by the hand, and they brought some seats, made according to their usage and very richly decorated and embroidered with gold in many designs, and Montezuma asked our Captain to be seated, and both of them sat down each on his chair. Then Montezuma began a very good speech, saying that he was greatly rejoiced to have in his house and his kingdom such valiant gentlemen as were Cortés and all of us. That two years ago he had received news of another Captain who came to Chanpoton, and likewise last year they had brought him news of another Captain who came with four ships, and that each time he had wished to see them, and now that he had us with him he was at our service, and would give us of all that he possessed; that it must indeed be true that we were those of whom his ancestors in years long past had spoken, saying that men would come from where the sun rose to rule over these lands, and that we must be those men, as we had fought so valiantly in the affairs at Potonchan and Tabasco and against the Tlaxcalans; for they had brought him pictures of the battles true to life.

Cortés answered him through our interpreters who always accompanied him, especially Doña Marina, and said to him that he and all of us did not know how to repay him the great favours we received from him every day. It was true that we came from where the sun rose, and were the vassals and servants of a great Prince called the Emperor Don Carlos, who held beneath his sway many and great princes, and that the Emperor having heard of him and what a great prince he was, had sent us to these parts to see him, and to beg them to become Christians, the same as our Emperor and all of us, so that his soul and those of all his vassals might be saved. Later on he would further explain how and in what manner this should be done, and how we worship one only true God, and who He is, and many other good things which he should listen to, such as he had already told to his ambassadors Tendile, and Pitalpitoque and Quintalbor when we were on the sand dunes. When this conference was over, the Great Montezuma had already at hand some very rich golden jewels, of many patterns, which he gave to our Captain, and in the same manner to each one of our Captains he gave trifles of gold, and three loads of mantles of rich feather work, and to the soldiers also he gave to each one two loads of mantles, and he did it cheerfully and in every way he seemed to be a great Prince. When these things had been distributed, he asked Cortés if we were all brethren and vassals of our great Emperor, and Cortés replied yes, we were brothers in affection and friendship, and persons of great distinction, and servants of our great King and Prince. Further polite speeches passed between Montezuma and Cortés, and as this was the first time he had come to visit us, and so as not to be wearisome, they ceased talking. Montezuma had ordered his stewards that, according to our own use and customs in all things, we should be provided with maize and [grinding] stones, and women to make bread, and fowls and fruit, and much fodder for the horses. Then Montezuma took leave of our Captain and all of us with the greatest courtesy, and we went out with him as far as the street. Cortés ordered us not to go far from our quarters for the present, until we knew better what was expedient. . . .

The next day Cortés decided to go to Montezuma's palace, and he first sent to find out what he intended doing and to let him know that we were coming. He took with him four captains, namely Pedro de Alvarado, Juan Velásquez de Leon, Diego de Ordás, and Gonzalo de Sandoval, and five of us soldiers also went with him.

When Montezuma knew of our coming he advanced to the middle of the hall to receive us, accompanied by many of his nephews, for no other chiefs were permitted to enter or hold communication with Montezuma where he then was, unless it were on important business. Cortés and he paid the greatest reverence to each other and then they took one another by the hand and Montezuma made him sit down on his couch on his right hand, and he also bade all of us to be seated on seats which he ordered to be brought.

Then Cortés began to make an explanation through our interpreters Doña Marina and Aguilar, and said that he and all of us were rested, and that in coming to see and converse with such a great Prince as he was, we had completed the journey and fulfilled the command which our great King and prince had laid on us. But what he chiefly came to say on behalf of our Lord God had already been brought to his [Montezuma's] knowledge through his ambassadors, Tendile, Pitalpitoque and Quintalbor, at the time when he did us the favour to send the golden sun and moon to the sand dunes; for we told them then that we were Christians and worshipped one true and only God, named Jesus Christ, who suffered death and passion to save us, and we told them that a cross (when they asked us why we worshipped it) was a sign of the other Cross on which our Lord God was crucified for our salvation, and that the death and passion which He suffered was for the salvation of the whole human race, which was lost, and that this our God rose on the third day and is now in heaven, and it is He who made the heavens and the earth, the sea and the sands, and created all the things there are in the world, and He sends the rain and the dew, and nothing happens in the world without

His holy will. That we believe in Him and worship Him, but that those whom they look upon as gods are not so, but are devils, which are evil things, and if their looks are bad their deeds are worse, and they could see that they were evil and of little worth, for where we had set up crosses such as those his ambassadors had seen, they dared not appear before them, through fear of them, and that as time went on they would notice this.

The favour he now begged of him was his attention to the words that he now wished to tell him; then he explained to him very clearly about the creation of the world, and how we are all brothers, sons of one father and one mother who were called Adam and Eve, and how such a brother as our great Emperor, grieving for the perdition of so many souls, such as those which their idols were leading to Hell, where they burn in living flames, had sent us, so that after what he [Montezuma] had now heard he would put a stop to it and they would no longer adore these Idols or sacrifice Indian men and women to them, for we were all brethren, nor should they commit sodomy or thefts. He also told them that, in course of time, our Lord and King would send some men who among us lead very holy lives, much better than we do, who will explain to them all about it, for at present we merely came to give them due warning, and so he prayed him to do what he was asked and carry it into effect.

As Montezuma appeared to wish to reply, Cortés broke off his argument, and to all of us who were with him he said: "with this we have done our duty considering it is the first attempt."

Montezuma replied—"Señor Malinche,* I have understood your words and arguments very well before now, from what you said to my servants at the sand dunes, this about three Gods and the Cross, and all those things that you have preached in the towns through which you have come. We have not made any answer to it because here throughout all time we have worshipped our own gods, and thought they were good, as no doubt yours are, so do not trouble to speak to us any more about them at present. Regarding the creation of the world, we have held the same belief for ages past, and for this reason we take it for certain that you are those whom our ancestors predicted would come from the direction of the sunrise. As for your great King, I feel that I am indebted to him, and I will give him of what I possess, for as I have already said, two years ago I heard of the Captains who came in ships from the direction

* Malinche, a term of respect, refers to Cortés in this case not to doña Marina.

in which you came, and they said that they were the servants of this your great King, and I wish to know if you are all one and the same.

Cortés replied, Yes, that we were all brethren and servants of our Emperor, and that those men came to examine the way and the seas and the ports so as to know them well in order that we might follow as we had done. Montezuma was referring to the expeditions of Francisco Hernández de Córdova and of Grijalva, when we first came on voyages of discovery, and he said that ever since that time he had wished to capture some of those men who had come so as to keep them in his kingdoms and cities and to do them honour, and his gods had now fulfilled his desires, for now that we were in his home, which we might call our own, we should rejoice and take our rest for there we should be well treated. And if he had on other occasions sent to say that we should not enter his city, it was not of his free will, but because his vassals were afraid, for they said that we shot out flashes of lightning, and killed many Indians with our horses, and that we were angry Teules, and other childish stories, and now that he had seen our persons and knew we were of flesh and bone, and had sound sense, and that we were very valiant, for these reasons he held us in much higher regard than he did from their reports, and he would share his possessions with us. Then Cortés and all of us answered that we thanked him sincerely for such signal good will, and Montezuma said, laughing, for he was very merry in his princely way of speaking: "Malinche, I know very well that these people of Tlaxcala with whom you are such good friends have told you that I am a sort of God or Teul, and that everything in my houses is made of gold and silver and precious stones, I know well enough that you are wise and did not believe it but took it as a joke. Behold now, Señor Malinche, my body is of flesh and bone like yours, my houses and palaces of stone and wood and lime; that I am a great king and inherit the riches of my ancestors is true, but not all the nonsense and lies that they have told you about me, although of course you treated it as a joke, as I did your thunder and lightning."

Cortés answered him, also laughing, and said that opponents and enemies always say evil things, without truth in them, of those whom they hate, and that he well knew that he could not hope to find another Prince more magnificent in these countries, and that not without reason had he been so vaunted to our Emperor. . . .

The Great Montezuma was about forty years old, of good height and well proportioned, slender, and spare of flesh, not very swarthy, but of the natural colour and shade of an Indian. He did not wear his hair long, but so as just to cover his ears, his scanty black beard was well shaped and thin. His face was somewhat long, but cheerful, and he had good eyes and showed in his appearance and manner both tenderness and, when necessary, gravity. He was very neat and clean and bathed once every day in the afternoon. He had many women as mistresses, daughters of Chieftains, and he had two great Cacicas as his legitimate wives, and when he had intercourse with them it was so secretly that no one knew anything about it, except some of his servants. He was free from unnatural offences. The clothes that he wore one day, he did not put on again until four days later. He had over two hundred chieftains in his guard, in other rooms close to his own, not that all were meant to converse with him, but only one or another, and when they went to speak to him they were obliged to take off their rich mantles and put on others of little worth, but they had to be clean, and they had to enter barefoot with their eyes lowered to the ground, and not to look up in his face. And they made him three obeisances, and said: "Lord, my Lord, my Great Lord," before they came up to him, and then they made their report and with a few words he dismissed them, and on taking leave they did not turn their backs, but kept their faces toward him with their eyes to the ground, and they did not turn their backs until they left the room. I noticed another thing, that when other great chiefs came from distant lands about disputes or business, when they reached the apartments of the Great Montezuma, they had to come barefoot and with poor mantles, and they might not enter directly into the Palace, but had to loiter about a little on one side of the Palace door, for to enter hurriedly was considered to be disrespectful.

For each meal, over thirty different dishes were prepared by his cooks according to their ways and usage, and they placed small pottery brasiers beneath the dishes so that they should not get cold. They prepared more than three hundred plates of the food that Montezuma was going to eat, and more than a thousand for the guard. When he was going to eat, Montezuma would sometimes go out with his chiefs and stewards, and they would point out to him which dish was best, and of what birds and other things it was composed, and as they advised him, so he would eat, but it was not often that he would go out to see the food, and then merely as a pastime.

I have heard it said that they were wont to cook for him the flesh of young boys, but as he had such a variety of dishes, made of so many things, we could not succeed in seeing if they were of human flesh or of other things, for they daily cooked fowls, turkeys, pheasants, native partridges, quail, tame and wild ducks, venison, wild boar, reed birds, pigeons, hares and rabbits, and many sorts of birds and other things which are bred in this country, and they are so numerous that I cannot finish naming them in a hurry; so we had no insight into it, but I know for certain that after our Captain censured the sacrifice of human beings, and the eating of their flesh, he ordered that such food should not be prepared for him thenceforth.

Let us cease speaking of this and return to the way things were served to him at meal times. It was in this way: if it was cold they made up a large fire of live coals of a firewood made from the bark of trees which did not give off any smoke, and the scent of the bark from which the fire was made was very fragrant, and so that it should not give off more heat than he required, they placed in front of it a sort of screen adorned with figures of idols worked in gold. He was seated on a low stool, soft and richly worked, and the table, which was also low, was made in the same style as the seats, and on it they placed the table cloths of white cloth and some rather long napkins of the same material. Four very beautiful cleanly women brought water for his hands in a sort of deep basin which they called "xicales," * and they held others like plates below to catch the water, and they brought him towels. And two other women brought him tortilla bread, and as soon as he began to eat they placed before him a sort of wooden screen painted over with gold, so that no one should watch him eating. Then the four women stood aside, and four great chieftains who were old men came and stood beside them, and with these Montezuma now and then conversed, and asked them questions, and as a great favour he would give to each of these elders a dish of what to him tasted best. They say that these elders were his near relations, and were his counselors and judges of law suits, and the dishes and food which Montezuma gave them they ate standing up with much reverence and without looking at his face. He was served on Cholula earthenware either red or black. While he was at his meal the men of his guard who were in the rooms near to that of Montezuma, never dreamed of making any noise or speaking aloud. They brought him fruit of all the different kinds that the land produced, but he ate very little of it. From time to time they brought him, in cup-shaped vessels of pure gold, a certain drink made from cacao which they said he took when he was going to visit his wives, and at the time he took no heed of it, but what I did see was that they brought over fifty great jugs of good cacao frothed up, and he drank of that, and the women served this drink to him with great reverence.

Sometimes at meal-times there were present some very ugly humpbacks, very small of stature and their bodies almost broken in half, who

* Gourds.

are their jesters, and other Indians, who must have been buffoons, who told him witty sayings, and others who sang and danced, for Montezuma was fond of pleasure and song, and to these he ordered to be given what was left of the food and the jugs of cacao. Then the same four women removed the table cloths, and with much ceremony they brought water for his hands. And Montezuma talked with those four old chieftains about things that interested him, and they took leave of him with the great reverence in which they held him, and he remained to repose.

As soon as the Great Montezuma had dined, all the men of the Guard had their meal and as many more of the other house servants, and it seems to me that they brought out over a thousand dishes of the food of which I have spoken, and then over two thousand jugs of cacao all frothed up, as they make it in Mexico, and a limitless quantity of fruit, so that with his women and female servants and bread makers and cacao makers his expenses must have been very great.

Let us cease talking about the expenses and the food for his household and let us speak of the Stewards and the Treasurers and the stores and pantries and of those who had charge of the houses where the maize was stored. I say that there would be so much to write about, each thing by itself, that I should not know where to begin, but we stood astonished at the excellent arrangements and the great abundance of provisions that he had in all, but I must add what I had forgotten, for it is as well to go back and relate it, and that is, that while Montezuma was at table eating as I have described, there were waiting on him two other graceful women to bring him tortillas, kneaded with eggs and other sustaining ingredients, and these tortillas were very white, and they were brought on plates covered with clean napkins, and they also brought him another kind of bread, like long balls kneaded with other kinds of sustaining food, and "pan pachol" for so they call it in this country, which is a sort of wafer. There were also placed on the table three tubes much painted and gilded, which held *liquidambar* mixed with certain herbs which they call *tabaco,* and when he had finished eating, after they had danced before him and sung and the table was removed, he inhaled the smoke from one of those tubes, but he took very little of it and with that he fell asleep.

Let us cease speaking about the service of his table and go back to our story. I remember that at that time his steward was a great Cacique to whom we gave the name of Tápia, and he kept the accounts of all the revenue that was brought to Montezuma, in his books which were made of paper which they call *Amal,* and he had a great house full of these books. Now we must leave the books and the accounts for it is outside our story, and say how Montezuma had two houses full of every sort of arms, many of them richly adorned with gold and precious stones. There were shields great and small, and a sort of broadswords, and others like two-handed swords set with stone knives which cut much better than our swords, and lances longer than ours are, with a fathom of blade with many knives set in it, which even when they are driven into a buckler or shield do not come out, in fact they cut like razors so that they can shave their heads with them. There were very good bows and arrows and double-pointed lances and others with one point, as well as their throwing sticks, and many slings and round stones shaped by hand, and some sort of artful shields which are so made that they can be rolled up, so as not to be in the way when they are not fighting, and when they are needed for fighting they let them fall down, and they cover the body from top to toe. There was also much quilted cotton armour, richly ornamented on the outside with many coloured feathers, used as devices and distinguishing marks, and there were casques or helmets made of wood and bone, also highly decorated with feathers on the outside, and there were other arms of other makes which, so as to avoid prolixity, I will not describe, and there were artisans who were skilled in such things and worked at them, and stewards who had charge of the arms.

Let us leave this and proceed to the Aviary, and I am forced to abstain from enumerating every kind of bird that was there and its peculiarity, for there was everything from the Royal Eagle and other smaller eagles, and many other birds of great size, down to tiny birds of many-coloured plumage, also birds from which they take the rich plumage which they use in their green feather work. The birds which have these feathers are about the size of the magpies in Spain, they are called in this country *Quezales,* and there are other birds which have feathers of five colours — green, red, white, yellow and blue; I don't remember what they are called; then there were parrots of many different colours, and there are so many of them that I forget their names, not to mention the beautifully marked ducks and other larger ones like them. From all these birds they plucked the feathers when the time was right to do so, and the feathers grew again. All the birds that I have spoken about breed in these houses, and in the setting season certain Indian men and women who look after the birds, place the eggs under them and clean the nests and feed them, so that each kind of bird has its proper food. In this house that I have spoken of there is a great tank of fresh water and in it there are other sorts of birds with long stilted legs, with body, wings and tail all red; I don't know their names, but in the Island of Cuba they are called *Ypiris,* and there are others something like them, and there are also in that tank many other kinds of birds which always live in the water.

Let us leave this and go on to another great house, where they keep many Idols, and they say that they are their fierce gods, and with them many kinds of carnivorous beasts of prey, tigers and two kinds of lions, and animals something like wolves which in this country they call jackals and foxes, and other smaller carnivorous animals, and all these carnivores they feed with flesh, and the greater number of them breed in the house. They give them as food deer and fowls, dogs and other things which they are used to hunt, and I have heard it said that they feed them on the bodies of the Indians who have been sacrificed. It is in this way: you have already heard me say that when they sacrifice a wretched Indian they saw open the chest with stone knives and hasten to tear out the palpitating heart and blood, and offer it to their Idols in whose name the sacrifice is made. Then they cut off the thighs, arms and head and eat the former at feasts and banquets, and the head they hang up on some beams, and the body of the man sacrificed is not eaten but given to these fierce animals. They also have in that cursed house many vipers and poisonous snakes which carry on their tails things that sound like bells. These are the worst vipers of all, and they keep them in jars and great pottery vessels with many feathers, and there they lay their eggs and rear their young, and they give them to eat the bodies of the Indians who have been sacrificed, and the flesh of dogs which they are in the habit of breeding. We even knew for certain that when they drove us out of Mexico and killed over eight hundred of our soldiers that they fed those fierce animals and snakes for many days on their bodies, as I will relate at the proper time and season. And those snakes and wild beasts were dedicated to those savage Idols, so that they might keep them company.

Let me speak now of the infernal noise when the lions and tigers roared and the jackals and the foxes howled and the serpents hissed, it was horrible to listen to and it seemed like a hell. Let us go on and speak of the skilled workmen he [Montezuma] employed in every craft that was practiced among them. We will begin with lapidaries and workers in gold and silver and all the hollow work, which even the great goldsmiths in Spain were forced to admire, and of these there were a great number of the best in a town named Azcapotzalco, a league from Mexico. Then for working precious stones and chalchihuites, which are like emeralds, there were other great artists. Let us go on to the great craftsmen in feather work, and painters and sculptors who were most refined; from what we see of their work to-day we can form a judgment of what they did then, for there are three Indians to-day in the City of Mexico named Marcos de Aquino, Juan de la Cruz and El Crespillo, so skilful in their work as sculptors and painters, that had they lived in the days of the ancient and famous Apelles, or of Michael Angelo Buonarotti, in our times, they would be placed in the same company. Let us go on to the Indian women who did the weaving and the washing, who made such an immense quantity of fine fabrics with wonderful feather work designs; the greater part of it was brought daily from some towns of the province on the north coast near Vera Cruz called Cotaxtla, close by San Juan de Ulua, where we disembarked when we came with Cortés.

In the house of the Great Montezuma himself, all the daughters of chieftains whom he had as mistresses always wore beautiful things, and there were many daughters of Mexican citizens who lived in retirement and wished to appear to be like nuns, who also did weaving but it was wholly of feather work. These nuns had their houses near the great Cue of Huichilobos and out of devotion to it, or to another idol, that of a woman who was said to be their mediatrix in the matter of marriage, their fathers placed them in that religious retirement until they married, and they were [only] taken out thence to be married.

Let us go on and tell about the great number of dancers kept by the Great Montezuma for his amusement, and others who used stilts on their feet, and others who flew when they danced up in the air, and others like Merry-Andrews, and I may say that there was a district full of these people who had no other occupation. Let us go on and speak of the workmen that he had as stone cutters, masons and carpenters, all of whom attended to the work of his houses, I say that he had as many as he wished for. We must not forget the gardens of flowers and sweet-scented trees, and the many kinds that there were of them, and the arrangement of them and the walks, and the ponds and tanks of fresh water where the water entered at one end and flowed out at the other; and the baths which he had there, and the variety of small birds that nested in the branches, and the medicinal and useful herbs that were in the gardens. It was a wonder to see, and to take care of it there were many gardeners. Everything was made in masonry and well cemented, baths and walks and closets, and apartments like summer houses where they danced and sang. There was as much to be seen in these gardens as there was everywhere else, and we could not tire of witnessing his great power. Thus as a consequence of so many crafts being practiced among them, a large number of skilled Indians were employed. . . .

As we had already been four days in Mexico and neither the Captain nor any of us had left our lodgings except to go to the houses and gardens, Cortés said to us that it would be well to go to the great Plaza and see the great Temple of Huichilobos, and that he wished to consult the Great Montezuma and have his approval. For this purpose he sent Jerónimo de

Aguilar and the Doña Marina as messengers, and with them went our Captain's small page named Orteguilla, who already understood something of the language. When Montezuma knew his wishes he sent to say that we were welcome to go; on the other hand, as he was afraid that we might do some dishonour to his Idols, he determined to go with us himself with many of his chieftains. He came out from his Palace in his rich litter, but when half the distance had been traversed and he was near some oratories, he stepped out of the litter, for he thought it a great affront to his idols to go to their house and temple in that manner. Some of the great chieftains supported him with their arms, and the tribal lords went in front of him carrying two staves like scepters held on high, which was the sign that the Great Montezuma was coming. (When he went in his litter he carried a wand half of gold and half of wood, which was held up like a wand of justice.) So he went on and ascended the great Cue accompanied by many priests, and he began to burn incense and perform other ceremonies to Huichilobos.

Let us leave Montezuma, who had gone ahead as I have said, and return to Cortés and our captains and soldiers, who according to our custom both night and day were armed, and as Montezuma was used to see us so armed when we went to visit him, he did not look upon it as anything new. I say this because our captain and all those who had horses went to Tlaltelolco on horseback, and nearly all of us soldiers were fully equipped, and many Caciques whom Montezuma had sent for that purpose went in our company. When we arrived at the great market place, called Tlaltelolco, we were astonished at the number of people and the quantity of merchandise that it contained, and at the good order and control that was maintained, for we had never seen such a thing before. The chieftains who accompanied us acted as guides. Each kind of merchandise was kept by itself and had its fixed place marked out. Let us begin with the dealers in gold, silver, and precious stones, feathers, mantles, and embroidered goods. Then there were other wares consisting of Indian slaves both men and women; and I say that they bring as many of them to that great market for sale as the Portuguese bring negroes from Guinea; and they brought them along tied to long poles, with collars round their necks so that they could not escape, and others they left free. Next there were other traders who sold great pieces of cloth and cotton, and articles of twisted thread, and there were *cacahuateros* who sold cacao. In this way one could see every sort of merchandise that is to be found in the whole of New Spain, placed in arrangement in the same manner as they do in my own country, which is Medina del Campo, where they hold the fairs, where each line of booths has its particular kind of merchandise, and so it is in this great market. There were those

who sold cloths of henequen and ropes and the *cotaras** with which they
are shod, which are made from the same plant, and sweet cooked roots,
and other tubers which they get from this plant, all were kept in one part
of the market in the place assigned to them. In another part there were
skins of tigers and lions, of otters and jackals, deer and other animals
and badgers and mountain cats, some tanned and others untanned, and
other classes of merchandise.

Let us go on and speak of those who sold beans and sage and other
vegetables and herbs in another part, and to those who sold fowls, cocks
with wattles, rabbits, hares, deer, mallards, young dogs and other things
of that sort in their part of the market, and let us also mention the fruiter-
ers, and the women who sold cooked food, dough and tripe in their own
part of the market; then every sort of pottery made in a thousand different forms from great water jars to little jugs, these also had a place to
themselves; then those who sold honey and honey paste and other dain-
ties like nut paste, and those who sold lumber, boards, cradles, beams,
blocks and benches, each article by itself, and the vendors of *ocote*† firewood, and other things of a similar nature. I must furthermore mention,
asking your pardon, that they also sold many canoes full of human ex-
crement, and these were kept in the creeks near the market, and this
they use to make salt or for tanning skins, for without it they say that
they cannot be well prepared. I know well that some gentlemen laugh at
this, but I say that it is so, and I may add that on all the roads it is a usual
thing to have places made of reeds or straw or grass, so that they may be
screened from the passers by, into these they retire when they wish to
purge their bowels so that even that filth should not be lost. But why do
I waste so many words in recounting what they sell in that great market,
for I shall never finish if I tell it all in detail. Paper, which in this country
is called *Amal,* and reeds scented with *liquidambar,* and full of tobacco,
and yellow ointments and things of that sort are sold by themselves, and
much cochineal is sold under the arcades which are in that great market
place, and there are many vendors of herbs and other sorts of trades.
There are also buildings where three magistrates sit in judgment, and
there are executive officers like *Alguacils* who inspect the merchandise.
I am forgetting those who sell salt, and those who make the stone
knives, and how they split them off the stone itself; and the fisherwomen
and others who sell some small cakes made from a sort of ooze which

---

*Sandals.
†Pitch-pine for torches.

they get out of the great lake, which curdles, and from this they make a bread having a flavour something like cheese. There are for sale axes of brass and copper and tin, and gourds and gaily painted jars made of wood. I could wish that I had finished telling of all the things which are sold there, but they are so numerous and of such different quality and the great market place with its surrounding arcades was so crowded with people, that one would not have been able to see and inquire about it all in two days.

Then we went to the great Cue, and when we were already approaching its great courts, before leaving the market place itself, there were many more merchants, who, as I was told, brought gold for sale in grains, just as it is taken from the mines. The gold is placed in thin quills of the geese of the country, white quills, so that the gold can be seen through, and according to the length and thickness of the quills they arrange their accounts with one another, how much so many mantles or so many gourds full of cacao were worth, or how many slaves, or whatever other thing they were exchanging.

Now let us leave the great market place, and not look at it again, and arrive at the great courts and walls where the great Cue stands. Before reaching the great Cue there is a great enclosure of courts, it seems to me larger than the plaza of Salamanca, with two walls of masonry surrounding it and the court itself all paved with very smooth great white flagstones. And where there were not these stones it was cemented and burnished and all very clean, so that one could not find any dust or a straw in the whole place. . . .

When we arrived there Montezuma came out of an oratory where his cursed idols were, at the summit of the great Cue, and two priests came with him, and after paying great reverence to Cortés and to all of us he said: "You must be tired, Señor Malinche, from ascending this our great Cue," and Cortés replied through our interpreters who were with us that he and his companions were never tired by anything. Then Montezuma took him by the hand and told him to look at his great city and all the other cities that were standing in the water, and the many other towns on the land round the lake, and that if he had not seen the great market place well, that from where they were they could see it better.

So we stood looking about us, for that huge and cursed temple stood so high that from it one could see over everything very well, and we saw the three causeways which led into Mexico, that is the causeway of Iztapalapa by which we had entered four days before, and that of Tacuba, along which later on we fled on the night of our great defeat, when Cuitlahuac the new prince drove us out of the city, as I shall tell later on, and that of Tepeaquilla, and we saw the fresh water that comes from Cha-pultepec which supplies the city, and we saw the bridges on the three causeways which were built at certain distances apart through which the water of the lake flowed in and out from one side to the other, and we be-held on that great lake a great multitude of canoes, some coming with supplies of food and others returning loaded with cargoes of merchan-dise; and we saw that from every house of that great city and of all the other cities that were built in the water it was impossible to pass from house to house, except by drawbridges which were made of wood or in canoes; and we saw in those cities Cues and oratories like towers and fortresses and all gleaming white, and it was a wonderful thing to be-hold; then the houses with flat roofs, and on the causeways other small towers and oratories which were like fortresses.

After having examined and considered all that we had seen we turned to look at the great market place and the crowds of people that were in it, some buying and others selling, so that the murmur and hum of their voices and words that they used could be heard more than a league off. Some of the soldiers among us who had been in many parts of the world, in Constantinople, and all over Italy, and in Rome, said that so large a market place and so full of people, and so well regulated and arranged, they had never beheld before.

Let us leave this, and return to our Captain, who said to Fray Bar-tolomé de Olmedo, who has often been mentioned by me, and who hap-pened to be near by him: "It seems to me, Señor Padre, that it would be a good thing to throw out a feeler to Montezuma, as to whether he would allow us to build our church here"; and the Padre replied that it would be a good thing if it were successful, but it seemed to him that it was not quite a suitable time to speak about it, for Montezuma did not appear to be inclined to do such a thing.

Then our Cortés said to Montezuma through the interpreter Doña Marina: "Your Highness is indeed a very great prince and worthy of even greater things. We are rejoiced to see your cities, and as we are here in your temple, what I now beg as a favour is that you will show us your gods and Teules. Montezuma replied that he must first speak with his high priests, and when he had spoken to them he said that we might en-ter into a small tower and apartment, a sort of hall, where there were two altars, with very richly carved boardings on the top of the roof. On each altar were two figures, like giants with very tall bodies and very fat, and the first which stood on the right hand they said was the figure of Huichilobos their god of War; it had a very broad face and monstrous and terrible eyes, and the whole of his body was covered with precious stones, and gold and pearls, and with seed pearls stuck on with a paste that they make in this country out of a sort of root, and all the body and head was covered with it, and the body was girdled by great snakes made of gold and precious stones, and in one hand he held a bow and in the other some arrows. And another small idol that stood by him, they said was his page, and he held a short lance and a shield richly decorated with gold and stones. Huichilobos had round his neck some Indians' faces and other things like hearts of Indians, the former made of gold and the latter of silver, with many precious blue stones.

There were some braziers with incense which they call copal, and in them they were burning the hearts of the three Indians whom they had sacrificed that day, and they had made the sacrifice with smoke and co-pal. All the walls of the oratory were so splashed and encrusted with blood that they were black, the floor was the same and the whole place stank vilely. Then we saw on the other side on the left hand there stood the other great image the same height as Huichilobos, and it had a face like a bear and eyes that shone, made of their mirrors which they call *Tezcat,* and the body plastered with precious stones like that of Huichilo-bos, for they say that the two are brothers; and this Tezcatepuca was the god of Hell and had charge of the souls of the Mexicans, and his body was girt with figures like little devils with snakes' tails. The walls were so clotted with blood and the soil so bathed with it that in the slaughter houses in Spain there is not such another stench.

They had offered to this Idol five hearts from that day's sacrifices. In the highest part of the Cue there was a recess of which the woodwork was very richly worked, and in it was another image half man and half lizard, with precious stones all over it, and half the body was covered with a mantle. They say that the body of this figure is full of all the seeds that there are in the world, and they say that it is the god of seed time and harvest, but I do not remember its name, and everything was cov-ered with blood, both walls and altar, and the stench was such that we could hardly wait the moment to get out of it.

They had an exceedingly large drum there, and when they beat it the sound of it was so dismal and like, so to say, an instrument of the infer-nal regions, that one could hear it a distance of two leagues, and they said that the skins it was covered with were those of great snakes. In that small place there were many diabolical things to be seen, bugles and trumpets and knives, and many hearts of Indians that they had burned in fumigating their idols, and everything was so clotted with blood, and there was so much of it, that I curse the whole of it, and as it stank like a slaughter house we hastened to clear out of such a bad stench and worse sight. Our Captain said to Montezuma through our interpreter, half laughing: "Señor Montezuma, I do not understand how such a great Prince and wise man as you are has not come to the conclusion, in your mind, that these idols of yours are not gods, but evil things that are called devils, and so that you may know it and all your priests may see it clearly, do me the favour to approve of my placing a cross here on the top of this tower, and that in one part of these oratories where your Huichilobos and Tezcatepuca stand we may divide off a space where we can set up an image of Our Lady (an image which Montezuma had already seen) and you will see by the fear in which these Idols hold it that they are deceiving you."

Montezuma replied half angrily, (and the two priests who were with him showed great annoyance,) and said: "Señor Malinche, if I had known that you would have said such defamatory things I would not have shown you my gods, we consider them to be very good, for they give us health and rains and good seed times and seasons and as many victories as we desire, and we are obliged to worship them and make sacrifices, and I pray you not to say another word to their dishonour."

When our Captain heard that and noted the angry looks he did not refer again to the subject, but said with a cheerful manner: "It is time for your Excellency and for us to return," and Montezuma replied that it was well, but that he had to pray and offer certain sacrifices on account of the great *tatacul,* that is to say sin, which he had committed in allowing us to ascend his great Cue, and being the cause of our being permitted to see his gods, and of our dishonouring them by speaking evil of them, so that before he left he must pray and worship.

Then Cortés said "I ask your pardon if it be so," and then we went down the steps, and as they numbered one hundred and fourteen, and as some of our soldiers were suffering from tumours and abscesses, their legs were tired by the descent.

I will leave off talking about the oratory, and I will give my impressions of its surroundings, and if I do not describe it as accurately as I should do, do not wonder at it, for at that time I had other things to think about, regarding what we had on hand, that is to say my soldier's duties and what my Captain ordered me to do, and not about telling stories. To go back to the facts, it seems to me that the circuit of the great Cue was equal to [that of] six large sites,* such as they measure in this country, and from below up to where a small tower stood, where they kept their idols, it narrowed, and in the middle of the lofty Cue up to its highest

* Solares. Solar is a town lot for house building.

point, there were five hollows like barbicans, but open, without screens, and as there are many Cues painted on the banners of the conquerors, and on one which I possess, any one who has seen them can infer what they looked like from outside, better that I myself saw and understood it. There was a report that at the time they began to build that great Cue, all the inhabitants of that mighty city had placed as offerings in the foundations, gold and silver and pearls and precious stones, and had bathed them with the blood of the many Indian prisoners of war who were sacrificed, and had placed there every sort and kind of seed that the land produces, so that their Idols should give them victories and riches, and large crops. Some of my inquisitive readers will ask, how could we come to know that into the foundations of that great Cue they cast gold and silver and precious chalchihuites and seeds, and watered them with the human blood of the Indians whom they sacrificed, when it was more than a thousand years ago that they built and made it? The answer I give to this is that after we took that great and strong city, and the sites were apportioned, it was then proposed that in [the place of] the great *Cue* we should build a church to our patron and guide Señor Santiago, and a great part of the site of the great temple of Huichilobos was occupied by the site of the holy church, and when they opened the foundations in order to strengthen them, they found much gold and silver and chalchihuites and pearls and seed pearls and other stones. And a settler in Mexico who occupied another part of the same site found the same things, and the officers of His Majesty's treasury demanded them saying that they belonged by right to His Majesty, and there was a lawsuit about it. I do not remember what happened except that they sought information from the Caciques and Chieftains of Mexico, and from Guatémoc, who was then alive, and they said that it was true that all the inhabitants of Mexico at that time cast into the foundations those jewels and all the rest of the things, and that so it was noted in their books and pictures of ancient things, and from this cause those riches were preserved for the building of the holy church of Santiago.

Let us leave this and speak of the great and splendid Courts which were in front of the [temple of] Huichilobos, where now stands [the church of] Señor Santiago, which was called Tlaltelolco, for so they were accustomed to call it.

I have already said that there were two walls of masonry [which had to be passed] before entering, and that the court was paved with white stones, like flagstones, carefully whitewashed and burnished and clean, and it was as large and as broad as the plaza of Salamanca. A little way apart from the great Cue there was another small tower which was also an Idol house, or a true hell, for it had at the opening of one gate a most terrible mouth such as they depict, saying that such there are in hell. The mouth was open with great fangs to devour souls, and here too were some groups of devils and bodies of serpents close to the door, and a little way off was a place of sacrifice all blood-stained and black with smoke, and encrusted with blood, and there were many great ollas and cántaros and tinajas * of water inside the house, for it was here that they cooked the flesh of the unfortunate Indians who were sacrificed, which was eaten by the priests. There were also near the place of sacrifice many large knives and chopping blocks, such as those on which they cut up meat in the slaughter houses. Then behind that cursed house, some distance away from it, were some great piles of firewood, and not far from them a large tank of water which rises and falls, the water coming through a tube from the covered channel which enters the city from Chapultepec. I always called that house "the Infernal Regions."

Let us go on beyond the court to another Cue where the great Mexican princes were buried, where also there were many Idols, and all was full of blood and smoke, and it had other doorways with hellish figures, and then near that Cue was another full of skulls and large bones arranged in perfect order, which one could look at but could not count, for there were too many of them. The skulls were by themselves and the bones in separate piles. In that place there were other Idols, and in every house or Cue or oratory that I have mentioned there were priests with long robes of black cloth and long hoods like those of the Dominicans, and slightly resembling those of the Canons. The hair of these priests was very long and so matted that it could not be separated or disentangled, and most of them had their ears scarified, and their hair was clotted with blood. Let us go on; there were other Cues, a little way from where the skulls were, which contained other Idols and places of sacrifice [decorated] with other evil paintings. And they said that those idols were intercessors in the marriages of men. I do not want to delay any longer telling about idols, but will only add that all round that great court there were many houses, not lofty, used and occupied by the priests and other Indians who had charge of the Idols. On one side of the great Cue there was another much larger pond or tank of very clear water dedicated solely to the service of Huichilobos and Tezcatepuca, and the water entered that pond through covered pipes which came from Chapultepec. Near to this were other large buildings such as a sort of nunnery where many of the daughters of the inhabitants of Mexico were

* Names of various large pottery vessels for holding water and cooking.

sheltered like nuns up to the time they were married, and there stood two Idols with the figures of women, which were the intercessors in the marriages of women, and women made sacrifices to them and held festivals so that they should give them good husbands.

I have spent a long time talking about this great Cue of Tlaltelolco and its Courts, but I say that it was the greatest temple in the whole of Mexico although there were many others, very splendid. Four or five parishes or districts possessed, between them, an oratory with its Idols, and as they were very numerous I have not kept count of them all. I will go on and say that the great oratory that they had in Cholula was higher than that of Mexico, for it had one hundred and twenty steps, and according to what they say they held the Idol of Cholula to be good, and they went to it on pilgrimages from all parts of New Spain to obtain absolution, and for this reason they built for it such a splendid Cue; but it is of another form from that of Mexico although the courts are the same, very large with a double wall. I may add that the Cue in the City of Texcoco was very lofty, having one hundred and seventeen steps, and the Courts were broad and fine, shaped in a different form from the others. It is a laughable matter that every province had its Idols and those of one province or city were of no use to the others, thus they had an infinite number of Idols and they made sacrifices to them all.

After our Captain and all of us were tired of walking about and seeing such a diversity of Idols and their sacrifices, we returned to our quarters, all the time accompanied by many Caciques and chieftains whom Montezuma sent with us. I will stop here and go on to say what more we did.

6

Things Fall Apart:
Toxcatl and the *Noche triste*

After installing themselves in the palaces, invited by Moctezuma, the Spaniards settled into a routine. Relations with Moctezuma remained cordial and visits between him and Cortés were done with considerable courtesy and formality. Meanwhile, the Spaniards began to reconnoiter the city, examining the markets, the temples, and the crowds. The Spaniards also built a small chapel for their prayers and discovered a secret vault filled with treasure in one of the temple walls. Bernal Díaz tells of this period in some detail. He also claims that some of the Spanish captains and soldiers prevailed upon Cortés to place Moctezuma under arrest in order to forestall any rebellion against them. The plans were already under way for this move when justification for it arrived from the coast. Word was brought of a battle near Vera Cruz in which the Totonacs supported by the Spaniards had resisted a Mexica army aimed at restoring the Totonacs to a tributary status. Cortés used the incident as an excuse to take Moctezuma hostage and to demand the execution of the Mexica captains responsible for the attack. With this audacious and treacherous act, barely a week after the Spanish entry into Tenochtitlan, Cortés seized the initiative, making Moctezuma a prisoner in his own city. While some of the other leaders like Cacamatzin, ruler of Texcoco, advocated resistance to the strangers, with Moctezuma still alive, many of the Mexica were reluctant to act against his wishes, although Cortés and Bernal Díaz both suggested that Moctezuma was himself secretly organizing a resistance. In any case, for dynastic, ethnic, and personal reasons, the Mexica city-states and the various factions inside Tenochtitlan were still not able to mount a resistance and Moctezuma retained his role as a Spanish captive and puppet, albeit a reluctant one.

At the end of April 1520, news arrived from Vera Cruz that a large expedition had been sent by Diego Velázquez, governor of Cuba, to arrest Cortés for his disobedience. Almost a thousand soldiers with artillery and horses had been sent against Cortés under Pánfilo Narváez.

Whereas divisions among the native peoples had until this moment hindered their actions against the Spaniards, divisions among the Europeans now threatened Cortés's program. Leaving a small garrison under Pedro de Alvarado in control of the palaces and of Moctezuma, and pretending that the newly arrived Spaniards were his friends (although Moctezuma's spies had probably informed him of the truth), Cortés marched with about two hundred men and many Tlaxcalan allies to meet this new threat. In a quick, surprise attack, Cortés routed Narváez and his forces. He then offered to let Narváez's men return to Cuba (in disgrace) or to join him in the conquest of a great and wealthy empire. By this stroke of good luck and skill, Cortés converted a potential disaster into reinforcements and marched back to Tenochtitlan with about 1,400 new recruits. Despite various promises he had made to win the support of the newcomers, a division developed between the men of the original band and those later recruited from Narváez's forces. That division would continue to plague Spanish operations.

Meanwhile in Tenochtitlan, the situation had darkened. Alvarado was brave but impulsive. The accounts of Bernal Díaz and those of the Nahua observers differ on what happened, but apparently in Cortés's absence, the Mexica approached Alvarado and asked permission to celebrate the festival of Toxcatl in honor of Huitzilopochtli. Permission was given, but during the festival when "song was linked to song" (see Figure 12), as the Nahua accounts retell it, Alvarado staged a surprise attack on the unarmed celebrants. Hundreds of the leading nobles and warriors were brutally slain and the city then rose in open revolt, surrounding the Spaniards in the temple precinct and placing them under siege. Alvarado forced Moctezuma to try to stop the siege but his authority was weakening. Cortés, learning of the situation, made a forced march back to Tenochtitlan and on June 24 reentered the city. No crowds of curious Mexica awaited the Spaniards this time, but rather abandoned streets and a sullen population. Moctezuma was already dead. Spanish and Nahua accounts differ on what had happened to the Mexica ruler. The Spanish versions claim that he was struck by a stone as he tried from a rooftop to dissuade his people from attacking. The Nahua accounts state that he was murdered by the Spaniards. In any case, his brother Cuitlahuac, lord of Iztapalapa, began to organize the resistance and was soon recognized as the new *tlatoani*. There is no dispute over what happened to the nobles who waited on Moctezuma in captivity. They were simply put to death by the Spaniards.

The Spanish position had become untenable, surrounded as they were in the heart of the city, besieged and cut off from food and water.

Figure 12. A Mexica festival. Warriors dance to the sound of the traditional drums.
Source: From the *Codex Tovar.* Courtesy of the John Carter Brown Library at Brown University, Providence, Rhode Island.

Bernal Díaz describes the conditions and the discussions on a plan of action. On the rainy night of June 30, 1520, Cortés, his men and allies stealthily broke out. Discovered, a savage battle ensued. Hundreds of Spaniards and thousands of Tlaxcalans were killed before the Spanish force reached the lakeshore. The escape from the city had been made but the event was always remembered by the Spaniards thereafter as the "*Noche triste*" (Sad Night).

FRANCISCO LÓPEZ DE GÓMARA

From *Istoria de la conquista de Mexico*

The question of responsibility for the Toxcatl massacre is addressed first in a chapter from Istoria de la conquista de Mexico *(Zaragoza, 1552) by Francisco López de Gómara, Cortés's secretary and biographer. Gómara had access to Cortés's private papers and his biography was always favorable to the conqueror's interests. Neither Bernal Díaz nor Cortés were in Tenochtitlan during the Toxcatl massacre so their accounts are based on hearsay rather than on their own observation.*

Francisco López de Gómara — cleric, Renaissance scholar, and author of great stylistic ability — became Cortés's confessor. His history of the conquest published in 1552 was essentially a defense and apologia *for Cortés and was, in fact, dedicated to Cortés's son. By this time Cortés was in disfavor because of his political ambitions and so López de Gómara's book, like Cortés's letters, was banned. Bernal Díaz particularly objected to its unceasing pro-Cortés stance, the artistic license of the author in reporting apparitions of various saints during the battles, and probably, most of all, by the fact that López de Gómara had published first. Still, López de Gómara knew how to tell a story, and even in the sixteenth century other Europeans were fascinated by the events in Mexico, as this modernization of an Elizabethan translation of the* Istoria *attests.*

Francisco López de Gómara, *Istoria de la conquista de Mexico*, in *Cortés: The Life of the Conqueror.* This excerpt is taken from an English translation, *The Pleasant Historie of the Conquest of the West India, now called New Spaine* (London, 1577), modernized by Stuart B. Schwartz.

Cortés procured to know the principal cause of the insurrection of the Mexican Indians, and having a general day of hearing, the charge being laid against them, some said, that it was through the letters and persuasion of Narvaez, others answered [that] their desire and meaning was to expel the strangers, according to agreement made, for in their skirmishes they cried nothing but "Get you hence, get you hence." Others said, that they pretended the liberty of Mutezuma, for in their combats they would say, "Let go our god and king, if you list not to be slain." Others said, that they [the Spaniards] were thieves and had robbed their gold and plate [silver] from them which was in value more than seven hundred thousand duckets. Others cried, "Here you shall leave the gold that you have taken from us." Others said that they could not abide the Tlaxcaltecas and other mortal enemies. Many believed that the mutiny was for throwing down their gods and idols. Each of these causes were sufficient to rebel, how much more altogether.

But the chiefest and most principal cause was, that after the departure of Cortés toward Narvaez, happened a solemn holiday which the Mexicans were wont to celebrate, and desiring to observe the same, as they were wont to do, they came and besought the captain Alvarado to grant them license and not to imagine that they were formed together to kill the Spaniards. Alvarado gave them license with [no] such conditions, that in their sacrifice there should be no blood spilt nor yet to wear [bear] any weapon.

At this feast five hundred Gentlemen and principal persons joined together in the great Temple: some do say that there were more than a thousand persons of great estate, but that night they made a marvelous great noise with cornets, shells, cloven bones, wherewith they made a strange music. They celebrated the feast, their naked bodies covered with tele [cloth] made and wrought with precious stones, collars, girdles, bracelets, and many other jewels of gold, silver and aliofar [mother of pearl] with gallant tufts of feathers on their heads. They danced a dance called *Mazeualiztli* which is to say desert [reward] with pain, and so they call [the term derived from] Mazauali a husbandman. This dance is like Netoriliztli which is another dance. The manner is that they lay out mats in the Temple yard, and with the sound of their drums called atabals they dance around, hand in hand, some singing and others answer, which songs were in honor and praise of the god or saint whose feast it is, hoping for this service to have rain, corn, health, victory, peace, children or any other thing that they may wish or desire.

These Indian gentlemen being occupied in their dancing and ceremonies, it fortuned that Pedro de Alvarado went to the Temple of

Figure 13. Cortés as kingmaker. Here, he crowns Ixlilxochitl as *tlatoani* of Texcoco. This was part of the Spanish policy of isolating Tenochtitlan by creating regimes friendly to Cortés among the other Nahua city-states.
Source: Diego Garcia Panes, *La Conquista,* ed. José Ignacio Echeagaray (Mexico City: San Angel Ediciones, 1976). These are selections from Garcia Panes's eighteenth-century work "Theatro de Nueva España" in the Biblioteca Nacional in Mexico City. Courtesy Biblioteca Nacional.

Uitzilopochtli to behold their doings, and whether his going was of his own accord or by the consent of his company I am not certain, although some say that he was advised how the mutiny was there conspired, as after did follow: others hold opinion that their only going to the Temple was to behold the marvelous and strange dance. And then seeing them so richly attired, they coveted their gold and jewels which they wore and besieged the Temple with ten Spaniards at each door, and the Captain entered in with fifty men, and without any Christian respect slew and murdered them all and took from them all their treasure. Although this fact seemed odious to Cortés, yet his own proceedings as time did them require, not knowing what need he might have of them [the culprits], but especially to avoid contention among his company.

From the *Florentine Codex* and the *Codex Aubin*

Miguel León-Portilla, the great Mexican scholar, gathered together a number of postconquest indigenous texts on the Toxcatl incident in his volume Broken Spears. *Included here are his renditions of the* Florentine Codex *accounts and a small section from the* Codex Aubin, *a manuscript postconquest collection of Nahuatl writings preserved in Paris. The indigenous sources give no indication that any "rebellion" was coordinated with the festival. These sources make the shock of these events clear.*

The Preparations for the Fiesta

The Aztecs begged permission of their king to hold the fiesta of Huitzilopochtli. The Spaniards wanted to see this fiesta to learn how it was celebrated. A delegation of the celebrants came to the palace where Motecuhzoma was a prisoner, and when their spokesman asked his permission, he granted it to them.

As soon as the delegation returned, the women began to grind seeds of the chicalote.* These women had fasted for a whole year. They ground the seeds in the patio of the temple.

*Argemone mexicana, an edible plant, also used in medicines.

Miguel León-Portilla, *The Broken Spears: The Aztec Account of the Conquest of Mexico,* 2nd ed. (Boston: Beacon Press, 1992), 71–78, 80–81.

The Spaniards came out of the palace together, dressed in armor and carrying their weapons with them. They stalked among the women and looked at them one by one; they stared into the faces of the women who were grinding seeds. After this cold inspection, they went back into the palace. It is said that they planned to kill the celebrants if the men entered the patio.

The Beginning of the Fiesta

Early the next morning, the statue's face was uncovered by those who had been chosen for that ceremony. They gathered in front of the idol in single file and offered it gifts of food, such as round seedcakes or perhaps human flesh. But they did not carry it up to its temple on top of the pyramid.

All the young warriors were eager for the fiesta to begin. They had sworn to dance and sing with all their hearts, so that the Spaniards would marvel at the beauty of the rituals.

The procession began, and the celebrants filed into the temple patio to dance the Dance of the Serpent. When they were all together in the patio, the songs and the dance began. Those who had fasted for twenty days and those who had fasted for a year were in command of the others; they kept the dancers in file with their pine wands. (If anyone wished to urinate, he did not stop dancing, but simply opened his clothing at the hips and separated his clusters of heron feathers.)

If anyone disobeyed the leaders or was not in his proper place they struck him on the hips and shoulders. Then they drove him out of the patio, beating him and shoving him from behind. They pushed him so hard that he sprawled to the ground, and they dragged him outside by the ears. No one dared to say a word about this punishment, for those who had fasted during the year were feared and venerated; they had earned the exclusive title "Brothers of Huitzilopochtli."

The great captains, the bravest warriors, danced at the head of the files to guide the others. The youths followed at a slight distance. Some of the youths wore their hair gathered into large locks, a sign that they had never taken any captives. Others carried their headdresses on their shoulders; they had taken captives, but only with help.

Then came the recruits, who were called "the young warriors." They had each captured an enemy or two. The others called to them: "Come, comrades, show us how brave you are! Dance with all your hearts!"

The Spaniards Attack the Celebrants

At this moment in the fiesta, when the dance was loveliest and when song was linked to song, the Spaniards were seized with an urge to kill the celebrants. They all ran forward, armed as if for battle. They closed the entrances and passageways, all the gates of the patio: the Eagle Gate in the lesser palace, the Gate of the Canestalk and the Gate of the Serpent of Mirrors. They posted guards so that no one could escape, and then rushed into the Sacred Patio to slaughter the celebrants. They came on foot, carrying their swords and their wooden or metal shields.

They ran in among the dancers, forcing their way to the place where the drums were played. They attacked the man who was drumming and cut off his arms. Then they cut off his head, and it rolled across the floor.

They attacked all the celebrants, stabbing them, spearing them, striking them with their swords. They attacked some of them from behind, and these fell instantly to the ground with their entrails hanging out. Others they beheaded: they cut off their heads, or split their heads to pieces.

They struck others in the shoulders, and their arms were torn from their bodies. They wounded some in the thigh and some in the calf. They slashed others in the abdomen, and their entrails all spilled to the ground. Some attempted to run away, but their intestines dragged as they ran; they seemed to tangle their feet in their own entrails. No matter how they tried to save themselves, they could find no escape.

Some attempted to force their way out, but the Spaniards murdered them at the gates. Others climbed the walls, but they could not save themselves. Those who ran into the communal houses were safe there for a while; so were those who lay down among the victims and pretended to be dead. But if they stood up again, the Spaniards saw them and killed them.

The blood of the warriors flowed like water and gathered into pools. The pools widened, and the stench of blood and entrails filled the air. The Spaniards ran into the communal houses to kill those who were hiding. They ran everywhere and searched everywhere; they invaded every room, hunting and killing.

The Aztecs Retaliate

When the news of this massacre was heard outside the Sacred Patio, a great cry went up: "Mexicanos, come running! Bring your spears and shields! The strangers have murdered our warriors!"

This cry was answered with a roar of grief and anger: the people shouted and wailed and beat their palms against their mouths. The captains assembled at once, as if the hour had been determined in advance. They all carried their spears and shields.

Then the battle began. The Aztecs attacked with javelins and arrows, even with the light spears that are used for hunting birds. They hurled their javelins with all their strength, and the cloud of missiles spread out over the Spaniards like a yellow cloak.

The Spaniards immediately took refuge in the palace. They began to shoot at the Mexicans with their iron arrows and to fire their cannons and arquebuses. And they shackled Motecuhzoma in chains.

The Lament for the Dead

The Mexicans who had died in the massacre were taken out of the patio one by one and inquiries were made to discover their names. The fathers and mothers of the dead wept and lamented.

Each victim was taken first to his own home and then to the Sacred Patio, where all the dead were brought together. Some of the bodies were later burned in the place called the Eagle Urn, and others in the House of the Young Men.

Motecuhzoma's Message

At sunset, Itzcuauhtzin climbed onto the roof of the palace and shouted this proclamation: "Mexicanos! Tlatelolcas! Your king, the lord Motecuhzoma, has sent me to speak for him. Mexicanos, hear me, for these are his words to you: 'We must not fight them. We are not their equals in battle. Put down your shields and arrows.'

"He tells you this because it is the aged who will suffer most, and they deserve your pity. The humblest classes will also suffer, and so will the innocent children who still crawl on all fours, who still sleep in their cradles.

"Therefore your king says: 'We are not strong enough to defeat them. Stop fighting, and return to your homes.' Mexicanos, they have put your king in chains; his feet are bound with chains."

When Itzcuauhtzin had finished speaking, there was a great uproar among the people. They shouted insults at him in their fury, and cried: "Who is Motecuhzoma to give us orders? We are no longer his slaves!" They shouted war cries and fired arrows at the rooftop. The Spaniards quickly hid Motecuhzoma and Itzcuauhtzin behind their shields so that the arrows would not find them.

The Mexicans were enraged because the attack on the captains had been so treacherous: their warriors had been killed without the slightest warning. Now they refused to go away or to put down their arms.

The Massacre According to the *Codex Aubin*

Motecuhzoma said to La Malinche: "Please ask the god to hear me. It is almost time to celebrate the fiesta of Toxcatl. It will last for only ten days, and we beg his permission to hold it. We merely burn some incense and dance our dances. There will be a little noise because of the music, but that is all."

The Captain said: "Very well, tell him they may hold it." Then he left the city to meet another force of Spaniards who were marching in this direction. Pedro de Alvarado, called The Sun, was in command during his absence.

When the day of the fiesta arrived, Motecuhzoma said to The Sun: "Please hear me, my lord. We beg your permission to begin the fiesta of our god."

The Sun replied: "Let it begin. We shall be here to watch it."

The Aztec captains then called for their elder brothers, who were given this order: "You must celebrate the fiesta as grandly as possible."

The elder brothers replied: "We will dance with all our might."

Then Tecatzin, the chief of the armory, said: "Please remind the lord that he is here, not in Cholula. You know how they trapped the Cholultecas in their patio! They have already caused us enough trouble. We should hide our weapons close at hand!"

But Motecuhzoma said: "Are we at war with them? I tell you, we can trust them."

Tecatzin said: "Very well."

Then the songs and dances began. A young captain wearing a lip plug guided the dancers; he was Cuatlazol, from Tolnahuac.

But the songs had hardly begun when the Christians came out of the palace. They entered the patio and stationed four guards at each entrance. Then they attacked the captain who was guiding the dance. One of the Spaniards struck the idol in the face, and others attacked the three men who were playing the drums. After that there was a general slaughter until the patio was heaped with corpses.

A priest from the Place of the Canefields cried out in a loud voice: "Mexicanos! Who said we are not at war? Who said we could trust them?"

The Mexicans could only fight back with sticks of wood; they were cut to pieces by the swords. Finally the Spaniards retired to the palace where they were lodged.

BERNAL DÍAZ

From *The True History of the Conquest of New Spain*

In his account, Bernal Díaz, who had gone with Cortés to attack Narváez, reported on the return to a Tenochtitlan in arms. Cortés, he reported, was furious with Alvarado but also with Moctezuma, whom he suspected had been in contact with Narváez. The intercession of various Spanish captains in favor of the captive ruler did not pacify him. It quickly became apparent that the Spaniards were besieged. Three excerpts are presented here; first, Díaz's account of the battle to control the major cue, *the pyramid and temple of Huitzilopochtli; second, the death of Moctezuma; and lastly the escape of the* Noche triste *and the disastrous (for the Spaniards and Tlaxcalans) fighting at the Tolteca canal.*

. . . We passed the night in dressing wounds and in mending the breaches in the walls that they [the enemy] had made, and in getting ready for the next day. Then, as soon as it was dawn, our Captain decided that all of us and Narvaez' men should sally out to fight with them and that we should take the cannon and muskets and crossbows and endeavour to defeat them, or at least to make them feel our strength and valour better than the day before. I may state that when we came to this decision, the Mexicans were arranging the very same thing. We fought very well, but they were so strong, and had so many squadrons which relieved each other from time to time, that even if ten thousand Trojan Hectors and as many more Roldans had been there, they would not have been able to break through them.

So that it may now be understood, I will relate how it happened. We noted [their] tenacity in fighting, but I declare that I do not know how to

Bernal Díaz, from *The True History of the Conquest of New Spain,* ed. A. P. Maudslay (London: Hakluyt Society, 1908), 230–48.

describe it, for neither cannon nor muskets nor crossbows availed, nor hand-to-hand fighting, nor killing thirty or forty of them every time we charged, for they still fought on in as close ranks and with more energy than in the beginning. Sometimes when we were gaining a little ground or a part of the street, they pretended to retreat, but it was [merely] to induce us to follow them and cut us off from our fortress and quarters, so as to fall on us in greater safety to themselves, believing that we could not return to our quarters alive, for they did us much damage when we were retreating.

Then, as to going out to burn their houses, I have already said in the chapter that treats of the subject, that between one house and another, they have wooden drawbridges, and these they raised so that we could only pass through deep water. Then we could not endure the rocks and stones [hurled] from the roofs, in such a way that they damaged and wounded many of our men. I do not know why I write thus, so lukewarmly, for some three or four soldiers who were there with us and who had served in Italy, swore to God many times that they had never seen such fierce fights, not even when they had taken part in such between Christians, and against the artillery of the King of France, or of the Great Turk, nor had they seen men like those Indians with such courage in closing up their ranks.

However, as they said many other things and gave explanations of them, as will be seen further on, I will leave the matter here, and will relate how, with great difficulty we withdrew to our quarters, many squadrons of warriors still pressing on us with loud yells and whistles, and trumpets and drums, calling us villains and cowards who did not dare to meet them all day in battle, but turned in flight.

On that day they killed ten or twelve more soldiers and we all returned badly wounded. What took place during the night was the arrangement that in two days' time all the soldiers in camp, as many as were able, should sally out with four engines like towers built of strong timber, in such a manner that five and twenty men could find shelter under each of them, and they were provided with apertures and loopholes through which to shoot, and musketeers and crossbowmen accompanied them, and close by them were to march the other soldiers, musketeers and crossbowmen and the guns, and all the rest, and the horsemen were to make charges.

When this plan was settled, as we spent all that day in carrying out the work and in strengthening many breaches that they had made in the walls, we did not go out to fight.

I do not know how to tell of the great squadrons of warriors who came to attack us in our quarters, not only in ten or twelve places, but in more than twenty, for we were distributed over them all and in many other places, and while we built up and fortified [ourselves], as I have related, many other squadrons openly endeavoured to penetrate into our quarters, and neither with guns, crossbows nor muskets, nor with many charges and sword-thrusts could we force them back, for they said that not one of us should remain [alive] that day and they would sacrifice our hearts and blood to their gods, and would have enough to glut [their appetites] and hold feasts on our arms and legs, and would throw our bodies to the tigers, lions, vipers and snakes, which they kept caged, so that they might gorge on them, and for that reason they had ordered them not to be given food for the past two days. As for the gold we possessed, we would get little satisfaction from it or from all the cloths; and as for the Tlaxcalans who were with us, they said that they would place them in cages to fatten, and little by little they would offer their bodies in sacrifice; and, very tenderly, they said that we should give up to them their great Lord Montezuma, and they said other things. Night by night, in like manner, there were always many yells and whistles and showers of darts, stones and arrows.

As soon as dawn came, after commending ourselves to God, we sallied out from our quarters with our towers (and it seems to me that in other countries where I have been,* in wars where such things were necessary, they were called "Buros" and "Mantas") with the cannon, muskets and crossbows in advance, and the horsemen making charges, but, as I have stated, although we killed many of them it availed nothing towards making them turn their backs, indeed if they had fought bravely on the two previous days, they proved themselves far more vigorous and displayed much greater forces and squadrons on this day. Nevertheless, we determined, although it should cost the lives of all of us, to push on with our towers and engines as far as the great Cue of Huichilobos.

I will not relate at length, the fights we had with them in a fortified house, nor will I tell how they wounded the horses, nor were they [the horses] of any use to us, because although they charged the squadrons to break through them, so many arrows, darts and stones were hurled at them, that they, well protected by armour though they were, could not prevail against them [the enemy], and if they pursued and overtook them, the Mexicans promptly dropped for safety into the canals and lagoons where they had raised other walls against the horsemen, and many other Indians were stationed with very long lances to finish killing them. Thus it benefited us nothing to turn aside to burn or demolish a

---

*The text says "donde me he hallado en guerra," but Bernal Díaz had not been in any wars except wars in America.

house, it was quite useless, for, as I have said, they all stood in the water, and between house and house there was a movable bridge, and to cross by swimming was very dangerous, for on the roofs they had such store of rocks and stones and such defences, that it was certain destruction to risk it. In addition to this, where we did set fire to some houses, a single house took a whole day to burn, and the houses did not catch fire one from the other, as, for one reason, they stood apart with the water between; and, for the other, were provided with flat roofs (azoteas); thus it was useless toil to risk our persons in the attempt, so we went towards the great Cue of their Idols. Then, all of a sudden, more than four thousand Mexicans ascended it, not counting other Companies that were posted on it with long lances and stones and darts, and placed themselves on the defensive, and resisted our ascent for a good while, and neither the towers nor the cannon or crossbows, nor the muskets were of any avail, nor the horsemen, for, although they wished to charge [with] their horses, the whole of the courtyard was paved with very large flagstones, so that the horses lost their foothold, and they [the stones] were so slippery that they [the horses] fell. While from the steps of the lofty Cue they forbade our advance, we had so many enemies both on one side and the other that although our cannon [shots] carried off ten or fifteen of them and we slew many others by sword-thrusts and charges, so many men attacked us that we were not able to ascend the lofty Cue. However with great unanimity we persisted in the attack, and without taking the towers (for they were already destroyed) we made our way to the summit.

Here Cortés showed himself very much of a man, as he always was. Oh! what a fight and what a fierce battle it was that took place; it was a memorable thing to see us all streaming with blood, and covered with wounds and others slain. It pleased our Lord that we reached the place where we used to keep the image of Our Lady, and we did not find it, and it appears, as we came to know, that the great Montezuma paid devotion to Her, and ordered it [the image] to be preserved in safety.

We set fire to their Idols and a good part of the chamber with the Idols Huichilobos and Tezcatepuca was burned. On that occasion the Tlaxcalans helped us very greatly. After this was accomplished, while some of us were fighting and others kindling the fire, as I have related, oh! to see the priests who were stationed on this great Cue, and the three or four thousand Indians, all men of importance. While we descended, oh! how they made us tumble down six or even ten steps at a time! And so much more there is to tell of the other squadrons posted on the battlements and recesses of the great Cue discharging so many darts and arrows that we could face neither one group of squadrons nor the other. We resolved to return, with much toil and risk to ourselves, to our quarters, our castles being destroyed, all of us wounded and sixteen slain, with the Indians constantly pressing on us and other squadrons on our flanks.

However clearly I may tell all this, I can never [fully] explain it to any one who did not see us. So far, I have not spoken of what the Mexican squadrons did who kept on attacking our quarters while we were marching outside, and the great obstinacy and tenacity they displayed in forcing their way in.

In this battle, we captured two of the chief priests, whom Cortés ordered us to convey with great care.

Many times I have seen among the Mexicans and Tlaxcalans, paintings of this battle, and the ascent that we made of the great Cue, as they look upon it as a very heroic deed. And although in the pictures that they have made of it, they depict all of us as badly wounded and streaming with blood and many of us dead they considered it a great feat, this setting fire to the Cue, when so many warriors were guarding it both on the battlements and recesses, and many more Indians were below on the ground and the Courts were full of them and there were many more on the sides; and with our towers destroyed, how was it possible to scale it? . . .

Let us return to the great attacks they made on us; Montezuma was placed by a battlement of the roof with many of us soldiers guarding him, and he began to speak to them [his people], with very affectionate expressions [telling them] to desist from the war, and that we would leave Mexico. Many of the Mexican Chieftains and Captains knew him well and at once ordered their people to be silent and not to discharge darts, stones or arrows, and four of them reached a spot where Montezuma could speak to them, and they to him, and with tears they said to him: "Oh! Señor, and our great Lord, how all your misfortune and injury and that of your children and relations afflicts us, we make known to you that we have already raised one of your kinsmen to be our Lord," and there he stated his name, that he was called Cuitlahuac, the Lord of Ixtapalapa, (for it was not Guatemoc, he who was Lord soon after,) and moreover they said that the war must be carried through, and that they had vowed to their Idols not to relax it until we were all dead, and that they prayed every day to their Huichilobos and Texcatepuca to guard him free and safe from our power, and that should it end as they desired, they would not fail to hold him in higher regard as their Lord than they did before, and they begged him to forgive them. They had hardly finished this speech when suddenly such a shower of stones and darts was discharged that (our men who were shielding him having neglected their duty [to shield him] for a moment, because they saw how the attack ceased while he spoke to them) he was hit by three stones, one on the head, another on the arm and another on the leg, and although they begged him to have the wounds dressed and to take food, and spoke kind words to him about it, he would not. Indeed, when we least expected it, they came to say that he was dead. Cortés wept for him, and all of us Captains and soldiers, and there was no man among us who knew him and was intimate with him, who did not bemoan him as though he were our father, and it is not to be wondered at, considering how good he was. It was stated that he had reigned for seventeen years and that he was the best king there had ever been in Mexico, and that he had conquered in person, in three wars which he had carried on in the countries he had subjugated. Let us continue.

I have already told about the sorrow that we all of us felt about it when we saw that Montezuma was dead. We even thought badly of the Fraile de la Merced because he had not persuaded him to become a Christian, and he gave as an excuse that he did not think that he would die of those wounds, but that he ought to have ordered them to give him something to stupefy him. At the end of much discussion Cortés ordered a priest and a chief from among the prisoners to go and tell the Cacique whom they had chosen for Lord, who was named Cuitlahuac, and his Captains, that the great Montezuma was dead, and they had seen him die, and about the manner of his death and the wounds his own people had inflicted on him, and they should say how grieved we all were about it, and that they should bury him as the great king that he was, and they should raise the cousin of Montezuma who was with us, to be king, for the inheritance was his, or one of his (Montezuma's) other sons, and that he whom they had raised to be king was not so by right, and they should negotiate a peace so that we could leave Mexico; and if they did not do so, now that Montezuma was dead, whom we held in respect and for that reason had not destroyed their city, we should sally out to make war on them and burn all their houses and do them much damage. So as to convince them that Montezuma was dead, he ordered six Mexicans who were high chieftains, and the priests whom we held as prisoners, to carry him out on their shoulders and to hand him [the body] over to the Mexican Captains, and to tell them what Montezuma had commanded at the time of his death, for those who carried him out on their backs were present at his death; and they told Cuitlahuac the whole truth, how his own people killed him with blows from three stones.

When they beheld him thus dead, we saw that they were in floods of tears and we clearly heard the shrieks and cries of distress that they gave for him, but for all this, the fierce assault they made on us with darts, stones and arrows never ceased, and then they came on us again with greater force and fury, and said to us: "Now for certain you will pay for the death of our King and Lord, and the dishonour to our Idols; and as for the peace you sent to beg for, come out here and we will settle how and in what way it is to be made," and they said many things about this and other matters that I cannot now remember and I will leave them unreported, and [they said] that they had already chosen a good king, and he would not be so fainthearted as to be deceived with false speeches like their good Montezuma, and as for the burial, we need not trouble about that, but about our own lives, for in two days there would not be one of us left;— so much for the messages we had sent them. With these words [they fell on us] with loud yells and whistles and showers of stones, darts and arrows, while other squadrons were still attempting to set fire to our quarters in many places.

When Cortés and all of us observed this, we agreed that next day we would all of us sally out from our camp and attack in another direction, where there were many houses on dry land, and we would do all the damage we were able and go towards the causeway, and that all the horsemen should break through the squadrons and spear them with their lances or drive them into the water, even though they [the enemy] should kill the horses. This was decided on in order to find out if by chance, with the damage and slaughter that we should inflict on them, they would abandon their attack and arrange some sort of peace, so that we could go free without more deaths and damage. Although the next day we all bore ourselves very manfully and killed many of the enemy and burned a matter of twenty houses and almost reached dry land, it was all of no use, because of the great damage and deaths and wounds they inflicted on us, and we could not hold a single bridge, for they were all of them half broken down. Many Mexicans charged down on us, and they had set up walls and barricades in places which they thought could be reached by the horses, so that if we had met with many difficulties up to this time, we found much greater ones ahead of us.

Let us leave it here, and go back to say that we determined to get out of Mexico. . . .

Now we saw our forces diminishing every day and those of the Mexicans increasing, and many of our men were dead and all the rest wounded, and although we fought like brave men we could not drive back nor even get free from the many squadrons which attacked us both by day and night, and the powder was giving out, and the same was happening with the food and water, and the great Montezuma being dead, they were unwilling to grant the peace and truce which we had sent to demand of them. In fact we were staring death in the face, and the bridges had been raised. It was [therefore] decided by Cortés and all of us captains and soldiers that we should set out during the night, when we could see that the squadrons of warriors were most off their guard. In order to put them all the more off their guard, that very afternoon we sent to tell them, through one of their priests whom we held prisoner and who was a man of great importance among them and through some other prisoners, that they should let us go in peace within eight days and we would give up to them all the gold; and this [was done] to put them off their guard so that we might get out that night.

. . . I will relate how the order was given to make a bridge of very strong beams and planks, so that we could carry it with us and place it where the bridges were broken. Four hundred Tlaxcalan Indians and one hundred and fifty soldiers were told off to carry this bridge and place it in position and guard the passage until the army and all the baggage had crossed. Two hundred Tlaxcalan Indians and fifty soldiers were told off to carry the cannon, and Gonzalo de Sandoval, Diego de Ordás, Francisco de Sauzedo, Francisco de Lugo and a company of one hundred young and active soldiers were selected to go in the van to do the fighting. It was agreed that Cortés himself, Alonzo de Ávila, Cristóbal de Olid, and other Captains should go in the middle and support the party that most needed help in fighting. Pedro de Alvarado and Juan Velásquez de Leon were with the rearguard, and placed in the middle between them [and tne preceding section] were two captains and the soldiers of Narvaez, and three hundred Tlaxcalans, and thirty soldiers were told off to take charge of the prisoners and of Doña Marina and Doña Luisa; by the time this arrangement was made, it was already night.

In order to bring out the gold and divide it up and carry it, Cortés ordered his steward named Cristóbal de Guzman and other soldiers who were his servants to bring out all the gold and jewels and silver, and he gave them many Tlaxcalan Indians for the purpose, and they placed it in the Hall. Then Cortés told the King's officers named Alonzo Dávila and Gonzalo Mejía to take charge of the gold belonging to His Majesty, and he gave them seven wounded and lame horses and one mare, and many friendly Tlaxcalans, more than eighty in number, and they loaded them with parcels of it, as much as they could carry, for it was put up into very broad ingots, as I have already said in the chapter that treats of it, and much gold still remained in the Hall piled up in heaps. Then Cortés called his secretary and the others who were King's Notaries, and said: "Bear witness for me that I can do no more with this gold. We have here in this apartment and Hall over seven hundred thousand pesos in gold, and, as you have seen, it cannot be weighed nor placed in safety. I now give it up to any of the soldiers who care to take it, otherwise it will be lost among these dogs [of Mexicans]."

When they heard this, many of the soldiers of Narvaez and some of our people loaded themselves with it. I declare that I had no other desire but the desire to save my life, but I did not fail to carry off from some small boxes that were there, four chalchihuites, which are stones very highly prized among the Indians, and I quickly placed them in my bosom under my armour, and, later on, the price of them served me well in healing my wounds and getting me food.

After we had learnt the plans that Cortés had made about the way in which we were to escape that night and get to the bridges, as it was somewhat dark and cloudy and rainy, we began before midnight to bring along the bridge and the baggage, and the horses and mare began their march, and the Tlaxcalans who were laden with the gold. Then the bridge was quickly put in place, and Cortés and the others whom he took with him in the first [detachment], and many of the horsemen, crossed over it. While this was happening, the voices, trumpets, cries and whistles of the Mexicans began to sound and they called out in their language to the people of Tlaltelolco, "Come out at once with your canoes for the Teules are leaving; cut them off so that not one of them may be left alive." When I least expected it, we saw so many squadrons of warriors bearing down on us, and the lake so crowded with canoes that we could not defend ourselves. Many of our soldiers had already crossed [the bridge] and while we were in this position, a great multitude of Mexicans charged down on us [with the intention of] removing the bridge and wounding and killing our men who were unable to assist each other; and as misfortune is perverse at such times, one mischance followed another, and as it was raining, two of the horses slipped and fell into the lake. When I and others of Cortés's Company saw that, we got safely to the other side of the bridge, and so many warriors charged on us, that despite all our good fighting, no further use could be made of the bridge, so that the passage or water opening was soon filled up with dead horses, Indian men and women, servants, baggage and boxes.

Fearing that they would not fail to kill us, we thrust ourselves ahead along the causeway, and we met many squadrons armed with long lances waiting for us, and they used abusive words to us, and among them they cried "Oh! villains, are you still alive?" and with the cuts and thrusts we gave them, we got through, although they then wounded six of those who were going along [with me]. Then if there was some sort of plan such as we had agreed upon it was an accursed one; for Cortés and the captains and soldiers who passed first on horseback, so as to save themselves and reach dry land and make sure of their lives, spurred on along the causeway, and they did not fail to attain their object, and the horses with the gold and the Tlaxcalans also got out in safety. I assert that if we had waited, (the horsemen and the soldiers, one for the other,) at the bridges, we should all have been put an end to, and not one of us would have been left alive; the reason was this, that as we went along the causeway, charging the Mexican squadrons, on one side of us was water and on the other azoteas,* and the lake was full of canoes so that we could do nothing. Moreover the muskets and crossbows were all left behind at the bridge, and as it was night time, what could we do beyond what we accomplished? which was to charge and give some sword-thrusts to those who tried to lay hands on us, and to march and get on ahead so as to get off the causeway.

Had it been in the day-time, it would have been far worse, and we who escaped did so only by the Grace of God. To one who saw the hosts of warriors who fell on us that night and the canoes [full] of them coming along to carry off our soldiers, it was terrifying. So we went ahead along the causeway in order to get to the town of Tacuba where Cortés was already stationed with all the Captains. Gonzalo de Sandoval, Cristóbal de Olid and others of those horsemen who had gone on ahead were crying out: "Señor Capitan, let us halt, for they say that we are fleeing and leaving them to die at the bridges; let us go back and help them, if any of them survive"; but not one of them came out or escaped. Cortés's reply was that it was a miracle that any of us escaped. However, he promptly went back with the horsemen and the soldiers who were unwounded, but they did not march far, for Pedro de Alvarado soon met them, badly wounded, holding a spear in his hand, and on foot, for they [the enemy] had already killed his sorrel mare, and he brought with him four soldiers as badly wounded as he was himself, and eight Tlaxcalans, all of them with blood flowing from many wounds.

While Cortés was on the causeway with the rest of the captains, we repaired to the courtyard in Tacuba. Many squadrons had already arrived from Mexico, shouting out orders to Tacuba and to the other town named Azcapotzalco, and they began to hurl darts, stones, and arrows [and attack] with their long lances. We made some charges and both attacked [them] and defended ourselves. . . .

*The flat roofs of the houses.

Let us go on and I will relate how, when we were waiting in Tacuba, many Mexican warriors came together from all those towns and they killed three of our soldiers, so we agreed to get out of that town as quickly as we could, and five Tlaxcalan Indians, who found out a way towards Tlaxcala without following the [main] road, guided us with great precaution until we reached some small houses placed on a hill, and near to them a Cue or Oratory [built] like a fort, where we halted. . . .

FRAY BERNARDINO DE SAHAGÚN
From the *Florentine Codex*

Before reading this Mexica account of Noche triste, *take a look at Figures 14 and 15 (from* Lienzo de Tlaxcala*) to see how the Tlaxcalan view is presented. There are some striking images of the battle to escape the city in which Cortés, doña Marina, and the Tlaxcalan warriors are carefully shown in European style; however, indigenous pictorial conventions like the symbols for temples and water are also used effectively. This selection by the city's defenders is drawn from the* Florentine Codex. *It reports the death of Moctezuma and then the fighting in the city. These descriptions convey the intensity of the battles from the Mexica point of view. It should be remembered that many of Sahagún's informants were Tlatelolcans, who had their own complaints against Moctezuma's leadership.*

Twenty-third chapter, where it is said how Moteucçoma and a great nobleman of Tlatelolco died, and the Spaniards threw their bodies out at the entryway of the house where they were.

Four days after people had been cast down from the temple, [the Spaniards] removed [the bodies of] Moteucçoma and Itzquauhtzin, who had died, to a place at the water's edge called Teoayoc [Place of the Divine Turtle], for an image of a turtle was there, carved in stone; the stone represented a turtle.

And when they were seen and recognized as Moteucçoma and Itzquauhtzin, they hastened to take Moteucçoma up in their arms and

James Lockhart, *We People Here: Nahuatl Accounts of the Conquest of Mexico,* Repertorium Columbianum, UCLA Center for Medieval and Renaissance Studies (Los Angeles: University of California Press, 1993), 150–56, even pages only.

Figure 14.   The siege of the Spaniards after the Toxcatl massacre.

Source: From Prospero Cahuartzi, ed., *Lienzo de Tlaxcala* (Mexico City: Libreria Antiquaria G. M. Echaniz, 1939).

brought him to the place called Copolco. Then they placed him on a pile of wood and set fire to it, ignited it. Then the fire crackled and roared, with many tongues of flame, tongues of flame like tassels, rising up. And Moteucçoma's body lay sizzling, and it let off a stench as it burned.

And when it was burning, some people, enraged and no longer with goodwill, scolded at him, saying, "This miserable fellow made the whole world fear him, in the whole world he was dreaded, in the whole world he inspired respect and fright. If someone offended him only in some small way, he immediately disposed of him. He punished many for imagined things, not true, but just fabricated tales." And there were many others who scolded him, moaning, lamenting, shaking their heads.

But Itzquauhtzin they put in a boat; they took his body in a boat until they got him here to Tlatelolco. They grieved greatly, their hearts were desolate; the tears flowed down. Not a soul scolded him or cursed him.

Figure 15. The escape of the *Noche triste*. The fight at the Tolteca canal.
Source: From *Lienzo de Tlaxcala*, ed. Prospero Cahuartzi (Mexico City: Libreria Antiquaria G. M. Echaniz, 1939).

They said, "The lord Tlacochcalcatl Itzquauhtzin has suffered travail, for he suffered and was afflicted along with Moteucçoma. What tribulations he endured on our behalf in the past, during all of Moteucçoma's time!" Then they outfitted him, equipping him with the lordly banner and other items of paper, and they gave him provisions. Then they took him and burned him in the temple courtyard at the place called Quauhxicalco. It was with great splendor that his body was burned.

After four days of fighting, for seven days the Spaniards were just enclosed in the house. But when the seven days were past, they came back out for a while to take a look, looking around here and there; they went as far as Maçatzintamalco. They gathered stalks of green maize, beginning to form ears. They just gathered the maize leaves as one does in war, going in great haste. Hardly had they got where they were going when they quickly went back into the building. When they had come out the sun was already off to one side, about to set.

Twenty-fourth chapter, where it is said how the Spaniards and Tlaxcalans came out and fled from Mexico by night.

When night had fallen and midnight had come, the Spaniards came out. They formed up, along with all the Tlaxcalans. The Spaniards went ahead, and the Tlaxcalans went following, bringing up the rear, like their wall of protection. [The Spaniards] went carrying a wooden platform [or platforms]; they laid it down at a canal and crossed over on it.

At this time it was drizzling and sprinkling, the rain was gently dripping down. They were able to cross some other canals, at Tecpantzinco, Tzapotla, and Atenchicalco. But when they got to Mixcoatechialtitlan, at the fourth canal, there they were seen coming out. It was a woman fetching water who saw them; then she shouted, saying, "O Mexica, come running, your enemies have come out, they have emerged secretly!" Then another person shouted, on top of [the temple of] Huitzilopochtli; his crying spread everywhere, everyone heard it. He said, "O warriors, o Mexica, your enemies are coming out, let everyone hasten with the war boats and on the roads!"

When it was heard, there was a clamor. Everyone scrambled; the operators of the war boats hastened and paddled hard, hitting one another's boats as they went in the direction of Mictlantonco and Macuilcuitlapilco. The war boats came upon them from both directions; the war boats of the Tenochca and the war boats of the Tlatelolca converged on them. And some people went on foot, going straight to Nonoalco, heading toward Tlacopan to try to cut them off there. Then the war-boat people hurled barbed darts at the Spaniards; from both sides the darts fell on them. But the Spaniards also shot at the Mexica, shooting back with iron bolts and guns. There were deaths on both sides. Spaniards and Tlaxcalans were hit, and Mexica were hit.

When the Spaniards reached Tlaltecayoacan, where the Tolteca canal is, it was as though they had fallen off a precipice; they all fell and dropped in, the Tlaxcalans, the people of Tliliuhquitepec, and the Spaniards, along with the horses, and some women. The canal was completely full of them, full to the very top. And those who came last just passed and crossed over on people, on bodies.

When they reached Petlacalco, where there was yet another canal, they passed gently, slowly, gradually, with caution, on the wooden platform. There they restored themselves, took their breath, regained their vigor. When they reached Popotlan, it dawned, light came. They began to go along with spirit, they went heading into the distance.

Then the Mexica went shouting at them, surrounding them, hovering about them. They captured some Tlaxcalans as they went, and some Spaniards died. Also Mexica and Tlatelolca were killed; there was death on both sides. They drove and pursued [the Spaniards] to Tlacopan. And when they had driven them to Tiliuhcan, to Xocotliiyohuican, at Xoxocotla, Chimalpopoca, son of Moteucçoma, died in battle. They came upon him lying hit by a barbed dart and struck [by some hand weapon]. At the same place died Tlaltecatzin, a Tepaneca lord who had been guiding the Spaniards, pointing out the way for them, conducting them, showing them the road.

Then they crossed the Tepçolatl (a small river); they forded and went over the water at Tepçolac. Then they went up to Acueco and stopped at Otoncalpolco, [where] wooden walls or barricades were in the courtyard. There they all took a rest and caught their breath, there they restored themselves. There the people of Teocalhueyacan came to meet them and guide them.

7

The Siege and Fall of Tenochtitlan

The final stage of the military conquest of Mexico took place in roughly a year, between the arrival of the Spaniards in Tlaxcala on July 11, 1520, after their flight from Tenochtitlan and their destruction of the Mexica capital and the surrender of the last emperor Cuahtemoc on August 13, 1521. During the first ten of those thirteen months, both the Mexica and the Spaniards maneuvered to find allies and to muster their forces. These months were filled with campaigns and battles around the valley of Mexico. The final siege of Tenochtitlan lasted about three months (Bernal Díaz says ninety-three days). It ended with the fall of Tenochtitlan.

The fighting in these last few months was bitter, and at the end it was often house-by-house combat. The Mexica had to contend not only with the reinforced Spanish troops and the thousands of native allies that accompanied them, but also with another enemy: epidemic disease in the form of smallpox. The Nahua accounts mention the effects of the disease that decimated the population and devastated their leadership. Cuitlahuac, the brother of Moctezuma who became the *tlatoani* when the latter died and who directed the attacks of the *Noche triste,* lived for only three months before succumbing to smallpox. He was then replaced by Cuahtemoc, who directed the final defense. Historian Ross Hassig has argued that the plague strengthened the Spanish position, although the native allies of the Spanish also suffered from its effects. Cortés exploited these gaps in the leadership of other cities by backing new leaders who were loyal to him. Meanwhile, Cuahtemoc tried to win support by lowering the tribute demands on the Mexica dependents, but his attempts only made Tenochtitlan seem weak. This contributed to the number of native groups which collaborated with the Spaniards.

As the Spaniards consolidated their position and more soldiers arrived on the coast, Cortés demonstrated considerable ability in cajoling, convincing, and bullying various cities into joining him for the final effort against Tenochtitlan. Key in this effort was the continued allegiance of Tlaxcala, which, even after the *Noche triste* when the Spaniards were at their weakest, maintained its loyalty.

The final battle for Tenochtitlan was a combined naval and land operation. First Cortés sought to isolate the city from its support. Texcoco, another major city on the shores of the lake and a traditional ally of Tenochtitlan, was in the midst of a dynastic crisis and civil war. Cortés was able to gain its loyalty without a battle. The Spaniards seized Iztapalapa but were later forced out again. Eventually, however, the Spaniards were able to win over or neutralize many of the lakeside towns and cities and to secure access to the coast by defeating Mexica armies operating outside the lake area. In the final battles, Tenochtitlan and its subdivision Tlatelolco were effectively left to fight on their own.

The city's peculiar location on an island in the midst of a lake had defensive advantages as long as the defenders could control access across the lake. Cortés realized this, and so upon return to Tlaxcala he began the construction of thirteen small (about forty feet long), shallow-draught ships, or brigantines. The timber for these was then dragged back to the lake by his native allies. These ships were then outfitted with small cannon, sails, and rigging that the Spaniards had saved from the original ships scuttled at Vera Cruz.[1] Although the Mexica developed various barriers and traps to impede the Spanish naval operations, once these ships were on the lake, the Mexica war canoes were outmatched. Cortés was able to cut the city off from its supply sources, tightening a noose around the throat of the city.

Meanwhile, the Mexica took advantage of the structure of their city with its many canals and its streets intersected by bridges. The Mexica would draw Spanish troops into the city and then cut off their retreat by removing the bridges over which they had crossed. The Spanish eventually learned to avoid these situations by not advancing beyond secured areas or by carrying small portable bridges along with their forces. When on the causeways, the Spanish found the mobility and effectiveness of their horses hampered and the Mexica war canoes effectively harassed the Spanish forces. On a number of occasions, Spanish forces were routed withstanding great losses. The spirited Mexica defense, however, was almost helpless against the Spanish brigantines, which could attack at any point and were not limited to the streets and cause-

---

[1] The naval aspects of the final siege are the subject of C. Harvey Gardiner, *Naval Power in the Conquest of Mexico* (Austin: University of Texas Press, 1956).

ways where the Mexica could plan their defense. In the final days of fighting, the Spaniards destroyed houses to eliminate their rooftops as platforms from which the Mexica could fire arrows or hurl stones. The Spaniards also used the rubble to fill in the water gaps created by the Mexica in the streets to cut off the enemy. The result of these tactics was the leveling of large parts of the city. Even Cortés regretted the loss. In a moment of explanation and self-justification he told his king why he had burned many of the palaces and great houses in an attempt to bring the Mexica to submission: "I was much grieved to do this," he wrote, "but since it was still more grievous to them I determined on burning them." Such tactics had little effect on the Mexica will to fight. The admiration of Cortés and Bernal Díaz for the bravery and resilience of the Mexica defenders is evident throughout their accounts.

This chapter includes both indigenous and Spanish accounts. Included here is an excerpt from the Tarascan neighbors of the Mexica, the Nahua accounts drawn from the *Florentine Codex,* and some elegies preserved in Nahuatl after the conquest about the fall of the city. The Spanish side is represented both by Bernal Díaz and by another conquistador, Francisco de Aguilar.

From *Chronicles of Michoacán*

This selection is taken from Chronicles of Michoacán. *It describes a Mexica approach to the cazonci, the ruler of their traditional enemies, the Tarascans of Michoacán, in a desperate search for allies. The Tarascans had already turned down such approaches, and the failure of this embassy underlines the way in which indigenous politics tipped the balance against the Mexica.*[1] *From the text it appears that the Tarascans conflated a number of approaches from the Mexica into the narrative of a single embassy.*

---

[1] On the Tarascan kingdom see Helen Perlstein Pollard, *Taríacuri's Legacy: The Prehistoric Tarascan State* (Norman: University of Oklahoma Press, 1993), and J. Benedict Warren, *The Conquest of Michoacán* (Norman: University of Oklahoma Press, 1985).

Eugene R. Crane and Reginald C. Reindorp, trans. and eds., *Chronicles of Michoacán* (Norman: University of Oklahoma Press, 1970), 60–63, 65–67.

The Arrival of the Spaniards

According to Don Pedro, who is now governor, Montezuma sent ten messengers from Mexico City to Taximaroa.[2] They brought a message for the Cazonci,[3] called Zuangua, father of the one who had just died, who was very old and who had been the Master of Taximaroa. When asked what they wanted they answered that they brought a message from Montezuma for the Cazonci in Mechuacán and for him alone. The Master of Taximaroa reported this to the Cazonci who ordered that they be received well but that they should not come at once. When they came before Zuangua they delivered gifts of turquoise, jerky, green feathers, ten round shields with golden rims, rich blankets, belts, and large mirrors. All the lords and sons of the Cazonci disguised themselves and put on some old blankets so that they would not be recognized, for they had heard that the Mexicans had come for them. The Mexicans sat down and the Cazonci called in an interpreter of the Mexican language, by the name of Nuritan, who was his Nahuatl interpreter. The Cazonci asked him what the Mexicans wanted and why they came. The Cazonci was calm, holding an arrow in his hand with which he struck the ground repeatedly. The Mexicans repeated their message. "The Master of Mexico, called Montezuma, sends us and some other Lords with orders to report to our brother the Cazonci about the strange people who have come and taken us by surprise. We have met them in battle and killed some two hundred of those who came riding deer and two hundred of those who were not mounted. Those deer wore coats of mail and carried something that sounds like the clouds, makes a great thundering noise and kills all those it meets leaving not one. They completely broke up our formation and killed many of us. They are accompanied by people from Tlaxcala, because these people have turned against us. We should have killed the people of Tezaico if it had not been for those who help them to keep us besieged and isolated in this city. If your sons had not come to help us, the ones called Tirimarasco, Anini, and Acuiche, bringing their people and defending us, we should have all died there."

Having heard the message Zuangua replied: "It is well, you are welcome. You have made your message known to our Gods Curicaveri and Xaratanga. At the moment I cannot send people because I have need of those whom you have named for they are busy conquering in the Four

[2] The Tarascan capital.
[3] Cazonci: Tarascan ruler.

Quarters.[4] Rest here a day or so and these my interpreters, Nuritan and Pivo, and two others will go with you. They shall confer with the people of whom you speak as soon as everyone has returned from the conquest."

The messengers went out and were given quarters, food, belts, blankets, leather war jackets, and clover-leaf wreaths. The Cazonci called his advisors and said to them: "What shall we do? This message they have brought me is serious. What has happened to us for the sun used to look with favor upon these two Kingdoms, Mexico and ours, and we never knew that there were any other people for we all served the same gods. What purpose would I have in sending people to Mexico for we are always at war when we approach each other and there is rancor between us. Remember that the Mexicans are very astute when they talk and very artful with the truth—I have no need of them as I said. Take heed lest it be a trick. Since they have not been able to conquer some villages, they want to take out their vengeance on us by killing us through treachery. They want to destroy us. As I said, let the Nahuatls and interpreters go for they are not boys to do boyish things and they will learn what it is all about." His advisors replied: "Sire, let it be as ordered by you who are King and Master. How can we contradict you? Let those whom you mention go at once."

He sent for rich blankets, gourd dishes, leather war jackets, for the bloody skirts and blankets of their gods and for some of everything produced in Mechuacán. These gifts he gave to the messengers to give to Montezuma just as Montezuma had sent similar gifts from Mexico for the local gods. The Nahuatls went with them to learn the truth, and the Cazonci sent war people by another road who captured three Otomis and asked them whether they had any news from Mexico. The Otomis replied: "The Mexicans have been conquered; we do not know who the conquerors are, but all Mexico City is foul with the odor of dead bodies. For this reason they are looking for allies who will free and defend them. We know how they have sent throughout the villages for help. It is true that they have gone for we know it. Take us to Mechuacán so they will give us blankets for we are freezing to death and we want to be subjects of the Cazonci." The capture of the three Otomis and the news they brought were reported to the Cazonci: "Sire, it is true. The Mexicans have been destroyed and the entire village smells of dead bodies. They are petitioning all the villages for help. This is what was reported also in Taximaroa for the chief *Capacapecho* verified it." Then the Cazonci

---

[4] A region of the Tarascan empire.

spoke, saying: "Welcome; we do not know what may become of the poor fellows we sent to Mexico. Let us wait for their return to learn the truth."

News from Mexico City and the Death of Zuangua

The messengers who had been sent to Mexico City returned, appeared before the Cazonci, greeted him and showed him more gifts of rich blankets and belts sent by Montezuma. Zuangua returned their greeting, saying that it was good to see them again and telling them that "long ago, on another occasion, our ancient ancestors went to Mexico City." Then he asked them about their journey and the messengers replied: "Sire, during the night we arrived by canoe in Mexico City and showed the gift you sent to Montezuma, who welcomed us. We explained your orders that we should go with his messengers, we told him that you had sent your people to the Four Quarters and that we came ahead against the day when the war people could come. We told him that we came to learn about these strange people who have come to our land, in order to be better advised. He welcomed us and said: 'Look at that mountain range over there. Behind it are the people who have come from Taxcala [Tlaxcala].' Then they took us by canoe to show us. We landed in Texcuco [Texcoco] and climbed to the top of a mountain. From there they pointed to a long, flat clearing occupied by the strangers and outlined a plan to us: 'You people from Mechuacán will come from that way over there and we shall go this other way to catch them between us and thus kill them all. Why should we not be successful since everyone flees from you people of Mechuacán, who are such great archers? You have seen them, now take this information to your Master and tell him that we plead with him not to break our agreement. This is what we say to him, our gods have told us that Mexico City will never be destroyed, nor will our houses be burned. Two Kingdoms only are appointed, Mexico and Mechuacán. Take heed for there is much work.' We answered: 'Let us return to Mexico City.' We returned, the lords came out to receive us and we took our leave from Montezuma who said to us: 'Return to Mechuacán for you have seen the land. Let us not desert the land which we wish to give to you. This matter which we beg of your Master, what answer can he give except that you will all come? Are we peradventure to be slaves? Are they to conquer Mechuacán? Let us all die here first and not let them go to your land. This is what you shall say to your Master. May you all come; there is plenty of food so that the people may have strength for the war: do not pity the people. Let us die quickly, if we do not win, and we shall make our dais of the people who die supposing the cowardly gods do not favor us. It has been a long time since they told our god that no one would destroy his Kingdom, and we have heard of no other Kingdom but this one and Mechuacán. So, return.' We departed and the Mexicans came some distance with us before saying goodby. This is the report we bring back."

Then the Cazonci, Zuangua, spoke: "Welcome back. It has been a long time since our old ancestors went to Mexico City and while I know not why they went, the reason for your going now is important. What the Mexicans said is serious business. For what purpose are we to go to Mexico? Each one of us might go only to die and we know not what they will say about us afterwards. Perchance they will sell us out to these people who are coming and will be the cause of our being killed. Let the Mexicans do their own conquering or let them all come join us with their captaincies. Let the strangers kill the Mexicans because for many days they have not lived right for they do not bring wood to the temples but instead, we have heard, they honor their gods only with songs. What good are songs alone? How are the gods to favor them if they only sing songs? We work much more than is customarily required for the needs of the gods. Now let us do a little better, nay more, bring in wood for the temples, perhaps they will forgive us, for the gods of the heavens have become angry with us. Why would the strangers come without cause? A god has sent them, that is why they came! The people must know their sins; recall them to their memory even though they may lay the blame for their sins on me, the King. The common people do not want to listen to me for I tell them to bring wood for the temples. They heed not my words and they lose count of the war people. Why should not our God Curicaveri and the Goddess Xaratanga become angry with us? Since Curicaveri has no children and Xaratanga has not given birth to any, they complain to Mother Cueravaperi. I shall admonish the people to try to do better because they will not forgive us if we have failed in anything." The lords answered: "You have spoken well, Sire; we shall tell the people this which you order." And they went to their houses and nothing more was learned.

At this time a plague of smallpox and hemorrhaging from the bowels struck all the people in the entire province. The bishop of the temples died, as did the old Cazonci Zuanga [Zuangua], leaving his sons Tangaxoan, otherwise known as Zincicha, the oldest, Tirimarasco, Azinche, and Anini.

Another embassy of ten Mexicans came to ask for help. Unfortunately, for their purpose, they arrived at a time when the people were mourning the death of the old Cazonci. The arrival of the Mexicans was

reported to Zincicha [Tangaxoan], the oldest son of the deceased Cazonci who ordered them taken to his father's houses where they were
welcomed. It was explained to the Mexicans that the Cazonci was not
there, that he had gone to rest. The oldest son called the old men into
consultation and asked what should be done about the petition which
the Mexicans brought. "We know not what their real intent is. Let them
follow my Father to the Inferno and present him with the petition there.
Tell them to prepare themselves because this is the custom." The Mexicans were so informed, and they replied that as the Master had ordered
it, it should be done, and they asked that it be done quickly, adding that
there was nowhere for them to go; they had voluntarily come to their
death. The Mexicans were made ready in the customary manner, after
being informed that they were taking their message to the dead Cazonci,
and were sacrificed in the temple of Curicaveri and Xaratanga. . . .

FRAY BERNARDINO DE SAHAGÚN

From the *Florentine Codex*

Included here are excerpts from Book Twelve of the Florentine Codex *as
translated in* We People Here. *The agonies of the defeat are apparent, beginning with the report of the smallpox epidemic that was spreading
through the city. These excerpts give particular attention to the places
where the battles took place and the specific conditions of the combat. Sometimes, as in the case of Tzilacatzin, the names and exploits of the warriors
involved are given as well as the victories and defeats. In one noteworthy
selection a retelling of the capture and sacrifice of the Spaniards is described in detail. Sahagún's informants for these accounts were men from
Tlatelolco, the quarter of Tenochtitlan which had once been a separate city
and was politically subordinate. The excerpts indicate the strength of local
pride and perhaps a Tlatelolcan bias against the political and military failure of Tenochtitlan. Just as the first arrival of the Spaniards had been accompanied by supernatural signs in the Nahua accounts, the final defeat is*

James Lockhart, *We People Here: Nahuatl Accounts of the Conquest of Mexico,* Repertorium
Columbianum, UCLA Center for Medieval and Renaissance Studies (Los Angeles: University of California Press, 1993), 180–84, 192–94, 198–200, 214–18, 242–44, 246–48,
even pages only, 185.

also presaged by an omen, a blood-colored sky. The Nahua texts do not fail to mention in matter-of-fact directness the Spanish actions after the surrender, the search for gold, and the taking of women and of slaves.

Twenty-ninth chapter, where it is said how, at the time the Spaniards left Mexico, there came an illness of pustules of which many local people died; it was called "the great rash" [smallpox].

Before the Spaniards appeared to us, first an epidemic broke out, a sickness of pustules. It began in Tepeilhuitl. Large bumps spread on people; some were entirely covered. They spread everywhere, on the face, the head, the chest, etc. [The disease] brought great desolation; a great many died of it. They could no longer walk about, but lay in their dwellings and sleeping places, no longer able to move or stir. They were unable to change position, to stretch out on their sides or face down, or raise their heads. And when they made a motion, that called out loudly. The pustules that covered people caused great desolation; very many people died of them, and many just starved to death; starvation reigned, and no one took care of others any longer.

On some people, the pustules appeared only far apart, and they did not suffer greatly, nor did many of them die of it. But many people's faces were spoiled by it, their faces and noses were made rough. Some lost an eye or were blinded.

This disease of pustules lasted a full sixty days; after sixty days it abated and ended. When people were convalescing and reviving, the pustules disease began to move in the direction of Chalco. And many were disabled or paralyzed by it, but they were not disabled forever. It broke out in Teotleco, and it abated in Panquetzaliztli. The Mexica warriors were greatly weakened by it.

And when things were in this state, the Spaniards came, moving toward us from Tetzcoco. They appeared from the direction of Quauhtitlan and made a halt at Tlacopan. There they gave one another assignments and divided themselves. Pedro de Alvarado was made responsible for the road coming to Tlatelolco. The Marqués considered the Tenochca great and valiant warriors.

And it was right in Nextlatilco, or in Ilyacac, that war first began. Then [the Spaniards] quickly reached Nonoalco, and the warriors came pursuing them. None of the Mexica died; then the Spaniards retreated. The warriors fought in boats; the war-boat people shot at the Spaniards, and their arrows sprinkled down on them. Then [the main force of the Mexica] entered [Nonoalco]. Thereupon the Marqués sent [his men] to-

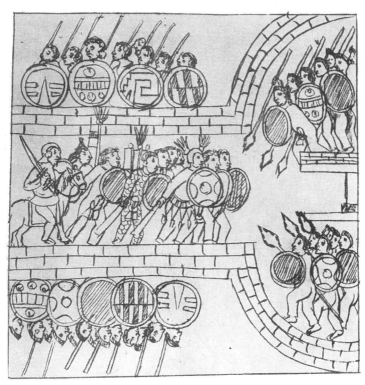

Figure 16.   Fighting in the final stages of the siege. Spaniards and their allies attack on the streets of Tenochtitlan.
Source: Relaciónes geográficas del Siglo XVI: Tlaxcala, ed. René Acuña (Mexico City: UNAM, 1984). Glasgow University Library, Department of Special Collections.

ward the Tenochca, following the Acachinanco road. Many times they skirmished, and the Mexica went out to face them.

Thirty-first chapter, where it is said how the Spaniards came with the brigantines, pursuing those who were in boats. When they were done contending with them, they drew close and reached all the houses.

And when they had finished adjusting [the guns], they shot at the wall. The wall then ripped and broke open. The second time it was hit, the wall went to the ground; it was knocked down in places, perforated, holes were blown in it. Then, like the other time, the road stood clear. And the warriors who had been lying at the wall dispersed and came fleeing; everyone escaped in fear. And then all the different people [who were on the side of the Spaniards] quickly went filling in the canals and making them level with stones, adobes, and some logs, with which they closed off the water.

And when the canals were stopped up, some horse[men] came, perhaps ten of them; they came going in circles, spinning, turning, twisting. Another group of horse[men] came following behind them. And some Tlatelolca who had quickly entered the palace that had been Moteucçoma's residence came back out in alarm to contend with the horse[men]. They lanced one of the Tlatclolca, but when they had lanced him, he was able to take hold of [the Spaniard's] iron lance. Then his companions took it from [the Spaniard's] hands, throwing him on his back and unhorsing him. When he fell to the ground, they struck him repeatedly on the back of the neck, and he died there.

Then the Spaniards sent everyone, they all moved together; they reached Quauhquiahuac [Eagle Gate]. As they went they took the cannon and its gear and set it down at Quauhquiahuac. (The reason it is so called is that an eagle stood there, carved of stone, some seven feet tall, and enclosing it were a jaguar standing on one side, and a wolf standing on the other, likewise carved in stone.) And when things were in this state the great warriors tried to take shelter behind the stone pillars; there were two rows of them, eight altogether. And the roof of the Coacalli was also full of warriors. None of them ventured to cross into the open.

And the Spaniards did not move at all; when they fired the cannon, it grew very dark, and smoke spread. Those who had been taking shelter behind the stone pillars fled; all who had been lying on the roof jumped down and ran far away. Then they brought the cannon up and set it down at the round stone [of gladiatorial sacrifice]. On top of [the temple of] Huitzilopochtli they were still trying to keep watch, beating the log drums, as though the air were full of them. Then two Spaniards climbed up and struck [the drummers]; after they had struck them they cast them aside, threw them down.

And those with scraped heads, all the warriors who were fighting in boats, came onto dry land, and only the youths who poled the others conducted the boats. And at this point the warriors inspected the passageways, with much running and shouting, saying "O warriors, let everyone come running!" . . .

Thirty-second chapter, where it is said how the Mexica left their altepetl in fear and came here when they dreaded the Spaniards.

And at this time the Tenochca came entering into Tlatelolco here, weeping and shouting. Many were the tears of the women; the men came accompanying their women, and some of them carried their children on their shoulders. In just one day they abandoned their altepetl. But the Tlatelolca still went to Tenochtitlan to fight.

And at this point Pedro de Alvarado hurled his forces at Ilyacac, toward Nonoalco, but they could do nothing; it was as though they had hit against a stone, because the Tlatelolca made great efforts. There was fighting on both sides of the road and in the water with war boats. When Alvarado tired, he returned and established himself in Tlacopan. But just two days later they sent out all the boats; at first only two came, then afterward all of them, and formed beside the houses in Nonoalco. Then they came onto dry land, and then they began to follow the narrow road between the houses; they came toward the center of them.

When the Spaniards landed it fell silent; not one of the people came out. But then Tzilacatzin, who was a great warrior and very valorous, hurled three stones he was carrying, huge round stones, wall stones or white stones; he had one in his hand and two on his shield. Then he went pursuing the Spaniards, scattering them, forcing them into the water. They went right into the water; those who went down in the water got thoroughly wetted.

(This Tzilacatzin had the warrior [rank] of Otomi, for which reason he wore the Otomi hairstyle, so he looked down on his enemies, even though they be Spaniards, thinking nothing of them. He inspired general fear. When our enemies saw Tzilacatzin, they would hunch down. They strove greatly to kill him, whether shooting him with iron bolts or with guns. But Tzilacatzin disguised himself in order not to be recognized. Sometimes he would put on [his own] device, with his lip pendant and his golden earplugs, and he would put on his shell necklace. He would go with his head uncovered, showing that he was an Otomi. But sometimes he put on only cotton upper armor and covered his forehead with a little narrow cloth. Sometimes to disguise himself he put on a feather hairpiece or wig, with eagle feathers tied at the back of the neck. This was the way in which those who threw people in the fire were attired; he went about looking like one of them, imitating them. He had golden arm bands on both sides, on both arms, shimmering, and he also had shining golden bands on the calves of his legs.)

Thirty-fifth chapter, where it is told how the Mexica took captives again — according to the count of the Spaniards they captured, there were fifty-three, as well as many Tlaxcalans and people of Tetzcoco, Chalco, and Xochimilco — and how they killed all of them before their former gods.

And at this point they let loose with all the warriors who had been crouching there; they came out and chased [the Spaniards] in the pas-

sageways, and when the Spaniards saw it they [the Mexica] seemed to
be intoxicated. Then captives were taken. Many Tlaxcalans, and people
of Acolhuacan, Chalco, Xochimilco, etc., were captured. A great abundance were captured and killed. They made the Spaniards and all the
others go right into the water. And the road became very slippery; one
could no longer walk on it, but would slip and slide. . . .

Then they took the captives to Yacacolco, hurrying them along, going
along herding their captives together. Some went weeping, some
singing, some went shouting while hitting their hands against their
mouths. When they got them to Yacacolco, they lined them all up. Each
one went to the altar platform, where the sacrifice was performed. The
Spaniards went first, going in the lead; the people of all the different altepetl just followed, coming last. And when the sacrifice was over, they
strung the Spaniards' heads on poles [on the skull rack]; they also
strung up the horses' heads. They placed them below, and the Spaniards' heads were above them, strung up facing east. But they did not
string up the heads of all the various [other] people from far away. There
were fifty-three of the Spaniards they captured, along with four horses.

Nevertheless, watch was kept everywhere, and there was fighting.
They did not stop keeping watch because of [what had happened]. The
people of Xochimilco went about in boats surrounding us on all sides;
there were deaths and captives taken on both sides.

And all the common people suffered greatly. There was famine; many
died of hunger. They no longer drank good, pure water, but the water
they drank was salty. Many people died of it, and because of it many
got dysentery and died. Everything was eaten: lizards, swallows, maize
straw, grass that grows on salt flats. And they chewed at colorin wood,
glue flowers, plaster, leather, and deerskin, which they roasted, baked,
and toasted so that they could eat them, and they ground up medicinal
herbs and adobe bricks. There had never been the like of such suffering. The siege was frightening, and great numbers died of hunger. And
bit by bit they came pressing us back against the wall, herding us together. . . .

Thirty-ninth chapter, where it is said how when [the Spaniards] had
forced the Mexica to the very wall, there appeared and was seen a blood-
colored fire that seemed to come from the sky. It appeared like a great
blazing coal as it came.

When night came, it rained and sprinkled off and on. It was very dark
when a fire appeared. It looked and appeared as if it was coming from the
sky, like a whirlwind. It went spinning around and around, turning on itself; as it went it seemed to explode into coals, some large, some small,

some just like sparks. It seemed to take on the aspect of a "wind-axe." It sputtered, crackled, and snapped. It circled the walls at the water, heading toward Coyonacazco, then it went into the midst of the water and disappeared there. No one struck his hand against his mouth, no one uttered a sound. . . .

Then they took Quauhtemoctzin in a boat. In it were only two people accompanying him, going with him: Tepotzitoloc, a seasoned warrior, and Iaztachimal, Quauhtemoctzin's page, with one person who poled them along, named Cenyaotl. When they were about to take Quauhtemoctzin, all the people wept, saying, "There goes the lord Quauhtemoctzin, going to give himself to the gods, the Spaniards."

Fortieth chapter, where it is said how the Tlatelolca and Tenochca and their ruler submitted to the Spaniards, and what happened when they were among them.

And when they had gotten him there and put him on land, all the Spaniards were waiting. They came to take him; the Spaniards grasped him by the hand, took him up to the roof, and stood him before the Captain, the war leader. When they stood him before him, he looked at Quauhtemoctzin, took a good look at him, stroked his hair; then they seated him next to him. And they fired off the guns; they hit no one, but they aimed over the people, the [shots] just went over their heads. Then they took a [cannon], put it in a boat, and took it to the home of Coyohuehuetzin. When they got there, they took it up on the roof. Then again they killed people; many died there. But [the Mexica] just fled, and the war came to an end.

Then everyone shouted, saying, "It's over! Let everyone leave! Go eat greens!" When they heard this, the people departed; they just went into the water. But when they went out on the highway, again they killed some people, which angered the Spaniards; a few of them were carrying their shields and war clubs. Those who lived in houses went straight to Amaxac, where the road forks. There the people divided, some going toward Tepeyacac, some toward Xoxohuiltitlan, some toward Nonoalco. But no one went toward Xoloco and Maçatzintamalco.

And all who lived in boats and on platforms [in the water] and those at Tolmayeccan just went into the water. The water came to the stomachs of some, to the chests of others, to the necks of others, and some sank entirely into the deep water. The little children were carried on people's backs. There was a general wail; but some rejoicing and amusing themselves as they went along the road. Most of the owners of boats left at night, though some left by day. They seemed to knock against one another as they went.

And along every stretch [of road] the Spaniards took things from people by force. They were looking for gold; they cared nothing for green-stone, precious feathers, or turquoise. They looked everywhere with the women, on their abdomens, under their skirts. And they looked everywhere with the men, under their loincloths and in their mouths. And [the Spaniards] took, picked out the beautiful women, with yellow bodies. And how some women got loose was that they covered their faces with mud and put on ragged blouses and skirts, clothing themselves in rags. And some men were picked out, those who were strong and in the prime of life, and those who were barely youths, to run errands for them and be their errand boys, called their *tlamacazque* [priests, acolytes]. Then they burned some of them on the mouth [branded them]; some they branded on the cheeks, some on the mouth.

And when the weapons were laid down and we collapsed, the year count was Three House, and the day count was One Serpent. . . .

FRANCISCO DE AGUILAR

Eighth Jornada

The Spanish selections on the final battles and fall concentrate on the strategy and tactics of the Spanish forces. Francisco de Aguilar, a conquistador who later repented of his actions and became a Franciscan friar, wrote a succinct journal of the conquest. An excerpt on the final siege from his account is included here.

Having rebuilt his army with men who had come over from the Islands, Captain Cortés marched with his troops toward Mexico and entered the great city of Texcoco, the seat of a dominion almost as large as that of Mexico. The city had eighty to a hundred thousand houses, or more, and the captain and his Spaniards were quartered there in some large and very beautiful rooms and courtyards.

They entered Texcoco without war having been waged by either side. The reason for this was that the lord of the city, whose name was Cuau-

Patricia de Fuentes, ed., *The Conquistadores: First-Person Accounts of the Conquest of Mexico* (Norman: University of Oklahoma Press, 1993), 158–62.

nacuxtli, and his brother Ixtlilxochitl, the captain general, had fortified themselves in Mexico together with their bravest warriors, so that there was no one in the city to give battle. Therefore no damage or injury was done to the people, nor was anything of theirs touched, except the provisions that they supplied voluntarily.

Then Captain Cortés ordered the brigantines constructed as quickly as possible, so that they could be used in fording the lake and entering Mexico, and they were completed in a short time. Meanwhile the captain applied himself to sending officers to the surrounding towns to persuade them to ally themselves peaceably, which they did, although all the lords and bravest warriors were in Mexico.

Upon finishing the brigantines, a deep canal was dug along a gully that went all the way to the lake. The brigantines were loaded with artillery, crossbowmen and harquebusiers, and seamen to man the oars, and after assigning captains to the ships Cortés went by land around the shore of the lake. He arrived with some of the men at the causeway that is called Coyoacan, and there with about two hundred men he made his camp. At the Tlatelolco causeway he stationed Captain Gonzalo de Sandoval, and at the Tacuba causeway Don Pedro de Alvarado, with a goodly number of men and Tlaxcalan Indians.

In this manner, with forces encircling the city, and with the brigantines which were a great help on the lake, the city began to be battered by land and by water. In addition great trouble was taken to cut off the fresh water supply from the springs of Chapultepec, which reached the city by conduits, and these were fiercely defended from all sides.

The Christians wounded some of the Indians, and great numbers of Indians were killed in the assaults on horseback and by the guns, harquebuses and crossbows. In spite of all this they put up their strong barricades, and opened causeways and canals, and defended themselves courageously. During the course of the war they also killed some of the Spaniards and captured alive one of them called Guzmán, who was Cortés' aide.

It happened that as some of the Spaniards were retreating the Indians forced them into a canal, where most of them died. Captain Cortés, who found himself alone, ran to help them and began pulling out those he could with his hands. So many Indians had rushed to the attack that they laid hold of him and were pushing him into the canal to drown him, when a brave soldier named Olloa appeared at his side. He cut off the hands and arms of the Indians who were holding the captain, and thus freed him and pulled him out.

The war was sustained fiercely by both sides, since on our side we had the help of many Tlaxcalan warriors, while the Mexicans [had the advantage of] their rooftops and high buildings from which they battered us, and by turns we were forced to retreat or were able to take the offensive. The brigantines and their captains and men fought very hard on the lake, and this was a pleasure to see because the Indian canoes, which covered the water, boldly attacked the brigantines. As soon as the Spaniards took any of the houses, which were all on the water, they had the Tlaxcalan Indians demolish and level them, for this gave more freedom to maneuver. And so they fought bravely, and the Indians defended themselves and killed or wounded some of the Spaniards.

When some of the Indian lords inside the city began to see the danger they were in, and the scarcity of supplies and lack of water, they decided to escape by night. One in particular was Ixtlilxochitl, captain general of Texcoco and brother of Cuaunacuxtli the lord of Texcoco. He appeared before Captain Cortés and offered himself and his allies, promising to aid him and the Christians in the war against his fellow people; and since he was very valiant, this was a great blow to the Mexicans. It must also have hurt them when on another night the lord who ruled Xochimilco and Cuitlahuac came over to our side, because his people, with their canoes, fought most cruelly against the Mexicans and contributed largely to their destruction. In addition to this, when the Christians were exhausted from war, God saw fit to send the Indians smallpox, and there was a great pestilence in the city because there were so many people there, especially women, and they had nothing more to eat. We soldiers could scarcely get about the streets because of the Indians who were sick from hunger, pestilence and smallpox. Also for these reasons they began to slacken in their fighting. Moreover, as they gradually retreated to some fortified houses on the water, we held the advantage, and our allies were able to devote themselves to leveling houses and buildings, which made it possible for us to take the whole city, since we could run our horses on level ground.

The Mexicans, almost vanquished, withdrew to their fortresses on the water, and since a great number of women were left among them, they armed them all and stationed them on the rooftops. The Spaniards were alarmed at seeing so many of the enemy again, whooping and shouting at them, and when they began killing them and saw they were women, there was dismay on both sides.

Captain Hernando Cortés, and Alderete the first royal treasurer, and the scrivener who was named Orduña, and several other gentlemen, reached the fortified house where Cuauhtemoc had already taken refuge. Cuauhtemoc, youthful lord of about eighteen years of age, was a person of great valor and courage. They sent word to him saying that since there was no place further to which he could retreat, he should surrender, and that the king would pardon him and grant him many privileges. He replied with great conceit and little shame: "I do not care to give myself up, for I prefer to see you all killed." And so at night we retired to our camp.

On the following morning they began fighting again, and a requisition was sent to Cuauhtemoc, but once more he refused to surrender. But two days before the requisition, the women and children had begun to come and give themselves up to the Spaniards, for they could see they were lost. Cuauhtemoc took to a small canoe, with only one paddler, and since it was night it happened that his canoe met with a brigantine commanded by Captain García Holguín. García Holguín captured him and presented him to Captain Hernando Cortés, thereby effecting a reconciliation with Cortés, who had not borne him good will.

This done, the Spaniards seized the house that had been Cuauhtemoc's stronghold, where they found a great quantity of gold and jewels, and other plunder. The Tlaxcalans who were assisting us in the war and the people who had left the city knew its ins and outs, so that when they went home again they were rich with the spoils they took. This house was seized on the day of Saint Hippolytus, which ended the war for the city, and we left to go to our camps. Captain Cortés was requested to settle in Tacuba, or Coyoacan or Texcoco, but he would never agree.

After the conquest of Mexico was over, Captain Hernando Cortés commanded that the Spaniards stay there in Mexico, where in a short time he began building a very beautiful and great city, which is the city of Mexico. . . .

BERNAL DÍAZ

From *The True History of the Conquest of New Spain*

In the final siege Cortés divided his forces into separate armies commanded by himself and his captains, Pedro de Alvarado, Cristóbal de Olid, and Gonzalo de Sandoval. Bernal Díaz was in Alvarado's camp and so in this

Bernal Díaz, from *The True History of the Conquest of New Spain,* ed. A. P. Maudslay (London: Hakluyt Society, 1908), 116–18, 128–30, 148–52, 179–84, 252–55.

excerpt he often had to write based on what he heard rather than what he saw. Included here first is a short section on the character, appearance, and personality of some of the Spanish captains and soldiers. The rest of the excerpt from Bernal Díaz describes the operations of the Spanish forces from the viewpoint of the common soldier involved in the bitter fighting of the final stages (see Figure 17). In fact, Bernal Díaz's True History *did not end with the fall of the city, but carried the story beyond to the conquest of the rest of the country and to his own history, which eventually took him to Guatemala.*

Figure 17. Mexica views of the final battles. Scenes depict (*clockwise*) Mexica war canoes on the lake; Spaniards and Nahua allies battling Mexica who are reduced to throwing stones; Mexica prepare to throw a captured cannon into the lake.

Source: Reproduced from Arthur J. O. Anderson and Charles E. Dibble, eds., *Florentine Codex,* Book 12 — *The Conquest of Mexico* (Santa Fe: School of American Research and University of Utah, 1975), plates 127, 128, 129. Courtesy Biblioteca Medicea Laurenziana.

. . . I wish now to record the age and appearance of Don Pedro de Alvarado, who was Comendador of Santiago and Adelantado and Governor of Guatemala, Honduras, and Chiapa. He was about thirty-four years old when he came here, of good size, and well proportioned, with a very cheerful countenance and a winning smile, and because he was so handsome the Mexican Indians gave him the name of "Tonatio," which means "the Sun." He was very active and a good horseman, and above all was very frankhearted and a good talker, and he was very neat in his attire but with rich and costly clothes. He wore a small gold chain round his neck with a jewel, and a ring with a good diamond. As I have already stated where he died and other things about him, I will say no more here.

The Adelantado Don Francisco de Montejo was of medium height and cheerful countenance; he liked merriment, and was a man of business and a good horseman, and was about thirty-five years old when he came. He was open-handed and spent more than his income; he was Adelantado and Governor of Yucatan and had other titles; he died in Castile.

Captain Gonzalo de Sandoval was a very valiant Captain, and was about twenty-four years of age when he came here; he was Chief Alguacil of New Spain and for a matter of ten months was Governor of New Spain together with the Treasurer, Alonzo de Estrada. He was not very tall but was very well made and robust, with a broad and deep chest, as were his shoulders. He was somewhat bowlegged, and was a very good horseman. His countenance tended towards the coarse, and his chestnut hair and beard were rather curly. His voice was not very clear, but slightly hesitating and lisping, more or less so. He was not a man of letters but of good average knowledge, nor was he covetous of anything but to be of good repute and act like a good and valiant Captain. In the wars which we waged in New Spain he always showed consideration for the soldiers who appeared to him to be behaving like men, and he protected and helped them. He was not a man to wear rich apparel but was always plainly clad. He owned the best horse, the best galloper and most easily turned to one side or the other, and they said that its like had never been seen in Castile or elsewhere. It was a chestnut with a star on its forehead and a white stocking on its near hind leg. It was named Motilla, and now when men dispute about good horses it is the custom to say in proof of excellence, "It is as good as was Motilla." I must stop talking about horses and say about this valiant Captain that he died in the town of Palos, when he went with Don Hernando Cortés to kiss the feet of His Majesty. It was about Gonzalo de Sandoval that the Marquis Cortés said to His Majesty, that besides the brave soldiers whom he had in his company, who were so valiant that one might name them amongst the most notable that the world had known, there was above them all Sandoval, who was already [fitted to be] the commander of many armies both in council and in action. He was a native of Medellin and a gentleman by birth, and his father was Alcalde of a fortress.

Let us go on to speak of another good Captain named Juan Velásquez de Leon, a native of Old Castile; he was about thirty-six years old when he came here. He was of good size and robust with good shoulders and chest, all well proportioned and upstanding. His countenance was a strong one and his beard was somewhat curly and well kept, his voice was harsh and coarse and he stuttered a little; he was very spirited and a good talker, and when at that time he had any possessions he shared them with his comrades. It is said that in the Island of Hispañola he killed a gentleman of importance, a rich man named Rívas Altias or Altas Rívas, in personal combat, and when he had killed him neither the Magistrates of that Island nor the Royal Audiencia were ever able to catch him to execute justice in the case, but although they went to arrest him he defended himself against the Alguacils, and he came to the Island of Cuba, and from Cuba to New Spain. He was a very good horseman and both on foot and on horseback was a very thorough man. He died at the bridges when we went fleeing from Mexico.

Diego de Ordás was a native of Campos de Valverde or Castro Verde; he was probably forty years old when he came here, and was Captain of sword and shield soldiers, for he was no horseman; he was brave and judicious. He was of good height and sturdy and had a very strong face with a thin blackish beard. In his speech he pronounced certain words imperfectly and with something of a stammer. He was frank and a good talker, a Comendador of [the order of] Santiago, and died in the affair of Marañon when he was Captain or Governor, but I do not know very well about that.

Captain Luis Marin was of fair size, robust and vigorous; he was bow-legged and his beard was reddish and his face long and pleasing, except that he had scars as though he had had smallpox. He was about thirty years old when he came here. He was a native of San Lucar, lisped a little like a Sevillano, was a good horseman, and a good talker; he died in the affairs of Michuacan.

Captain Pedro de Ircio was of middle height and limped, he had a cheerful face and talked to excess, and so it would come about that he was always telling stories about Don Pedro Giron and the Conde de Hurueña; he was cunning and so we called him "Sour grapes" without works, and without having done anything worth recording he died in Mexico. . . .

As Cortés and all our captains and soldiers understood that without the launches we could not advance along the causeways to fight [our way] to Mexico, he sent four of them to Pedro de Alvarado,* and he left six at his own camp (which was that of Cristóbal de Olid)† and he sent two launches to Gonzalo de Sandoval at the Tepeaquilla Causeway, and he ordered the smallest one not to be sent any more on the lake lest the canoes should upset it, for it was of small burden, and he ordered the people and sailors that were in it to be distributed among the other twelve, for there were already twenty men badly wounded among those who manned them.

When we saw ourselves reinforced with these launches in our camp at Tacuba Pedro de Alvarado ordered two of them to go on one side of the causeway and two on the other side, and we began to fight very successfully, for the launches vanquished the canoes which were wont to attack us from the water, and so we had an opportunity to capture several bridges and barricades, and while we were fighting, so numerous were the stones from the slings and the javelins and arrows that they shot at us that although all the soldiers were well protected by armour they were injured and wounded, and not until night parted us did we cease contending and fighting.‡

I wish to say that from time to time the Mexicans changed about and relieved their squadrons [as we could tell] by the devices and distinguishing marks on their armour. Then, as to the launches, they were checked by the darts, arrows and stones with which they were attacked from the Azoteas which fell thicker than hail, and I do not know how to describe it here nor would anyone be able to understand it except those who were present, for they were more numerous than hail stones, and quickly covered the causeway. Then, whenever we left a bridge or barricade unguarded after having captured it with much labour, they would retake and deepen it that same night, and construct stronger defences

* Cortés had broken a way through the Iztapalapa Causeway so that the launches could pass to the west side.

† This is misleading, Cristóbal de Olid's camp was at Coyoacan, but Olid himself and some of his men had joined Cortés at Acachinanco, on the causeway where the six launches were now stationed.

‡ On June 9th a general assault was ordered from all three causeways, but Bernal Díaz does not especially allude to it. On that day Cortés reached the great Plaza of Mexico, but retired to his camp on the Iztapalapa Causeway at night.

and even make hidden pits in the water, so that the next day when we were fighting, and it was time for us to retire, we should get entangled [among the defences] and fall into the pits and they would be able to vanquish us from their canoes, for they had also got ready many canoes for the purpose, stationed in places where our launches could not see them, so that when we were in distress in the pits some [were prepared] to fall upon us by land, and others by water. To prevent the launches from coming to our assistance, they had fixed many stakes hidden in the water so that they should get impaled on them. In this way we fought every day,* I have already said before that the cavalry were of little use on the causeways for if they charged or gave chase to the squadrons that fought with us the Mexicans at once threw themselves into the water, and other squadrons were posted behind breastworks, which they had raised on the causeway, waiting [for the horsemen] with long lances or scythes made very long with the arms captured at the time of the great defeat which they inflicted on us in Mexico. With these lances and great showers of arrows and javelins shot from the lake they wounded and killed the horses before the horsemen could do damage to the enemy. In addition to this those who owned horses did not want to risk them, for at that time a horse cost eight hundred pesos and some even cost more than a thousand, and they could accomplish nothing to speak of, as they could overtake very few of the enemy on the causeway.

. . . I want to say that at this time the Mexicans were quite close to us as we kept watch, and they too had their sentinels and changed them in watches, and it was in this way; they lighted great fires that burned all night through, but those who were on guard stood away from the fires and from afar we were not able to distinguish them, and although on account of the brightness of the wood that was always burning we could not see the Indians who were watching, yet we could always tell when they were changing guard, for then they came to feed the fire. On many nights, as it rained heavily at that season it happened that their fire was put out, and they rekindled it without making any noise nor a word spoken among them, for they understood one another by means of whistles.

I wish to say that very often our musketeers and crossbowmen when we knew that they [the enemy] were going to change guard threw stones and shot arrows at a venture at groups of them, but they did them

---

*Cortés ordered a general assault on June 16th, which was carried out, although Bernal Díaz makes no especial mention of it. On this day Cortés destroyed the palaces round the Plaza in Mexico and then retired to his camp.

no harm, because they were in a place which even if we had wished to get at them in the night we should not have been able to reach them on account of another great and very deep opening of the canal, which they had made by hand and of the barricades and walls they had raised, and they also shot at us volleys of javelins and arrows.

Let us stop speaking about keeping watch and say how each day we advanced along the causeway fighting in the most regular order and we captured the opening, which I have spoken of, where they kept guard; but such was the multitude of the enemy who came against us every day, and the javelins, arrows and stones they shot, that they wounded us all, although we proceeded with the greatest caution and were well armoured.

Then after having passed all the day fighting, when it was growing late and there was no opportunity for a further advance, only of turning back in retreat, that would be the [very] time they held many squadrons in readiness, believing that with the great energy of their attacks as we retired, they would be able to rout us, for they came on as fierce as tigers and fought us hand to hand. As soon as we found out this plan of theirs, we made the following arrangement for retreating; the first thing we did was to get our friends the Tlaxcalans off the causeway, for as they were very numerous, they longed with our support to get to blows with the Mexicans, and as the Mexicans were cunning, they wished nothing better than to see us entangled with our friends, thus they made fierce attacks on us from two or three directions, so as to enclose us in the middle and intercept some of us, and, with the many Tlaxcalans who embarrassed us, prevent us from fighting on all sides, and this was the reason that we got them [the Tlaxcalans] off the causeway to where we could place them in safety. As soon as we found ourselves no longer hampered by them, we retreated to our camp without turning our backs, but always facing the enemy, some of the crossbowmen and musketeers shooting and others loading, and with our four launches in the lake, two on each side of the causeway, protecting us against the fleets of canoes and the many stones from the azoteas and houses which were destined to be pulled down. Yet with all this caution every one of us ran great personal risk until we reached our ranchos. There we at once treated our wounds with oil and bandaged them with native cloth, and supped on the tortillas they had brought us from Tacuba, and on herbs, and such as had them, on Tunas. Then we at once mounted guard at the water-opening which I have mentioned, and the next morning we promptly returned to fight, for we could do nothing else, for however early in the morning it might be, battalions of the enemy were there ready to attack us, and they even reached our camp and shouted abuse at us, and in such manner we underwent our hardships. . . .

. . . At that time many companies of Mexicans came to the causeway and wounded the horsemen as well as all of us, and they gave Sandoval a good blow with a stone in the face. Then Pedro de Alvarado and other horsemen went to his assistance. As so many squadrons approached I and twenty other soldiers faced them, and Sandoval ordered us to retreat little by little so that they should not kill the horses, and because we did not retreat as quickly as he wished he said to us with fury "Do you wish that through your selfishness they should kill me and all these horsemen? For the love of me, dear brothers, do fall back," at that moment the enemy again wounded him and his horse. Just then we cleared our allies off the causeway, and [we retreated] little by little keeping our faces [to the enemy] and not turning our backs, as though to form a dam. Some of the crossbowmen and musketeers were shooting and others loading their guns for they did not fire them off all together, and the horsemen made charges, and Pedro Moreno Medrano, already mentioned by me, loaded and fired his cannon, yet, notwithstanding the number of Mexicans that the balls were sweeping away, we could not fend them off, on the contrary they kept on following us thinking that this very night they would carry us off to be sacrificed.

When we had retreated near to our quarters and had already crossed a great opening where there was much water, the arrows, javelins and stones could no longer reach us. Sandoval, Francisco de Lugo and Andrés de Tápia were standing with Pedro de Alvarado each one relating what had happened to him and what Cortés had ordered, when again there was sounded the dismal drum of Huichilobos and many other shells and horns and things like trumpets and the sound of them all was terrifying, and we all looked towards the lofty Cue where they were being sounded, and saw that our comrades whom they had captured when they defeated Cortés were being carried by force up the steps, and they were taking them to be sacrificed. When they got them up to a small square in [front of] the oratory, where their accursed idols are kept, we saw them place plumes on the heads of many of them and with things like fans [in their hands?] they forced them to dance before Huichilobos, and after they had danced they immediately placed them on their backs on some rather narrow stones which had been prepared as [places for] sacrifice, and with stone knives they sawed open their chests and drew out their palpitating hearts and offered them to the idols that were there, and they kicked the bodies down the steps, and Indian butchers who were waiting below cut off the arms and feet and flayed [the skin off] the faces, and prepared it afterwards like glove leather with the beards on, and kept those for the festivals when they celebrated drunken orgies, and the flesh they ate in *chilmole*. In the same way they sacrificed all the others and ate the legs and arms and offered the hearts and blood to their idols, as I have said, and the bodies, that is their entrails and feet, they threw to the tigers and lions which they kept in the house of the carnivores which I have spoken about in an earlier chapter.

When we saw those cruelties all of us in our camp and Pedro de Alvarado and Gonzalo de Sandoval and all the other captains (let the interested readers who peruse this, note what ills we suffered from them [the Mexicans]) said the one to the other "thank God that they are not carrying me off to day to be sacrificed."

It should also be noted that we were not far away from them, yet we could render them no help, and could only pray God to guard us from such a death.

Then, at the moment that they were making the sacrifices, great squadrons of Mexicans fell on us suddenly and gave us plenty to do on all sides and neither in one way or the other could we prevail against them.

And they cried: — "Look, that is the way in which you will all have to die, for our gods have promised it to us many times." Then the words and threats which they said to our friends the Tlaxcalans were so injurious and evil that they disheartened them, and they threw them roasted legs of Indians and the arms of our soldiers and cried to them: — "Eat of the flesh of these Teules and of your brothers for we are already glutted with it, and you can stuff yourselves with this which is over, and observe that as for the houses which you have destroyed, we shall have to bring you to rebuild them much better with white stone and well worked masonry, so go on helping the Teules, for you will see them all sacrificed."

There was another thing that Guatemoc ordered to be done when he won that victory, he sent to all the towns of our allies and friends and to their relations, the hands and feet of our soldiers and the flayed faces with the beards, and the heads of the horses that they had killed, and he sent word that more than half of us were dead and he would soon finish us off, and he told them to give up their friendship [with us] and come to Mexico and if they did not give it up promptly, he would come and destroy them, and he sent to tell them many other things to induce them to leave our camp and desert us, and then we should be killed by his hands.

As they still went on attacking us both by day and by night, all of us in our camp kept watch together, Gonzalo de Sandoval and Pedro de

Alvarado and the other captains keeping us company during our watch, and although during the night great companies of warriors came [against us] we withstood them. Both by day and night half the horsemen remained in Tacuba and the other half were on the causeway.

There was another greater evil that they did us; no matter how carefully we had filled in [the water spaces] since we advanced along the causeway, they returned and opened them all and constructed barricades stronger than before. Then our friends of the cities of the lake who had again accepted our friendship and had come to aid us with their canoes believed that they "came to gather wool and went back shorn" for many of them lost their lives and many more returned wounded, and they lost more than half of the canoes they had brought with them, but, even with all this, thenceforward they did not help the Mexicans, for they were hostile to them, but they carefully watched events as they happened. . . .

As I have said Cortés not only saw that the Catapult was useless but was angry with the soldier who advised him to have it made, and in consequence of Guatemoc and his Captains not wishing for peace of any sort, he ordered Gonzalo de Sandoval to invade that part of the City where Guatemoc had taken refuge with all the flower of his Captains and the most distinguished persons that were in Mexico, and he ordered him not to kill or wound any Indians unless they should attack him, and even if they did attack him, he was only to defend himself and not do them any other harm, but he should destroy their houses and the many defences they had erected in the lake. Cortés ascended the great Cue of Tlatelolco to see how Sandoval advanced with the launches, and at that time Pedro de Alvarado, Francisco Verdugo, Luis Marin and other soldiers were there with Cortés.

Sandoval advanced with great ardour upon the place where the Houses of Guatemoc stood, and when Guatemoc saw himself surrounded, he was afraid that they would capture him or kill him, and he had got ready fifty great piraguas* with good rowers so that when he saw himself hard pressed he could save himself by going to hide in some reed beds and get from thence to land and hide himself in another town, and those were the instructions he had given his captains and the persons of most importance who were with him in that fortified part of the city, so that they should do the same.

When they saw that the launches were getting among the houses they

* Canoes.

embarked in the fifty canoes, and they had already placed [on board] the property and gold and jewels of Guatemoc and all his family and women, and he had embarked himself and shot out into the lake ahead, accompanied by many Captains. As many other canoes set out at the same time, the lake was full of them, and Sandoval quickly received the news that Guatemoc was fleeing, and ordered all the launches to stop destroying the houses and fortifications and follow the flight of the canoes, and to have a care that they kept track of where Guatemoc was going, and not to molest him or do him any injury but try to capture him without using violence. As a certain García Holguín a friend of Sandoval, was captain of a launch which was very fast and a good sailor and was manned by good rowers Sandoval ordered him to follow in the direction in which they told him that Guatemoc was fleeing with his great piraguas, and instructed him not to do him [Guatemoc] any injury whatever beyond capturing him in case he should overtake him, and Sandoval went in another direction with other launches which kept him company. It pleased our Lord God that García Holguín should overtake the canoes and piraguas in which Guatemoc was travelling, and from the style and the awnings and the seat he was using he knew that it was Guatemoc the great Lord of Mexico, and he made signals for them to stop, but they would not stop, so he made as though he were going to discharge muskets and crossbows. When Guatemoc saw that, he was afraid and said "Do not shoot, I am the king of this City and they call me Guatemoc, and what I ask of you is not to disturb my things that I am taking with me nor my wife nor my relations, but carry me at once to Malinche." When Holguín heard him he was greatly delighted, and with much respect he embraced him and placed him in the launch, him and his wife and about thirty chieftains and seated him in the poop on some mats and cloths, and gave him to eat of the food that he had brought with him, and he touched nothing whatever in the canoes that carried his [Guatemoc's] property but brought it along with the launch. By this time Gonzalo de Sandoval had ordered all the launches to assemble together, and he knew that Holguín had captured Guatemoc and was carrying him to Cortés, and when he heard it he told the rowers on board his launch to make all the speed possible and he overtook Holguín and claimed the prisoner, and Holguín would not give him up and said that he had captured him and not Sandoval, and Sandoval replied that that was true, but that he was the Captain General of the launches, and that García Holguín sailed under his command and banner, and it was because he was his friend and his launch the fastest that he had ordered him to follow after Guatemoc, to capture him, and that to him as his General he must give up his prisoner. Still Holguín contended that he did not wish to do so, and at that moment another launch went in great haste to Cortés (who was very close by in Tlatelolco, watching from the top of the Cue how Sandoval was advancing) to demand a reward for the good news, and they told Cortés of the dispute which Sandoval was having with Holguín over the capture of the prisoner. When Cortés knew of it he at once dispatched Captain Luis Marin and Francisco de Verdugo to summon Sandoval and Holguín to come as they were in their launches without further discussion, and to bring Guatemoc and his wife and family with all [signs of] respect, and that he would settle whose was the prisoner and to whom was due the honour of it [the capture].

While they were bringing him, Cortés ordered a guest chamber to be prepared as well as could be done at the time, with mats and cloths and seats, and a good supply of the food which Cortés had reserved for himself. Sandoval and Holguín soon arrived with Guatemoc, and the two captains between them led him up to Cortés, and when he came in front of him he paid him great respect, and Cortés embraced Guatemoc with delight, and was very affectionate to him and his captains. Then Guatemoc said to Cortés "Señor Malinche, I have surely done my duty in defence of my City, and I can do no more and I come by force and a prisoner into your presence and into your power, take that dagger that you have in your belt and kill me at once with it" and when he said this he wept tears and sobbed and other great Lords whom he had brought with him also wept. Cortés answered him through Doña Marina and Aguilar our interpreters, very affectionately, that he esteemed him all the more for having been so brave as to defend the City, and he was deserving of no blame, on the contrary [this circumstance] must be more in his favour than otherwise.

What he wished was that he [Guatemoc] had made peace of his own free will before the city had been so far destroyed, and so many of his Mexicans had died, but now, that both had happened there was no help for it and it could not be mended, let his spirit and the spirit of his Captains take rest, and he should rule in Mexico and over his provinces as he did before. Then Guatemoc and his Captains said that they accepted his favour, and Cortés asked after his wife and other great ladies, the wives of other Captains who, he had been told, had come with Guatemoc. Guatemoc himself answered and said that he had begged Gonzalo de Sandoval and García Holguín that they might remain in the canoes while he came to see what orders Malinche gave them. Cortés at once sent for them and ordered them all to be given of the best that at that time there was in the camp to eat, and as it was late and was beginning to rain, Cortés arranged for them to go to Coyoacan, and took Guatemoc and all his family and household and many chieftains with him and he ordered Pedro de Alvarado, Gonzalo de Sandoval and the other captains each to go to his own quarters and camp, and we went to Tacuba, Sandoval to Tepeaquilla and Cortés to Coyoacan. Guatemoc and his captains were captured on the thirteenth day of August at the time of vespers on the day of Señor San Hipólito in the year one thousand five hundred and twenty-one, thanks to our Lord Jesus Christ and our Lady the Virgin Santa Maria, His Blessed Mother, Amen.

It rained and thundered and lightning flashed that afternoon and up to midnight heavier rain fell than usual. After Guatemoc had been captured all the soldiers turned as deaf as if some one had stood shouting from the top of a belfry with many bells clanging and in the midst of their ringing all of a sudden they had ceased to sound. I say this purposely, for during all the ninety-three days that we were besieging this city, both by night and day, some of the Mexican Captains kept on uttering so many shouts and yells, whilst they were mustering the squadrons and warriors who were to fight on the causeway, and others were calling out to those in the canoes who were to fight with the launches, and with us on the bridges, again others to those driving in piles and opening and deepening the water openings and bridges and making breastworks, or those who were making javelins and arrows, or to the women preparing rounded stones to hurl from the slings, while from the oratories and towers of the Idols, the accursed drums, trumpets and mournful kettledrums never ceased sounding, and in this way both by night and by day, there was such a great din that we could not hear one another. On the capture of Guatemoc, the shouts and all the clamour ceased, and it is for this reason I have said that up to then we seemed to be standing in a belfry. . . .

From *Cantares mexicanos*

In addition to the Nahua narratives contained in Sahagún's Florentine Codex, *this selection includes some Nahua poetry from the* Cantares mexicanos, *which bemoan the loss of Tenochtitlan.*[1] *These poems or elegies were*

[1]A modern translation and analysis of the *cantares* is John Bierhorst, trans. and ed., *Cantares Mexicanos: Songs of the Aztecs* (Stanford: Stanford University Press, 1985).

Miguel León-Portilla, *The Broken Spears: The Aztec Account of the Conquest of Mexico,* 2nd ed. (Boston: Beacon Press, 1992), 71–78, 80–81.

included by the Nahuatl scholar Miguel León-Portilla in his book The Broken Spears, *and they serve as a fitting conclusion to the tragedy of the conquest and the loss it represented.*

THE FALL OF TENOCHTITLAN

Our cries of grief rise up
and our tears rain down,
for Tlatelolco is lost.
The Aztecs are fleeing across the lake;
They are running away like women.

How can we save our homes, my people?
The Aztecs are deserting the city:
the city is in flames, and all
is darkness and destruction.

Motelchiuhtzin the Huiznahuacatl,
Tlacotzin the Tlailotlacatl,
Oquitzin the Tlacatecuhtli
are greeted with tears.

Weep, my people:
know that with these disasters
we have lost the Mexican nation.
The water has turned bitter,
our food is bitter!
These are the acts of the Giver of Life. . . .

The Aztecs are besieged in the city;
the Tlatelolcas are besieged in the city!

The walls are black,
the air is black with smoke,
the guns flash in the darkness.
They have captured Cuauhtemoc;
they have captured the princes of Mexico.

The Aztecs are besieged in the city;
the Tlatelolcas are besieged in the city!

After nine days, they were taken to Coyoacan:
Cuauhtemoc, Coanacoch, Tetlepanquetzaltzin.
The kings are prisoners now,

Tlacotzin consoled them:
"Oh my nephews, take heart!
The kings are prisoners now;
They are bound with chains."

The king Cuauhtemoc replied:
"Oh my nephew, you are a prisoner;
they, have bound you in irons,

"But who is that at the side of the Captain-General
Ah, it is Doña Isabel, my little niece!
Ah, it is true: the kings are prisoners now!

"You will be a slave and belong to another:
the collar will be fashioned in Coyoacan,
where the quetzal feathers will be woven.
Ah, it is Doña Isabel, my little niece.
Ah, it is true: the kings are prisoners now!"

FLOWERS AND SONGS OF SORROW

Nothing but flowers and songs of sorrow
are left in Mexico and Tlatelolco,
where once we saw warriors and wise men.

We know it is true
that we must perish,
for we are mortal men.
You, the Giver of Life,
You have ordained it.

We wander here and there
in our desolate poverty.
We are mortal men.
We have seen bloodshed and pain
where once we saw beauty and valor.

We are crushed to the ground;
we lie in ruins.
There is nothing but grief and suffering
in Mexico and Tlatelolco,
where once we saw beauty and valor.

Have you grown weary of your servants?
Are you angry with your servants,
O Giver of Life?

8

Aftermath: Tradition and Transformation

The fall of Tenochtitlan signaled both an end and a beginning. Cortés decided to make the ancient city, now in ruins, the site of his new capital. From there expeditions were sent out to pacify or take control of the rest of the country: Cristóbal de Olid to Michoacán, Pedro de Alvarado to Guatemala, Olid again to Honduras, Beltran Nuno de Guzmán to Pánuco (northeastern Mexico). The Zapotecs, the Maya, and other native peoples offered resistance, but within a decade or so most of central Mexico and large parts of the rest of what the Castilians called New Spain were under colonial rule. The Spaniards set about creating institutions to bring indigenous life and culture under control, to establish an ordered Christian society, and to make the new provinces or kingdoms profitable to the Spanish king and to the victors as "colonies," although that word was never used at the time. *Encomiendas* or grants of native labor or tribute were awarded to many conquistadors despite royal objections at first. Disputes over these grants and their effects plagued colonial society for a generation. A royal court of appeals or *audiencia* was established in 1528; royal fiscal officers set up a system of taxes and tribute; in 1528 a bishop, Juan de Zumárraga, was appointed to establish the Church on an ordered basis; and in 1535 the first viceroy, the energetic and able Antonio de Mendoza, arrived to begin his service as the direct royal representative and chief administrator. Perhaps most important, beginning in 1524 groups of missionaries, first the Franciscans and then the Dominicans and Augustinians, initiated the task of proselytization and conversion of the indigenous peoples.

The main personalities of the conquest suffered various fates. Cortés was amply rewarded for his victories. In 1529 he was given a noble title as Marqués (Marquis) del Valle, a grant that gave him the control of extensive lands and vassals and made him fabulously wealthy. In his remaining years, he was often in conflict with the king over the extent of his powers and authority in New Spain. Ruthless men of private ambition were ideal for winning conquests but made kings uneasy thereafter. He died near Seville in 1547. Doña Marina, who had borne Cortés a son, eventually married another conquistador and bore a number of children. Pedro de Alvarado went on to conquer Guatemala and then died fighting native nomadic people in New Spain in 1542. Olid was assassinated by his companions in Honduras after breaking with Cortés's authority, much as the latter had done to Velázquez. Bernal Díaz ended his days in 1584 as a respected if not very wealthy citizen of Guatemala where he had settled. Cuahtemoc, the last independent Mexica leader, was executed by Cortés in 1525, supposedly suspected of fomenting rebellion.

By the 1550s and 1560s the generation of the conquest was dying off and their legacy was still in the process of definition and transformation. At first, indigenous contact with Spanish rule was primarily through institutions such as the church, the law courts, or the *encomienda* but over time cultural, linguistic, and personal contacts transformed the nature of their relationships. Nahua society proved remarkably resilient and adaptable. Old distinctions of rank did not immediately disappear, indigenous ways were adapted to Spanish institutions, and in some ways life continued on much as before. To some extent this was also because the *altepetl* organization and the old rank distinctions and tribute arrangements could be adapted to Spanish demands easily and it served colonial purposes to leave them intact.[1]

The military victory and defeat of the Mexica was simply one of a number of conquests that took place in Mexico in the sixteenth century. The spiritual conquest, the conversion of indigenous peoples to Christianity, had been a goal and justification from the very beginning, but with the arrival of missionaries, a great utopian effort had begun. Many of the early friars believed that the souls taken from the church by the Devil in Europe were providentially being restored to the church in Mexico. (They pointed out that Cortés and the initiator of the Protestant Reformation, Martin Luther, had been born in the same year.) This led to a great program of missionary activity and church construction and also to the study of indigenous language and culture as an adjunct to this effort. The work of Bernardino de Sahagún is simply an outstanding example of the result. But the euphoria of the early mass conversions and the elimination of the old imperial cults of sacrifice and temple

---

[1]This is made clear in a number of recent studies. See, for example, Rebecca Horn, *Postconquest Coyoacan: Nahua-Spanish Relations in Central Mexico, 1519–1650* (Stanford: Stanford University Press, 1997), and Robert Haskett, *Indigenous Rulers: An Ethnohistory of Town Government in Colonial Cuernavaca* (Albuquerque: University of New Mexico Press, 1991). On the Spanish demands and their effect, see Charles Gibson, *The Aztecs under Spanish Rule* (Stanford: Stanford University Press, 1964).

pyramids eventually gave way to an understanding that the victories over the minds and hearts of men and women were neither easy nor clearly defined. Here too, sometimes to the dismay of the missionaries, indigenous society proved resilient and adaptable.

Still another conquest, the biological conquest, accompanied and transformed these processes. The horrific impact of epidemic disease, already apparent during the final siege of Tenochtitlan, catastrophically decimated native populations, thereby upsetting existing social and political arrangements as the ruling dynasties died out and the number of peasant tributaries shrank. The "great dying" in the sixteenth century, especially after the great plague of 1576–81, eventually contributed to a flagging of missionary vigor and perhaps led converts to question the new religion. Meanwhile, as the human population contracted, Spanish livestock rapidly multiplied, often occupying newly vacated fields. Eventually, Spanish farms and ranches began to appropriate and incorporate the old communal lands leading to a never-ending series of disputes over land and water rights.[2] Along with the livestock came the flora of Europe: citrus trees, wheat, barley, and a vast variety of other plants that transformed the landscape and ecology of Mexico as well. These new crops and animals changed diets and agricultural practices, at times producing negative consequences. Great herds of hoofed animals grew faster than the vegetation could accommodate them. In some places this resulted in degradation of the environment with broad social impacts.[3]

Accompanying all these "conquests" was a growing social interaction between Spaniards and natives, more intense to be sure in the cities and large towns where Europeans concentrated, but expanding continually into many regions and social situations. These encounters, at first institutional, became increasingly personal and generalized. From the very moment of the military conquest, sexual relations, forced or consensual, had also taken place. Alvarado, Cortés, and other of the leading conquistadors fathered children with native women. Those who had relations with high-born noble women sometimes married them as well. Formal unions between Spanish commoners and Indian women were more the norm. A generation of "mestizo" children appeared, progeny that eventually changed the face of a Mexico no longer composed of a Spanish conqueror caste, an indigenous ruling class, and a peasant mass, but now complicated by people of mixed origins, identities, and

[2] Woodrow Boarh, *Justice by Insurance* (Berkeley: University of California Press, 1983).
[3] Elinor G. K. Melville, *A Plague of Sheep: Environmental Consequences of the Conquest of Mexico* (Cambridge: Cambridge University Press, 1994).

cultures as well as by an ever more complicated social hierarchy. The great question that remains in colonial history is how, at the local level, this process of social transformation was worked out as new identities and affiliations were created in a context of continuing traditions of ethnic, linguistic, and social practices.

The documents in this chapter deal with both Spanish and indigenous perceptions of the process of change and transformation. Bernal Díaz provides a clear Spanish justification of the conquest and its effects on native peoples. In order to govern and convert after the conquest, the Spaniards sought to gather information from the indigenous peoples. What they collected often reveals previous practices but also indigenous ways of perceiving and thinking about the world which continued long after the conquest. Included here are documents from the *Codex Mendoza* and the *Relaciones geográficas* that illustrate this process. For their part the indigenous peoples adapted new skills like their command of alphabetic writing for their own communal and personal interests. One of the important ways in which they employed these skills was in shaping the memory of the events of the conquest. As illustrations of this process two variant versions of an event, the death of Cuauhtemoc, are presented. Finally, two versions of the whole trajectory of the conquest written by the descendants of those who survived it demonstrate the selective and creative nature of writing history.

BERNAL DÍAZ

From *The True History of the Conquest of New Spain*

While Bernal Díaz was often candid about his desire for wealth and women, he like many other conquistadors sought to justify his actions by his role in the spreading of Christianity. In this passage he reviews the impact of the conquest on native life and extols the participation of native peoples in the church and their acquisition of European culture. From his description, little appears of the continuation of indigenous traditions and beliefs or the oppression of the colonial regime.

Bernal Díaz, from *The True History of the Conquest of New Spain,* ed. A. P. Maudslay (London: Hakluyt Society, 1908), 265–70.

After getting rid of the idolatries and all the evil vices they practised, it pleased our Lord god that with his holy aid and with the good fortunes and the holy Christianity of our most Christian Emperor Don Carlos of Glorious Memory, and of our King and Lord the felicitous and invincible King of Spain, our Lord Don Felipe, his much loved and cherished son (May god grant him many years to live with an increase of more kingdoms, so that he may enjoy them in this his holy and happy [life]-time), there were baptized, after we conquered the country, all, both men and women, and children who have since been born, whose souls formerly went, lost, to the Infernal regions. Now there are many and good monks of [the order of] Señor San Francisco and of Santo Domingo and of other Orders, who go among the pueblos preaching, and, when a child is of the age our holy Mother Church of Rome ordains, they baptize it. Furthermore, through the holy sermons preached, the Holy Gospel is firmly planted in their hearts, and they go to Confession every year, and some of them, who have most knowledge of our holy faith, receive the Sacrament. In addition to this they have their Churches richly adorned with altars and all pertaining to the holy divine worship, with crosses and candlesticks and wax tapers and chalice and patens and silver plates, some large and some small, and censers all worked in silver. Then, in rich pueblos, they have copes, chasubles, and fontals, and often in moderate [sized] pueblos they are of velvet, damask and satin, and of taffeta of various colours and workmanship, and the arms of the crosses are elaborately embroidered with gold and silk, and the crosses of the dead are of black satin, and figured on them is a death's head with its ugly likeness and the bones, and the pall of the bier itself is sometimes good and at other times not so good. Then the necessary bells [vary] with the rank of each pueblo. There is no lack of choir singers with well harmonised voices such as tenors, trebles, contraltos, and basses, and in some pueblos there are organs, and nearly all of them have flutes, oboes, sackbuts and lutes. As for trumpets, shrill and deafening, there are not as many in my country, which is Old Castile, as there are in this province of Guatemala. It is a thing to be grateful for to God, and for profound consideration, to see how the natives assist in celebrating a holy Mass, especially when it is chanted by the Franciscans and Dominicans who have charge of the curacy of the pueblo where it is celebrated. There is another good thing they do [namely] that both men, women and children, who are of the age to learn them, know all the holy prayers in their own languages and are obliged to know them. They have other good customs about their holy Christianity, that when they pass near a sacred altar or Cross they bow their heads with humility, bend their knees, and say the prayer "Our Father," which we Conquistadores have taught them, and they place lighted wax candles before the holy altars and crosses, for formerly they did not know how to use wax in making candles. In addition to what I have said, we taught them to show great reverence and obedience to all the monks and priests, and, when these went to their pueblos, to sally forth to receive them with lighted wax candles and to ring the bells, and to feed them very well. This they do with the monks, and they paid the same attentions to the priests, but after they had seen and known some of these and the covetousness of the rest, and that they committed irregularities in the pueblos, they took no [further] notice of them and did not want them as Curas in their pueblos, but Franciscans and Dominicans. It does not mend matters that the poor Indians say to a prelate that they do not hear him or . . . but what more there is to be said about this subject had better remain in the inkpot, and I will return to my story. Besides the good customs reported by me they have others both holy and good, for when the day of Corpus Christi comes, or that of Our Lady, or other solemn festivals when among us we form processions, most of the pueblos in the neighbourhood of this city of Guatemala come out in procession with their crosses and lighted wax tapers, and carry on their shoulders, on a litter, the image of the saint who is the patron of the pueblo, as richly [adorned] as they are able, and they come chanting litanies and other prayers and playing on their flutes and trumpets. The same thing they do in their own pueblos when the day comes for these solemn festivals. They have the custom of making offerings, on Sundays and at Easter * and especially on All Saints Day, and about this custom of making offerings the secular priests hurry them up in their parishes by such means that the Indians cannot possibly forget, for two or three days before the festival takes place they order them to prepare for the offering. The Monks also [seek] offerings, but not with so great solicitude.

Let us get on, and state how most of the Indian natives of these lands have successfully learned all the trades that there are among us in Castile, and have their shops of the trades, and artisans, and gain a living by it. There are gold and silver smiths, both of chased and of hollow work, and they are very excellent craftsman, also lapidaries and painters. Carvers also do most beautiful work with their delicate burins of iron, especially in carving jades, and in them depict all the phases of the holy passion of our Lord Redeemer and Saviour Jesus Christ, such that, if one had not seen them, one would never believe that Indians had done. It seems in my judgment that the most renowned painter, such as was

* Domingos y Pascuas — Pascua is not only Easter, but any festival lasting three days.

Apelles in ancient times, or in our times a certain Berruguete and Michael Angelo or the other modern now lately become famous, who is a native of Burgos, who has as great a reputation as Apelles, could not emulate with their most skilful pencils the works of art in jade, nor the reliquaries, which are executed by three Mexican Indian craftsmen of that trade, named Andrés de Aquino, Juan de la Cruz, and El Crespillo. In addition to this nearly all the sons of Chieftains are usually grammarians, and would have become expert, if the holy synod had not commanded them to abandon that which the very reverend Archbishop of Mexico had ordered to be done.

Many sons of Chieftains know how to read and write, and to compose books of plain chant, and there are craftsmen in weaving satin and taffeta and making woolen cloth, from veintecuatrenos * to sackcloth, and cotton cloths and rugs. They are carders, woolcombers, and weavers in the same manner as there are in Segovia and in Cuenca, and others are hat makers and soap makers. There are only two crafts they have not been able to undertake, although they have tried: these are to make glass, and to become druggists, but I believe them to be so intelligent that they will acquire them very well. Some of them are surgeons and herbalists. They understand conjuring and working puppets and make very good guitars, indeed they were craftsmen by nature before we came to New Spain. Now they breed cattle of all sorts, and break in oxen, and plough the land, and sow wheat, and thresh harvest, and sell it, and make bread and biscuit, and they have planted their lands and hereditaments with all the trees and fruits which we have brought from Spain, and sell the fruit which they produce. They have planted so many trees that, because the peaches are not good for the health, and the banana plantations give them too much shade, they have cut and are cutting down many of them and putting in quinces and apples and pears, which they hold in higher esteem.

Let us go on, and I will speak of the laws which we have shown them how to guard and execute, and how every year they are to choose the Alcaldes ordinaries and Regidores, Notaries, Alguacils, Fiscals, and Mayordomos, and have their municipal houses (Cabildos) where they meet two days in the week, and they place doorkeepers in them, and give judgment and order debts to be paid which are owed by one to another. For some criminal acts they flog and chastise, and if it is for a death or something atrocious they remit it [the case] to the Governors, if there is no Royal Audiencia. According to what people, who know very well, have

---

*A technical term for a narrow band of twenty-four threads.

told me, in Tlaxcala, Texcoco, Cholula, Oaxaca and Tepeaca and in other great cities, when the Indians hold Court (Cabildo), Macebearers with gilt maces precede those who are Governors and Alcaldes (the same as the Viceroys of New Spain take with them), and justice is done with as much propriety and authority as among ourselves, and they appreciate and desire to know much of the laws of the kingdom.

In addition to this, many of the Caciques are rich, and possess horses, and bring good saddles with trappings, and ride abroad through the cities and towns and places where they are going for amusement, or of which they are natives, and bring Indians and pages to accompany them. In some pueblos, they even play at tilting with reeds and have bull fights, and they tilt at the ring, especially on Corpus Christi day or the day of San Juan or Señor Santiago, or of Our Lady of August, or at the removal* of the Saint of the pueblo from the Church. There are many who wait for the bulls although they are fierce, and many of them are horsemen, especially in a pueblo named Chiapa of the Indians, and, even those who are not Caciques, nearly all of them own horses, and some own herds of mares and mules, and use them to bring in firewood and maize and lime and other things of the kind which they sell in the Plazas, and many of them are carriers in the same way as we have in our Castile.

Not to waste more words, they carry on all trades very perfectly — and even know how to weave tapestry cloths.

I will stop talking further on this subject and will tell of many other grandeurs which, through us, there have been and still are in New Spain.

---

* Probably the round of visits paid by the image of the saint to the various Cofradias.

From the *Codex Mendoza*

The Codex Mendoza *was commissioned by Viceroy Mendoza and produced from 1541 to 1542 under the direction of Francisco Gualpuyogualcatl, the head of the painter's guild of Mexico City. In it, he and other indigenous artists painted a history of the Mexica: an explanation of their*

Frances F. Berdan and Patricia Rieff Anawalt, eds., *The Codex Mendoza*, 4 vols. (Berkeley: University of California Press, 1992), iv, 98–100; 132–35. fls. 42v; 63v. Plates appear in Volume 3: 101, 135; descriptions appear in Volume 4: 99, 133.

political system and social rankings, a listing of tribute obligations, and ex-
planations of various aspects of preconquest culture. To the indigenous pic-
tographs, explanations in Spanish were added (apparently by the Spanish
cleric Juan González) and separate sheets of commentary were written as
well. The manuscript was sent to Spain but lost to French pirates. It even-
tually ended up in the hands of the French humanist André Thévet, who
later sold it to the English scholar Richard Hakluyt.

This document, produced a generation after the conquest, displays the
continuing indigenous artistic conventions and traditions and a memory
of the past, but the combination of the traditional figures with a Spanish
gloss or commentary denotes the culturally mixed nature of the project. In
the two plates shown here, we see in Figure 18 a portion of a tribute list in
which the glyphs for the subject towns are listed in a column along the left
margin of the page and then the tribute required of each is presented in a
row across the page. In Figure 19 the duties of preconquest priests and the
rank of warriors have been recorded and explained. The English commen-
taries and glosses have been taken from the excellent edition by Frances F.
Berdan and Patricia Rieff Anawalt.

Figure 18. (*opposite*) Inventory of the items given in tribute to the Lords of
Mexico.

The number of towns of the hot lands drawn and named is seven, etc. The things
they gave in tribute to the lords of Mexico are the following:

First, two large strings of greenstones, rich stones;
Also one thousand four hundred bundles of rich feathers of blue, red, green, turquoise-
  blue, red, and green, which are drawn in six bundles;
Also eighty complete bird skins, of rich turquoise-blue feathers and purple breasts, of the
  colors drawn;
Also another eighty complete skins of the said birds;
Also eight hundred bundles of rich yellow feathers;
Also eight hundred bundles of rich, long green feathers, called *quetzalli;*
Also two lip plugs of clear amber, decorated with gold;
Also two hundred loads of cacao;
Also forty jaguar skins, 40 skins;
Also eight hundred rich bowls for drinking cacao;
Also two large pieces of clear amber of the size of a brick — all of which they gave in trib-
  ute every six months.

Source: Courtesy Bodleian Library, Oxford University.

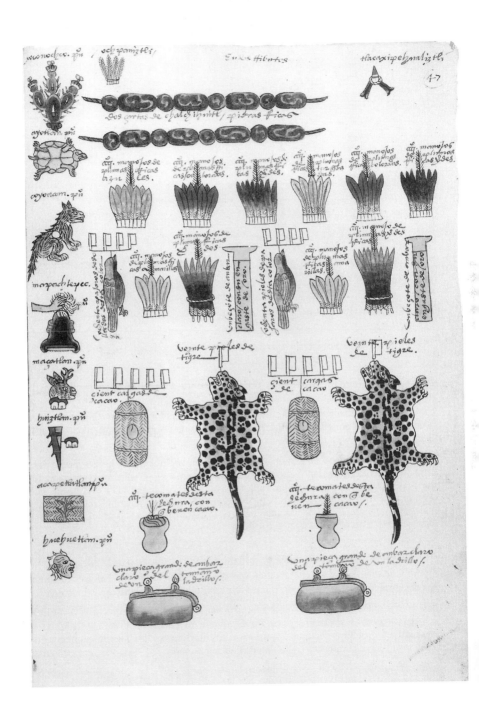

Figure 19. (*opposite*) Warriors being elevated to various ranks by the Lords of Mexico.

Explanation of the first part: In this part, there is a statement for each one of the figures, explaining what the priests are doing. Therefore, there is no need here to repeat what is stated there.

Explanation of the second part: In this part, in each one of the figures, there is a statement [embodied in the figures] of the warrior costumes represented. These warrior costumes identified the warriors according to rank, [the warriors] rising in higher authority with each rank, by the number of captives they captured in warfare. According to the previous discussion, with their warrior costumes and clothing, the warriors demonstrate the perquisites and ranks that warriors achieved. First rank.

Explanation of the third part, of the second rank that brave Mexicans would achieve: The lords of Mexico made them leaders, according to the warrior costumes represented in the figures, and the color of the clothing that was given to them for having captured the number of captives, as shown in the drawings with their titles and explanations.

Explanation of the fourth part, of the third rank of the valiant Mexicans, according to the warrior costumes represented: The lords of Mexico made them leaders because of their merits and number of captives captured in warfare. And thus they went rising into higher ranks, always with more perquisites and greater titles and honor.

Source: Courtesy Bodleian Library, Oxford University.

The Shape of the Land: The Codex Mendoza and the Relaciónes geográficas

One of the most dramatic ways in which the differences between indigenous and European views of the world can be seen is in their representation of space. Mesoamerican maps were not so much concerned with dimensions and topography as with recording social, political, and historical events and realities in relationship to a particular place.

The indigenous cartographic tradition was transformed and adapted after the conquest. Some fifty years or so following the fall of the Mexica Empire, the Spanish king, Philip II, wished to get a better idea of the nature and potential of his various possessions. To that end he set up a commission to gather information. It prepared a questionnaire and sent it to the Americas. The responses, called Relaciones geográficas, were returned from many places in the empire. In New Spain they were prepared in many communities, providing local histories, descriptions of present conditions, and a wealth of other information. Often, accompanying maps were prepared by indigenous mapmakers who still worked in traditional ways using glyphs and symbols to indicate water, hills, buildings, and other features and who continued to encode histories in their maps. The drawings were influenced by some European conventions and forms, but from Spain's point of view, since the maps were not geographically accurate, they were of little use. These maps, however, reveal that indigenous concepts of space and place persisted and with varying degrees of European influence (see Figures 20, 21, and 22). The elements that made up the community rather than topography continued to be the focus of indigenous cartography.

Figure 20. (*opposite*) Tenochtitlan. In this map from the *Codex Mendoza,* the classic elements of Mesoamerican mapmaking are visible. Tenochtitlan is represented divided into its four quarters by diagonal canals. Within the city, the ten leaders of the original clans (*calpulli*) are shown along with the glyph of an eagle on a cactus, the symbol for Tenochtitlan. The city is enclosed in a lake, which here is represented as a rectangular border. Below, the early conquests of neighboring towns are shown by the traditional symbols of prisoners taken and temples burned. The representation of history and social organization is as important as place in this map.

Source: From *The Codex Mendoza,* reprinted in Barbara Mundy, *The Mapping of New Spain* (Chicago: University of Chicago Press, 1996), xv. Courtesy of Benson Latin American Collection, The General Libraries, The University of Texas at Austin.

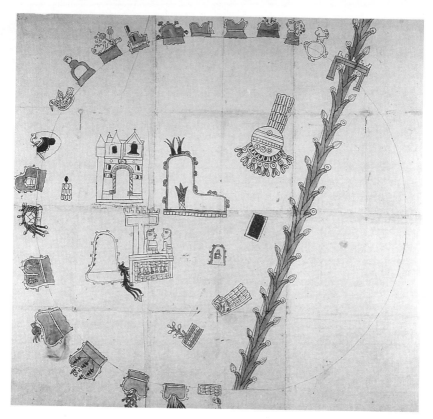

Figure 21. Amoltepec. This map from the *Relación geográfica* of Amoltepec was drawn long after the conquest, about 1580, but it still uses basically indigenous conventions to represent space. Here the traditional symbol for a stream sets one boundary while a semicircle of glyphs representing the names of different places which marked the limits of the community serve to define the other boundaries. Within this border the church and the palace of the ruler are represented along with glyphs for the names of places within the *altepetl*.

Source: Relación geográfica of Amoltepec, from Barbara E. Mundy, *The Mapping of New Spain* (Chicago: University of Chicago Press, 1996), plate 6. Courtesy of Benson Latin American Collection, The General Libraries, The University of Texas at Austin.

Figure 22. Guaxtepec. The map of Guaxtepec from the *Relación geográfica* was also done around 1580. It includes a glyph identifying the name of the town Guaxtepec (hill of the Guatzin tree) and indigenous symbols for streams and springs, but it also displays a network of roads and churches used to mark settlements.

Source: Relación geográfica of Guaxtepec, 1580, from Barbara Mundy, *The Mapping of New Spain* (Chicago: University of Chicago Press, 1996), plate 2. Courtesy of Benson Latin American Collection, The General Libraries, The University of Texas at Austin.

DON DOMINGO DE SAN ANTÓN MUÑÓN CHIMALPAHÍN

The Death of Cuauhtemoc

Not only did indigenous peoples continue to record things in their traditional ways, they also learned to write their own languages using the European alphabet. Nahuatl, Maya, Mixtec, Purepecha (Tarascan), and other languages were adapted in this way. Municipal councils in indigenous towns often kept their records in their native language and thereby a tradition of writing developed. Eventually, a generation of educated indigenous and mestizo historians developed who recorded the histories of their local communities, often extending that story back into the ancient past, but also including a record of more recent events. There was no single indigenous interpretation of the conquest, and the various histories reflected a broad variety of interests.

In this selection, an indigenous interpretation of the death of Cuauhtemoc, the last independent tlatoani *of Tenochtitlan, is presented. It is written by don Domingo de San Antón Muñón Chimalpahín, one of that generation of indigenous and mestizo historians who emerged in the years following the conquest. Born in 1579 to a family with perhaps distant claims to nobility in the region of Chalco to the south of Mexico-Tenochtitlan, he was sent as a youth to live in the capital. He worked for many years as the manager of a church and he read and studied the history of the region. He apparently knew most of the indigenous elite of the city. Chimalpahín wrote about his native Chalco in the annals tradition and he paid particular attention to the ties of lineage and genealogy of the indigenous elite. In this short excerpt on the death of Cuauhtemoc we see these concerns expressed in his defense of the last Mexica ruler.*

The year Three House, 1521. At this time the lord Quauhtemoctzin was installed as ruler of Tenochtitlan in Izcalli in the ancient month count, and in [the month of] February in the Christian month count, when the Spaniards still occupied Tlaxcala. He was a son of Ahuitzotzin.

Arthur J. O. Anderson and Susan Schroeder, trans. and eds., *Codex Chimalpahín: Society and Politics in Mexico Tenochtitlan, Tlatelolco, Texcoco, Culhuacan and other Nahua Altepetl in Central Mexico* (Norman: University of Oklahoma Press, 1997), 167–89.

And in this same said year, Three House, in Toçoztontli in the ancient month count and in April in the Christian month count, the great lords named above, sons of the lord Moteucçoma Xocoyotl, were killed. The first was named Tzihuacpopoca; the second was named Xoxopehualloc; the third was named Tzihuactzin; the fourth was named Tecuecuenotl; the fifth was named Axayaca; the sixth was named Totlehuicol. They were killed on Quauhtemoctzin's orders.

And Ahuitzol's son named Atlixcatzin Tlacateccatl begot and from him issued one son named don Diego Cahualtzin, as well as a second, named don Martín Ezmalintzin. And don Diego Cahualtzin begot two sons. The first was named don Diego Atlixcatzin; the second was named don Antonio de Mendoza Tlacacuitlahuatzin Temazcalxollotzin.

And the son of Axayacatzin, ruler of Tenochtitlan, named Teçoço-mocth Aculnahuacatl, begot two sons. The first was named don Diego Huanitzin who later became ruler of Tenochtitlan. The second was named don Carlos Oquiztzin, a great lord of Tenochtitlan. However, don Diego Huanitzin had first been ruler of Ectapec at the time that the Spaniards arrived, and don Carlos Oquiztzin was ruler in Azcapotzalco Mexicapan.

The year Seven House, 1525. At this time they falsely accused the ruler Quauhtemoctzin and the other rulers. Those who made false accusations were the Tlatelolca and the Michhuaque at Huey Mollan when don Hernando Cortés, Marquis del Valle, took them there. And thus did they falsely accuse the rulers, Quauhtemoctzin, ruler of Tenochtitlan, and Tetlepanquetzatzin, ruler of Tlacopan: they falsely claimed that it was said that they would once more make war upon the Spaniards. The one who falsely accused them was a resident of Tlatelolco named Cotztemexi.

And when the Marquis heard the false statement, he at once baptized the rulers Quauhtemoctzin, Tetlepanquetzatzin, and Tlacotzin Cihua-coatl. And when they were baptized, here is what their names became: the name of the first became don Hernando Quauhtemoctzin; the name of the second became don Pedro Tetlepanquetzatzin; the name of the third became don Juan Velásquez Tlacotzin Cihuacoatl. And when they had baptized don Hernando Quauhtemoctzin and don Pedro Tetlepan-quetzatzin, then in a trial the Marquis condemned both rulers. They died in Huey Mollan. They hanged them on a ceiba tree.

Title of Acalan-Tixel

This selection is drawn from the Chontal Maya-speaking region of Tabasco through which Cortés traveled on his way to Guatemala after the fall of Tenochtitlan. This account is really part of a título, *a type of document found throughout Mesoamerica in which indigenous communities sought to use history and genealogy to back up their claims to land, water, or other rights. Here, the Maya lord emphasizes his cooperation with the Spaniards as a way of claiming legitimacy for his family and community.*

... Therefore the Captain said to them, "Let the ruler come, for I wish to see him. I do not come to make war; I wish only to go and see the whole country. I will be good to him if he receives me well." This he said to the men who had come on behalf of their ruler, who returned to tell their ruler Paxbolonacha, who was in the *cah*[1] of Itzamkanac. All the rulers of the province's *cahob*[2] were thus gathered together — this was for the second time — and he said to them, "Fine! I shall go and see and hear what he wants, the Castilian man who has come." And so the ruler Paxbolonacha went. And the Capitán del Valle went out to meet him with many gifts — honey, turkeys, maize, copal, and a great quantity of fruit. Then he said to Ruler Paxbolon, "I have come here to your lands, for I am sent by the lord of the earth [*u yum cab*], the emperor [*enperador*] seated on his throne in Castile; he sends me to see the land and those who live in it, not for the purpose of wars. I wish only to ask for the way to Ulua, to the land where gold and plumage and cacao come from, as I have heard." Then he [Paxbolonacha] replied that it would be good if he left, but that he should come first to his land, to his home, to his *cah,* where they would discuss what would be best. "Let us rest first," the Capitán del Valle then told him; therefore they rested for twenty days. The ruler [*ahau*] Cuauhtemoc was there, having come with him [Cortés] from Mexico. And it happened that he said to the aforementioned ruler Paxbolonacha, "My lord ruler, these Castilian [TAT:72v] men will one day give you much misery and kill your people. In my opin-

[1] cah: Town or community.
[2] cahob: Towns (pl.).

Matthew Restall, *Maya Conquistador* (Boston: Beacon Press, 1998), 63–65.

TOWN COUNCIL OF HUEJOTZINGO

ion we should kill them, for I bring many officers and you also are many." This is what Cuauhtemoc said to Paxbolonacha, ruler of the people of Tamactun, who, upon hearing this speech of Cuauhtemoc's, replied that he would first think about what he wished to do about his speech. And, in considering his speech fully, he observed that the Castilian men behaved well, that they neither killed a single man nor beat a single man, and that they wished only to be given honey, turkey hens, maize, and various fruits, day after day. Thus he concluded, "I cannot therefore display two faces, two hearts, to the Castilian men." But Cuauhtemoc, the aforementioned ruler from Mexico, continued to press him about it, for he wished to kill the Castilian men. Because of this, the ruler Paxbolonacha told the Capitán del Valle, "My lord Capitán del Valle, this ruler Cuauhtemoc who is with you, observe him so that he does not revolt and betray you, for three or four times he talked to me about killing you." Upon hearing these words the Capitán del Valle seized him [Cuauhtemoc] and had him bound in chains. He was in chains for three days. Then they baptized him. It is not known what his baptismal name was; some say he was named don Juan and some say he was named don Hernando. After he was named, his head was cut off, and it was impaled on a ceiba tree in front of the pagan temple [*otot ciçin,* devil's home] at Yaxdzan. . . .

TOWN COUNCIL OF HUEJOTZINGO
Letter to King Philip II

The ancient attachments to the altepetl *died hard. Moreover, there were often good political or economic reasons to emphasize these ancient identities and traditional claims to land and water rights or to the old ways of doing things. In this letter of 1560, written in Nahuatl, from the indigenous town council of Huejotzingo, an* altepetl *that had allied with Cortés, the municipal councillors emphasize their community's services and compare them favorably to those of Tlaxcala. Notice too the formulas of subservience in address now applied to Philip II of Spain rather than to an indigenous ruler. Despite the flourishes, the objective of the letter is quite practical.*

Arthur J. O. Anderson, Frances Berdan, and James Lockhart, eds., *Beyond the Codices: The Nahua View of Colonial Mexico* (Berkeley: University of California Press, 1976), 179–91.

Our lord sovereign, you the king don Felipe our lord, we bow low in great reverence to your high dignity, we prostrate and humble ourselves before you, very high and feared king through omnipotent God, giver of life. We do not deserve to kiss your feet, only from afar we bow down to you, you who are most high and Christian and very pleasing to God our Lord, for you are his true representative here on earth, you who govern us and lead us in things of Christianity. All of us creatures and subjects of the life-giving God, we vassals and servants of your majesty, we people here, we who dwell here in New Spain, all together we look to you, our eyes and hearts go out toward you; we have complete confidence in you in the eyes of our Lord God, for he put us in your hands to guard us, and he assigned us to you for us to be your servants and your helpers. By our Lord God and by your very honored and very high majesty, remember us, have compassion with us, for very great is the poverty and affliction visited on us who dwell here in New Spain.

Our lord sovereign, king don Felipe our lord, with our words we appear and stand before you, we of Huejotzingo who guard for you your city — we citizens, I the governor and we the alcaldes and councilmen and we the lords and nobles, your men and your servants. Very humbly we implore you: Oh unfortunate are we, very great and heavy sadness and affliction lie upon us, nowhere do your pity and compassion extend over us and reach us, we do not deserve, we do not attain your rulership. And all the while since your subjects the Spaniards arrived among us, all the while we have been looking toward you, we have been confidently expecting that sometime your pity would reach us, as we also had confidence in and were awaiting the mercy of your very revered dear father the ruler of the world, don Carlos the late emperor. Therefore now, our lord sovereign, we bow humbly before you; may we deserve your pity, may the very greatly compassionate and merciful God enlighten you so that your pity is exercised on us, for we hear, and so it is said to us, that you are very merciful and humane towards all your vassals; and as to the time when you pity someone, when before you appears a vassal of yours in poverty, so it is said, then you have pity on him with your very revered majesty, and by the grace of omnipotent God you do it for him. May we now also deserve and attain the same, for every day such poverty and affliction reaches us and is visited on us that we weep and mourn. Oh unfortunate are we, what will happen to us, we your poor vassals of Huejotzingo, we who live in your city? If you were not so far away, many times we would appear before you. Though we greatly wish and desire to reach you and appear before you, we are unable, because we are very poor and do not have what is needed for the journey on the boat nor things to eat nor anything to pay people in order to be able to reach you. Therefore now we appear before you only in our words; we set before you our poor prayer. May you only in your very great Christianity and very revered high majesty attend well to this our prayer.

Our lord sovereign, before anyone told us of or made us acquainted with your fame and your story, most high and feared universal king who rules all, and before we were told or taught the glory and name of our Lord God, before the faith reached us, and before we were Christians, when your servants the Spaniards reached us and your captain general don Hernando Cortés arrived, although we were not yet acquainted with the omnipotent, very compassionate holy Trinity, our Lord God the ruler of heaven and possessor of earth caused us to deserve that in his mercy he enlightened us so that we took you as our king to belong to you and become your people and your subjects; not a single town surpassed us here in New Spain in that first and earliest we threw ourselves toward you, we gave ourselves to you, and furthermore no one intimidated us, no one forced us into it, but truly God caused us to deserve that voluntarily we adhered to you so that we gladly received the newly arrived Spaniards who reached us here in New Spain, for we left our homes behind to go a great distance to meet them; we went twenty leagues to greet captain general don Hernando Cortés and the others whom he led. We received them very gladly, we embraced them, we saluted them with many tears, though we were not acquainted with them, and our fathers and grandfathers also did not know them; but by the mercy of our Lord God we truly came to know them. Since they are our neighbors, therefore we loved them; nowhere did we attack them. Truly we fed them and served them; some arrived sick, so that we carried them in our arms and on our backs, and we served them in many other ways which we are not able to say here. Although the people who are called and named Tlaxcalans indeed helped, yet we strongly pressed them to give aid, and we admonished them not to make war; but though we so admonished them, they made war and fought for fifteen days. But we, when a Spaniard was afflicted, without fail at once we managed to reach him; [there was no one else]. We do not lie in this, for all the conquerors know it well, those who have died and some now living.

And when they began their conquest and war-making, then also we well prepared ourselves to aid them, for out came all of our war gear, our arms and provisions and all our equipment, and we not merely named someone, we went in person, we who rule, and we brought all our nobles and all of our vassals to aid the Spaniards. We helped not only in warfare, but also we gave them everything they needed; we fed and clothed them, and we would carry in our arms and on our backs those whom they wounded in war or who were very ill, and we did all the tasks in preparing for war. And so that they could fight the Mexica with boats, we worked hard; we gave them the wood and pitch with which the Spaniards made the boats. And when they conquered the Mexica and all belonging to them, we never abandoned them or left them behind in it. And when they went to conquer Michoacan, Jalisco, and Colhuacan, and there at Pánuco and there at Oaxaca and Tehuantepec and Guatemala, (we were) the only ones who went along while they conquered and made war here in New Spain until they finished the conquest; we never abandoned them, in no way did we prejudice their war-making, though some of us were destroyed in it [nor was there a single one of our subjects left?], for we did our duty very well. But as to those Tlaxcalans, several of their nobles were hanged for making war poorly; in many places they ran away, and often did badly in the war. In this we do not lie, for the conquerors know it well.

Our lord sovereign, we also say and declare before you that your fathers the twelve sons of St. Francis reached us, whom the very high priestly ruler the Holy Father sent and whom you sent, both taking pity on us so that they came to teach us the gospel, to teach us the holy Catholic faith and belief, to make us acquainted with the single deity God our Lord, and likewise God favored us and enlightened us, us of Huejotzingo, who dwell in your city, so that we gladly received them. When they entered the city of Huejotzingo, of our own free will we honored them and showed them esteem. When they embraced us so that we would abandon the wicked belief in many gods, we forthwith voluntarily left it; likewise they did us the good deed (of telling us) to destroy and burn the stones and wood that we worshipped as gods, and we did it; very willingly we destroyed, demolished, and burned the temples. Also when they gave us the holy gospel, the holy Catholic faith, with very good will and desire we received and grasped it; no one frightened us into it, no one forced us, but very willingly we seized it, and they gave us all the sacraments. Quietly and peacefully we arranged and ordered it among ourselves; no one, neither nobleman nor commoner, was ever tortured or burned for this, as was done on every hand here in New Spain. (The people of) many towns were forced and tortured, were hanged or burned because they did not want to leave idolatry, and unwillingly they received the gospel and faith. Especially those Tlaxcalans pushed out and rejected the fathers, and would not receive the faith, for many of the high nobles were burned, and some hanged, for combating the advocacy and service of our Lord God. But we of Huejotzingo, we your poor vassals, we never did anything in your harm, always we served you in every command you sent or what at your command we were ordered. Very quietly, peacefully we take and grasp it all, though only through the mercy of God do we do it, since it is not within our personal power. Therefore now, in and through God, may you hear these our words, all that we say and declare before you, so that you will take pity on us, so that you will exercise on us your rulership to console us and aid us in (this trouble) with which daily we weep and are sad. We are afflicted and sore pressed, and your town and city of Huejotzingo is as if it is about to disappear and be destroyed. Here is what is being done to us: now your stewards the royal officials and the prosecuting attorney Dr. Maldonado are assessing us a very great tribute to belong to you. The tribute we are to give is 14,800 pesos in money, and also all the bushels of maize.

Our lord sovereign, never has such happened to us in all the time since your servants and vassals the Spaniards came to us, for your servant don Hernando Cortés, late captain general, the Marqués del Valle, in all the time he lived here with us, always greatly cherished us and kept us happy; he never disturbed nor agitated us. Although we gave him tribute, he assigned it to us only with moderation; even though we gave him gold, it was only very little; no matter how much, no matter in what way, or if not very pure, he just received it gladly. He never reprimanded us or afflicted us, because it was evident to him and he understood well how very greatly we served and aided him. Also he told us many times that he would speak in our favor before you, that he would help us and inform you of all the ways in which we have aided and served you. And when he went before you, then you confirmed him and were merciful to him, you honored and rewarded him for the way he had served you here in New Spain. But perhaps before you he forgot us. How then shall we speak? We did not reach you, we were not given audience before you. Who then will speak for us? Unfortunate are we. Therefore now we place ourselves before you, our sovereign lord. And when you sent your representatives, the Presidente and Bishop don Sebastián Ramírez, and the judges, Licentiate Salmerón, Licentiates Ceinos, Quiroga, and Maldonado, they well affirmed and sustained the orders you gave for us people here, us who live in New Spain. In many things they aided us and lightened the very great tribute we had, and from many things that were our tasks they always delivered us, they pardoned us all of it. And we your poor vassals, we of Huejotzingo who dwell in your city, when Licentiate Salmerón came to us and entered the city of Huejotzingo, then he saw how troubled the town was with our tribute in gold, sixty pieces that we gave each year, and that it troubled us because gold does not appear here, and is not to be found in our province, though we searched for it everywhere; then at once Licentiate Salmerón pardoned it on your behalf, so that he made a replacement and substitution of the money. He set our tribute in money at 2,050 pesos. And in all the time he thus assessed us, all the time we kept doing it, we hastened to give it to you, since we are your subjects and belong to you; we never neglected it, we never did poorly, we made it all up. But now we are taken aback and very afraid and we ask, have we done something wrong, have we somehow behaved badly and ill toward you, our lord sovereign, or have we committed some sin against almighty God? Perhaps you have heard something of our wickedness and for that reason now this very great tribute has fallen upon us, seven times exceeding all we had paid before, the 2,000 pesos. And we declare to you that it will not be long before your city of Huejotzingo completely disappears and perishes, because our fathers, grandfathers, and ancestors knew no tribute and gave tribute to no one, but were independent, and we nobles who guard your subjects are now truly very poor. Nobility is seen among us no longer; now we resemble the commoners. As they eat and dress, so do we; we have been very greatly afflicted, and our poverty has reached its culmination. Of the way in which our fathers and grandfathers and forebears were rich and honored, there is no longer the slightest trace among us.

O our lord sovereign king, we rely on you as on God the one deity who dwells in heaven, we trust in you as our father. Take pity on us, have compassion with us. May you especially remember those who live and subsist in the wilds, those who move us to tears and pity; we truly live with them in just such poverty as theirs, wherefore we speak out before you so that afterwards you will not become angry with us when your subjects have disappeared or perished. There ends this our prayer.

We cannot write here for you the very many ways in which your city of Huejotzingo is poor and stricken; we are leaving that to our dear father Fray Alonso de Buendía, son of St. Francis, if God the one deity wills that he should arrive safely before you. He will be able to tell you much more about our anguish and poverty, since he learned and saw it well while he was prior here in the city of Huejotzingo for two years. We hope that he will tell and read this to you, for we have much confidence in him and have placed ourselves completely in his hands. This is all with which we come and appear before you. This letter was done in the city of Huejotzingo on the 30th day of the month of July, in the year of the birth of our Lord Jesus Christ 1560.

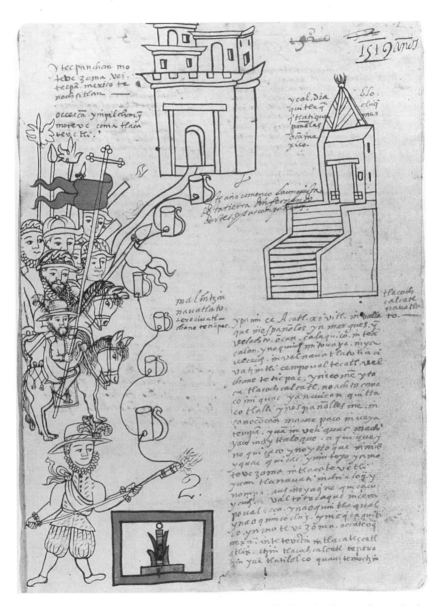

Figure 23. The march on Tenochtitlan. Here the Spaniards are shown igniting explosive charges to the palace of Moctezuma above the glyph for the year One Reed.

Source: Constantino Medina Lima, ed., *Libro de los guardianes y gobernadores de Cuauhtinchan (1519–1640)* (Mexico City: CIESAS, 1995), 28–33. Courtesy Universidad Autonoma Nacional de Mexico.

239

Your poor vassals who bow down humbly to you from afar,
Don Leonardo Ramírez, governor. Don Mateo de la Corona, alcalde.
Diego Alameda, alcalde. Don Felipe de Mendoza, alcalde. Hernando de
Meneses. Miguel de Alvarado. Alonso Pimentel, Augustín Osorio. Don
Francisco Vázquez. Don Diego de Chaves. Juan de Almo[. . .]. Diego de
Niza. Agustín de Santo Tomás. Diego Suárez. Toribio de San [Cristó]bal
Motolinia.

The Annals of Cuauhtinchan

Year-by-year chronologies or annals remained a common form of history in various parts of New Spain. In the town of Cuauhtinchan (Puebla) a book of annals covering the years 1519 to 1640 was written in Nahuatl using the Spanish alphabet but also integrating various preconquest symbols and some pictorial representations (see Figure 21). In this selection a brief synopsis of the conquest is given. Basic elements from other indigenous and perhaps Spanish accounts are recognizable here, but it is also clear that the author(s) conflated or combined events while preserving a vision of those momentous happenings in a way that made sense to those who followed in the next generation.

The Book of the Guardians and Governors of Cuauhtinchan, 1519–1640 . . .

When the Spaniards were seen, when the people of Castile came, it was said to Moctezuma: "Oh, Lord, we have gone to the seashore to see it. They cause terror with the fire they throw, it is frightening, their smell causes fright, their fire tubes and bad odor. And they come seated on their deer, they come looking to the sides and their fetlocks and hooves make a frightening noise when they step. The soldiers come adorned with shields, their swords, lances, and pennants divided in two, their helmets. Their feet are wrapped in skins, their shoes are covered. It is very frightening to see how [the horses] run. Their drum is carried by a man, he plays it and spins it in a marvelous manner. Their flags are varied, red, yellow and white; their swords all have points like stones that kill. Thus

Constantino Medina Lima, ed., *Libro de los guardianes y gobernadores de Cuauhtinchan (1519–1640)* (Mexico City: CIESAS, 1995), 28–33. The excerpt from this work has been translated from the Spanish by the author of this volume.

[the horses] have their withers covered. Their deer appear and go in the vanguard and the great soldiers are all covered with iron, on their heads are helmets and their musical instruments are curved and have a mouthpiece like a malacate. When they begin to cast fire [shoot] they form lines. It is horrible. You will scream if you hear it; they place soil [in the cannon] so that it thunders. This we saw exactly with our own eyes." And Moctezuma was greatly concerned when he heard that they were great warriors. Then he said to his warriors, "They have gained grace. Have no fear if they come." Then he ordered that deer and rabbits be hunted to greet don F(H)ernando Cortés. And when they arrived in Mexico he put collars of jade on them, he greeted them.

[One Reed] 1519

The Spaniards set fire and burnt the house of the devil [The Templo Mayor] there in Mexico. The Great Palace of Mexico-Tenochtitlan. In another place is the house of the noble *tlacateuctli* Moctezuma.

This year Fernando Cortés and his companions began the conquest of this land.

Malintzin, teuccihuatl, the interpreter of Nahuatl, from Teticpac. *Tlacochcalcatl,* interpreter of Nahuatl.

In the year One Reed the Marqués and the Spaniards arrived. First they entered there in Texcalan. In olden times it was said that a woman cempoaltecatl [from Cempoala], inhabitant of Teticpac came as an interpreter of Nahuatl. The so-called *Tlacochcalcatl* was the other [interpreter] who the Spaniards had previously taken prisoner when they first came to discover these lands and from there returned from the coast. This was when it was learned of those that had been seen, those who had come.

This is when they learned of the fame of the *tlacateuctli* Moctezuma. He ordered that they await him. Those who went returned in haste. The Cempoalans came rapidly and did not eat or sleep in order to report to Moctezuma that they [the Spaniards] still lived and it was in the presence of the lords, Altlicatzin the *tlacatecatl,* Tepehuatzin, the *tlacochcalcatl,* and Quauhtemoctzin of Tlatelolco.

Year One Reed

At the end of the mentioned year, One Reed, the Castillians entered Mexico for the first time. They left from Tlaxcala to Cholula, there they assassinated many people, then they digressed to Popocatépetl, to Amecameca, to all of Chalco, Mizquic, Cuitláhuac [today Tláhuac], Xochimilco, Culhuacán, Coyoacán, Mexicatzinco, Iztacalco and Iztapalapa. The lords [*tlatoque*] and the peasants surrendered themselves peacefully. The Tlaxcalans guided them and showed them the way.

On arriving in Mexico, they marched in an ordered formation. When they arrived Moctezuma came out accompanied by Atlixcatzin, the *tlcatecatl,* and by Tepeuatzin, the *Tlacochcalcatl,* and for this the Marqués dismounted to embrace [Moctezuma] who put a collar on his neck and greeted him and said, "You have tired yourself, it is some time since you came and we knew you would come. You have come to your town, you have come to see your servants (*macehualtin*)." They rested. Later they joined hands and went to the Palace.

The Marqués said he wished to see the way in which they celebrated the festival of the people for which they called together beforehand once they had arranged it. Then the dance began because it was a festival day and the Spaniards fell on them; first they killed the musician, then the rest of the people.

After they had killed the people, the Mexicans became angry. Thus began the war and for this they killed the Spaniards who went to Texcoco. Other warriors were then sent from Castile, they constructed their ships and stoned [fired on] the Mexicans, killing them.

Then a certain kind of plague [*acazauatl*][1] spread and killed many people.

This year the conquest began.

The Year Two Flint

Three years before the Castilians had come. In the year Three House many soldiers arrived and they completed their ships. Then Spaniards and the Tlaxcalans arrived.

They went out from Cuauhtitlán and they established themselves in Tlacopan, there they took up their positions; then they divided. The work of Pedro de Alvarado was on the road from Tlatelolco. And the Marqués set up in Coyoacán and on the road to Acachinanco, the one that comes from Mexico-Tenochtitlan. Thus the Marqués who was a great man took up a position; the *tenochcatl* was a great soldier.

The Marqués and his soldiers went first to conquer Nextlatilco and Yliyacac; afterwards they arrived at Nonalco where they were turned back and pursued by the warriors.

---

[1] Smallpox.

They began the war in canoes; the Spaniards, the Mexicans, and the Tlaxcalans fought. No Indian could win in the water and so all their women fought.

In Tlatelolco Saint James appeared three times to help the Spaniards; because of this now they have raised the temple [church] of Saint James there.

This year they completed the conquest of the city of Mexico, the thirteenth of August, Leo X was the Pontiff in Rome and the king of Spain was the Emperor Charles V.

Chronology of the Conquest of Tenochtitlan (1485–1584)

1485 Birth of Hernando (Hernán) Cortés.

1496 Birth of Bernal Díaz del Castillo.

1502 Moctezuma II, called the Younger (*Xocoyotl*), becomes *tlatoani* or ruler of Tenochtitlan.

1511–14 Conquest of Cuba.

1517 *February to April* Hernández de Córdoba sails from Cuba to Yucatan and encounters the Maya peoples.

1518 *May to November* Governor of Cuba, Diego Velázquez, sends second expedition to Yucatan under Juan de Grijalva.

1519 Governor Velázquez sends new expedition under Hernán Cortés.

February 10 Cortés sails for Yucatan.
Founding of Vera Cruz.

June 3 Spaniards reach Cempoala.

September 2–20 Spaniards battle Tlaxcalans.

c. October 15 Massacre at Cholula.

November 8 Spaniards enter Tenochtitlan.

November 14 Moctezuma is seized.

1520

early May Cortés marches against Pánfilo de Narváez.

c. May 16 Toxcatl festival; Pedro de Alvarado massacres celebrants.

June 24 Cortés reenters Tenochtitlan.

June 29 Moctezuma is killed.
Cuitlahuac is chosen *tlatoani*.

June 30–July 31 *Noche triste*—Spaniards and allies escape Tenochtitlan with great losses.

July 12 Fleeing Spaniards reach Tlaxcala and are well received.

July–December Recovery of Spanish forces; isolation of Tenochtitlan, Spanish expeditions to win allies and supporters.

October   Plague devastates Tenochtitlan.

December 4   Cuitlahuac dies from smallpox.

1521

February   Cuahtemoc becomes *tlatoani*.

February–April   Cortés campaigns around the lake.

May 10–13   Siege of Tenochtitlan begins.

May 26   Water to the city is cut off.

May 31   Fight for Iztapalapa.

June 1   Spaniards begin to enter Tenochtitlan.

June 16   Palaces of Moctezuma burned.

June 30   Spaniards set back between Tenochtitlan and Tlatelolco.

July 18   Mexica propose peace if Spaniards leave.

July 20–25   Main plaza of Tenochtitlan cleared of Mexica resistance.

July 27   Alvarado sets fire to temple of Tlatelolco.

August 7   Desperate fighting in Tlatelolco.

August 13   Starving defenders trapped, capture of Cuahtemoc and surrender of the city.

1522–23   Cortés's first three letters published in Seville.

1525   Cuahtemoc executed by Cortés.

1529   Cortés receives title Marqués del Valle.

1535   First Viceroy of Mexico arrives; Cortés's power is weakened.

1540–41   *Relación de Michoacán* is completed.

1547   Cortés dies in Spain.

1552   Francisco López de Gómara's *Historia de las Indias y conquista de Mexico* is published in Valladolid, Spain.

1568   Bernal Díaz completes first draft of *Historia verdadera de la conquista de la nueva España*.

1579   Domingo Francisco de San Antón Muñón Chimalpahín is born.

1584   Bernal Díaz dies.

Questions for Consideration

1. Is history always written by the winners? If so, how do we recapture the "other side" in the past?
2. How might have indigenous women viewed the conquest?
3. What is a "true" history?

1. FOREBODINGS AND OMENS

1. Why did indigenous people associate the Spanish arrival with omens? Did Europeans have a similar tradition of looking for natural and supernatural signs of great events?
2. Why did European authors incorporate the indigenous stories of omens in their accounts?

2. PREPARATIONS

1. Why might have Guerrero and Aguilar chosen to respond differently to Cortés's appeal to return?
2. Should the early Spanish expeditions be thought of as "explorations" or business ventures?
3. What is the role of religion in the Spanish expedition and in the Spanish explanation of events of the conquest?

3. ENCOUNTERS

1. What is Cortés's evaluation of the land and the people? What reasons does he have for presenting the new land in this way?
2. How do the Spanish and Nahua descriptions and understandings of the first meetings differ? What aspects of behavior most preoccupy the Spaniards and the Nahuas?

4. THE MARCH INLAND: TLAXCALA AND CHOLULA

1. Do the accounts of Andrés de Tapia and Bernal Díaz differ in any important ways? Do you think the Spaniards would have described the actions of European enemies in the same way?

2. In what ways do the Nahua descriptions of the Tlaxcalans and the Spaniards differ? What is the image of the Tlaxcalans conveyed in the Mexica account?

3. Can you identify European and indigenous artistic conventions in the *Lienzo de Tlaxcala*? What are the possible advantages or limitations of depending on pictorial elements or nonalphabetic writing systems to convey information?

5. TENOCHTITLAN

1. In what ways are the descriptions of Mexica culture influenced by European preconceptions and beliefs?

2. What was the role of doña Marina in the meeting of Cortés and Moctezuma?

6. THINGS FALL APART: TOXCATL AND THE *NOCHE TRISTE*

1. Reading the contrasting indigenous and Spanish accounts of the arrival of Pánfilo de Narváez and the Toxcatl massacre, do you think that the Mexica had planned a rebellion?

2. What role might Tlaxcalan informants have played in stimulating Pedro de Alvarado to action?

3. What effect did the differences in military technology have on the fighting in Tenochtitlan? How did the Mexica adapt to the challenge of Spanish arms?

4. How can the two distinct versions of the death of Moctezuma be explained?

7. THE SIEGE AND FALL OF TENOCHTITLAN

1. What was the role of Cortés's indigenous allies and why did they join the Spaniards? What does their decision tell us about the politics of central Mexico?

2. What factors besides politics and technology contributed to the Mexica defeat?

8. AFTERMATH: TRADITION AND TRANSFORMATION

1. In what ways did indigenous culture demonstrate resilience after the conquest?

2. What role did religion play in Spanish motivations and indigenous responses?

3. Did the conquest represent a radical change in indigenous history or were Spaniards and the colonial state incorporated into indigenous life as other conquerors had been before?

Biographical Notes

Aguilar, Francisco de (1479–1571) A conquistador with Cortés who at the age of fifty became a Dominican friar. He later wrote a brief account of the conquest.

Aguilar, Gerónimo de (1481?–1539) Arriving from Spain, he settled in Santo Domingo. Lost in a shipwreck in 1511, he was washed ashore in Yucatan where the Maya held him captive until the arrival of Cortés in 1519. During these years he learned the Maya language, and after Cortés freed him, he served as a translator for the Spanish.

Alvarado, Pedro de (1485–1541) A member of both Grijalva's (1518) and Cortés's (1519) expeditions to Mexico from Cuba, he served as a commander in one of Cortés's three armies during the conquest. He was responsible for the Toxcatl Massacre in Tenochtitlan while Cortés was away and was called "Tonatiuh," the Aztec sun god, by the Aztec because of his blond hair. He commanded the conquests into Guatemala.

Cacamatzin (*Cacama*) Ruler of Texcoco during the conquest of Mexico.

Carlos V (Charles V) (1500–1558) Holy Roman Emperor from 1519–56 and the king of Spain as Charles I from 1516–56.

Chimalpahín, Domingo Francisco de San Antón Muñón (1570?–1630?) A native of Chalco. He wrote an extensive history of his region in the late sixteenth century, today known as the *Codex Chimalpahín*. His account is noticeably anti-Mexica, which shows the lingering effects of previous indigenous hostility.

Cortés, Hernán (*Hernando Cortés–Díaz del Castillo*) (1485?–1547) Born in Medellín, Spain, he arrived in Hispaniola in 1504. After participating in the conquest of the island, he led the third expedition to Mexico in 1519 and, with the fall of Tenochtitlan two years later, conquered Mexico in 1521.

Cortés, Martín Son of Hernán Cortés and Malinche (doña Marina).

Cuauhtémoc (*Guatémoc-Díaz del Castillo; Quauhtemoctzin–Lockhart*) The eleventh and final *tlatoani* of Tenochtitlan. The son of Ahuitzol (eighth Aztec ruler) and grandson of Moctezuma I (fifth Aztec ruler), he ruled from December 1520 until Tenochtitlan was conquered by Cortés in August 1521. He was killed by the Spaniards in 1525.

Cuitlahuac (Mexica ruler, September 16, 1520–December 4, 1520)
The son of Axayacatl (sixth Mexica ruler, 1468–81), Cuitlahuac was the ruler of Ixtapalapa before succeeding his brother, Moctezuma Xocoyotl (I), in 1520. After ruling for only eighty days, he died of smallpox in December of 1520.

Díaz del Castillo, Bernal (1495–1583) Arriving in the New World from Spain in 1514, he was a member of all three expeditions to Mexico (Córdoba 1517, Grijalva 1518, Cortés 1519). A soldier in Cortés's army, he eventually wrote a history of the conquest in response to another book (by López de Gómara) on the conquest that he felt was incorrect.

Durán, Diego (1537?–1588) Born in Seville, he arrived in the New World in 1542, entered the Dominican Order in 1556, and thereafter chronicled both Nahua religion and history in some of the most revealing and detailed books ever written during this period.

Grijalva, Juan de (1480?–1527) Nephew of the governor of Hispaniola, Diego Velázquez (1514–1524). Grijalva assisted his uncle in the conquest of Hispaniola from 1511–14. In 1518 he led the second expedition to Mexico on order from Velázquez.

Guerrero, Gonzalo Presumably lost in a shipwreck with Gerónimo de Aguilar in 1511, he washed ashore in Yucatan and was captured by the Maya. After marrying a local woman, he achieved high status in Maya society and refused to join Cortés after he landed in Yucatan in 1519. He allegedly died fighting alongside the Maya in a battle against Cortés's forces.

Itzcoatl The fourth Mexica ruler, he ruled from 1426–40. He was one of three nobles responsible for the founding of the Triple Alliance in 1428, which gave the Mexica independence from vassalage and also established their empire.

Hernández de Córdoba, Francisco After assisting Velázquez in the conquest of Hispaniola (1511–14), he led the first expedition of exploration in 1517 and discovered the Yucatan. He died in the same year from wounds received in a skirmish with the Maya during the expedition.

Las Casas, Bartolomé de (1484–1576) Born in Seville, he arrived in Hispaniola in 1502 and participated in the conquest of the island (1511–14). After witnessing the massacre of the native community, he entered the Dominican Order, after which he devoted his life to the protection and defense of the indigenous peoples. He published several books defending them, including *Short Account of the Destruction of the Indies* (1542).

López de Gómara, Francisco (1511–1566) After Cortés returned to Spain, Gómara became his personal secretary and financial advisor. Using both Cortés's written documents and memoirs of the conquest as well as the many stories he would retell, López de Gómara wrote a history of the conquest of Mexico, even though he never set foot in the Americas. Heralding

Cortés as a hero, this is the book that inspired Díaz del Castillo to tell his own, "true," version of the conquest.

Malinche (*Malintzin, doña Marina, baptized as Marina*) A Nahua slave of a Maya cacique, she was given to Cortés by the Maya after their defeat at Potonchan. Speaking both Nahuatl and Yucatec Maya, she (and the ex-Maya captive Gerónimo de Aguilar) became crucial interpreters for Cortés as he entered the world of the Mexica. She was also the mother of Cortés's illegitimate son, Martín.

Mendoza, Antonio de (1494–1552) Of elite Spanish nobility and a diplomat in the Spanish court, he was personally selected by King Charles I in 1535 to serve as the first viceroy of New Spain and as president of the *audiencia*. He arrived in Mexico later that year and remained the viceroy of New Spain until 1551.

Moctezuma Ilhuicamina (I) (*Moteczoma–Durán; Motecçoma–Lockhart; Montezuma–Díaz del Castillo; Motecuhzoma–León Portilla*) The fifth Mexica *tlatoani,* he ruled from 1440–68. He was the son of the second Mexica ruler, Huitzilhuitl (1397–1417), and the grandfather of Moctezuma II (1502–20), the ruler when Cortés arrived in Mexico.

Moctezuma Xocoyotl (II) (*Moteczoma–Durán; Motecçoma–Lockhart; Montezuma–Dían del Castillo; Motecuhzoma–León Portilla*) The ninth Mexica ruler, he ruled from 1502–20. The son of Axacatl (sixth Mexica ruler) and the grandson of Moctezuma I (fifth Mexica ruler), he died on June 29, 1520, while being held hostage by the Spanish in his own palace.

Narváez, Pánfilo de (1480–1528?) In 1520 he was placed in command of a large fleet by Governor Diego Velázquez and ordered to sail from Hispaniola to Mexico to capture and return Cortés. After landing on the Veracruz coast in late April of 1520, his forces were defeated and captured by Córtes on May 28, 1520. Cortés used the captured men and supplies to reinforce his own armies by taking them back to Tenochtitlan.

Olid, Cristóbal de (1488–1524) Along with Alvarado and Sandoval, a commander of one of Cortés's three armies during the siege of Tenochtitlan and the conquest of Mexico. He later rebelled against Cortés after conquering Honduras much as Cortés had done to Diego Velázquez.

Olmedo, Bartolomé de A Mercedarian friar who sailed to Mexico from Cuba with Cortés and accompanied him to Tenochtitlan, he performed some of the first baptisms of Nahua nobility in Mexico.

Sahagún, Bernardino de (1499?–1590?) A Franciscan friar who arrived in the New World in 1529, he spent the rest of his life studying, documenting, and chronicling Nahua culture, history, language, and religion. He used interviews with Nahua elders in central Mexico to collect his information. His lifelong work, known today as the *Florentine Codex,* is the most detailed and thorough work on Nahua life and culture that exists today.

Sandoval, Gonzalo de (1498–1529?)   Along with Olid and Alvarado, a commander of one of Cortés's three armies during the siege of Tenochtitlan and the conquest of Mexico. Loyal to Cortés until his death, he served as co-governor of New Spain for a short period after the conquest.

Tangaxoan (see Zincicha)

Tlacaelel (1410s?–1480s?)   Nephew of Itzcoatl (fourth Mexica ruler), he served as commanding general of the Triple Alliance after 1428 and held the advisory position of *Cihuacoatl*—a sort of prime minister—to a number of Mexica rulers. Although the reach of his power has been disputed, it is certain that he was a central figure in the political and military expansion of the Mexica Empire throughout the fifteenth century.

Velázquez, Diego de (1465–1524)   Accompanied Columbus on his second voyage to the New World in 1493 and later conquered Cuba in 1511–14 becoming its first governor. In 1517 he ordered the first exploratory expedition by Córdoba, the result of which was the discovery of Mexico. In 1518 he authorized the second expedition to Mexico by Grijalva, and in 1519 the third by Cortés. In the following year, 1520, he ordered an unsuccessful expedition to Mexico by Narváez in order to capture Cortés. He died in Cuba in 1524.

Xicotencatl the Elder (*Xicotenga–Díaz del Castillo*)   Father of the rebellious Tlaxcalan general Xicotencatl the Younger. Having lived through the increasing pressures of the surrounding Mexica Empire, he saw the Spanish as a potential force for the Tlaxcalans to join to overthrow the Mexica and free themselves from the pressures of that dominating empire. He successfully lobbied for an alliance between the Spanish and Tlaxcalans.

Xicotencatl the Younger (*Xicotenga–Díaz del Castillo*)   Son of Xicotencatl the Elder, he was a Tlaxcalan general who resisted Cortés's arrival in Tlaxcala. Vehemently opposed to the Spanish invasion, he remained so even after the alliance was formed with them, and was eventually hanged in Texcoco by Cortés for allegedly planning a revolt with the Mexica against the Spanish.

Zincicha/Tangaxoan   Ruler (or *cazonci*) of the Tarascan Empire in present day Michoacán during the siege of Tenochtitlan. He was the son of the previous Tarascan ruler, Zuangua.

Zuangua   Ruler (or *cazonci*) of the Tarascan Empire before the arrival of the Spanish in Mexico.

Zumárraga, Juan de (1468–1548)   A Spanish friar of the Franciscan Order, he became the first bishop of New Spain in 1528.

Zurita, Alonzo de (1511?–1585?)   Arriving in New Spain in 1548, he became a royal judge of the *audiencia* in Mexico City. Twenty years later, he returned to Spain in 1568. Sympathetic to the plight of the native peoples, he wrote a *Brief and Summary Relation of the Lords of New Spain*.

Glossary of Spanish Terms

adelantado a border commander. A military leader given administrative control over the lands he conquers

alcalde municipal official with judicial powers within the municipal council; also acted as a magistrate, or justice of the peace

audiencia high court of justice. The *audiencia* of New Spain governed the country from the mid-1520s until the arrival of the viceroy in 1535. After the establishment of the viceroy, it functioned as a court of appeals or supreme court.

brigantine small, agile, usually square-masted ship used by Cortés in the final siege of Tenochtitlan. The brigantines were equipped with both oars and sails.

cabecera "head town," a city or town usually governed by its own local ruler and the locus of regional government for the area

cabildo local municipal or town council, headed by the *alcalde* mayor

caravel a small seagoing sailing ship used in the Old World, usually with two or three masts

corregidor royal judges and bureaucrats who were appointed as municipal officials in New Spain with various responsibilities and duties, the most important usually being the collection of taxes; they also had the ability to act as magistrates when necessary and presided over the cabildos in the towns of their residence

Council of Indies Spanish council in Madrid whose purpose was to oversee the affairs and development of the New World colonies

cue Spanish term often used by Bernal Díaz del Castillo meaning "temple"

encomienda a Spanish grant of rights to labor of a particular number of natives living within a specified area

regidor alderman; member of a municipal council

tamenes/tememes Spanish corruption of "*tlameme*," a human carrier or porter used to carry objects in ancient central Mexico

Glossary of Nahuatl Terms

A NOTE ON PRONUNCIATION

Nahuatl, the language of the Mexica, Tlaxcalans, and other Nahua peoples, is a living language still spoken in Mexico. It has changed in many ways since the conquest, but its basic structure and pronunciation remain similar to its form in the sixteenth century. Spaniards who first tried to write down what they heard in Nahuatl often only approximated the sounds and sometimes found the Spanish alphabet inadequate to the task. Pronunciation will be made easier for modern readers if it is remembered that:

x is pronounced as sh   (Mexica = Meshica)
tl is pronounced like English "atlas"   (Tlaxcala, Tlaloc) and at the end of a word the *l* is almost silent (Nahuatl = Nahuat(l))

acazauatl   smallpox

altepetl   city or city-state

atlatl   spearthrower used to throw small darts and spears

Aztlán   legendary name of the mythical home of the Mexica people

cacique/cacica   a Taino word meaning ruler, brought from the Indies to Mexico by the Spanish and used to refer to native rulers in Mexico and Latin America in general

calmecac   Mexica school for the priesthood, usually reserved for the children of Mexica nobles and elites. It also functioned to train future Mexica military and political leaders as well as warriors.

calpulli   Nahuatl term meaning "big house" which referred to the core territorial unit of social organization usually related to a neighborhood or barrio-like section of the town or city; often likened to a clan system

Camaxtli   "god of the hunt," the tribal patron deity of Tlaxcala and Huexotzingo

cazonci   Tarascan word for ruler

254

chinampas   rectangular plots of silt constructed in a lake by building dirt-filled enclosures, on which multiple harvests could be made in a single year. Similar to hydroponic agriculture; also called "floating gardens."

Cihuacoatl   "woman-snake," an earth goddess deity of the Mexica pantheon; also the title of the first advisor of the Mexica ruler

Huitzilipochtli   the tribal patron deity of the Mexica who in legend led them from Aztlán to the central valley of Mexico. He was the god of war and god of the hunt and he shared the largest temple in the ceremonial precinct in Tenochtitlan with Tlaloc, the god of rain. He is one of the first gods the Spanish attempted to destroy, possibly because of the heavy human sacrifices that the Mexica dedicated to him.

Ixtaccíhuatl   one of two mountains to the east of Tenochtitlan/Mexico City through which Cortés and his army passed en route to the Mexica capital

macehualtin   social class of peasant commoners

pipiltin   nobility; elite social class of Mexica society

pochteca   long-distance merchants and traders who also often served as spies

Popocatépetl   one of two mountains to the east of Tenochtitlan/Mexico City through which Cortés and his army passed en route to the Mexica capital. It is the highest peak in Mexico, exceeding 17,000 feet above sea level.

Quetzalcoatl   one of the great ancient gods of Mesoamerica, literally "plumed or feathered serpent." He was the god of priests and merchants and was revered by the Nahua for bringing language and civilization to Mexico. The Nahua also confused him with the historical ruler of Tula, Ce Acatl Topiltzin Quetzalcoatl, who left Mexico and sailed east, vowing to return. When Cortés arrived in Veracruz, the Mexica initially believed him to be the returning god, but soon after realized that he was not.

telpochcalli   Mexica school for the training of warriors, usually reserved for the sons of commoners. Each *calpulli* contained its own school, and many of the students in the school would accompany their mentors on war campaigns to carry weapons and supplies.

Tenochtitlan   the capital city of the Mexica founded on an island in Lake Texcoco around 1325 after they were forced onto the island by enemy city-states. A century later, in 1428, the Mexica defeated their rivals on the lake shore, and over the next decades the city became the most powerful in preconquest central Mexico. It was laid siege and conquered from 1519–21 by Cortés and his Spanish army.

tepustles   term used by Nahua to refer to iron bullets and cannonballs

***Tezcatlipoca* (*Tezcatepuca-Díaz del Castillo*)** literally "smoking mirror," one of the great ancient gods of Mesoamerica. He was the god of rulers, sorcerers, and warriors, and also the god of the night sky and divination. He was the deity to which the Toxcatl festival was devoted when the Spanish massacred the Mexica participants in the courtyard.

tlacateuctli signifies the Mexica ruler or king; similar to *tlatoani*

tlacochcalcatl a military commander, used as an honorific term in the annals of Cuauhtinchan to refer to Gerónimo de Aguilar, Cortés's rescued translator who spoke both Spanish and Maya

tlacuilo a trained Nahua artist-scribe, known as "master of the red and black ink," who produced books, codices, and lienzos for use by the priesthood, rulers, and nobility

Tlaloc one of the great ancient gods of Mesoamerica and an important deity to the Nahua. He was the god of rain and lightning for the Mexica and shared the Great Temple of Tenochtitlan in the ceremonial precinct with Huitzilopochtli.

tlameme a human carrier or porter used to carry objects in ancient central Mexico

tlatoani (*tlatoque*, pl.) literally "speaker," dynastic ruler of a Nahua altepetl

Xiutecuhtli mythical fire-serpent, also the god of fire, commonly associated with youthful warriors or rulers

Xochipilli literally "flower prince," he is the Mexica god of sport and leisure and is usually associated with festivity and harvest. In many respects he is the male form of Xochiquetzal.

Xochiquetzal literally "flower quetzal," she symbolized young female sexual power and pleasure, and was also the goddess of young mothers

xochiyaoyotl literally "war of flowers"; a ritual combat between two mesoamerican polities for religious reasons in which prisoners were taken for the purpose of sacrifice

Selected Bibliography

The following items were particularly helpful in the preparation of this book and provide an introduction to the rapidly growing literature in this field.

PRIMARY SOURCES

Alva Ixlilxochitl, Fernando de. *Obras historicas.* Ed. Edmundo O'Gorman. 2 vols. Mexico: UNAM, 1975.

Anderson, Arthur, and Susan Schroeder, trans. and eds. *Codex Chimalpahín.* 2 vols. Norman: University of Oklahoma Press, 1996.

Anderson, Arthur J. O., Frances Berdan, and James Lockhart. *Beyond the Codices: The Nahua View of Colonial Mexico.* UCLA Latin American Series. Los Angeles: University of California Press, 1976.

Berdan, Frances F., and Patricia Rieff Anawalt, eds. *The Codex Mendoza.* 4 vols. Berkeley: University of California Press, 1992.

Bierhorst, John, trans. and ed. *History and Mythology of the Aztecs: The Codex Chimalpopoca.* Tucson: University of Arizona Press, 1992.

Cortés, Hernán. *Letters from Mexico.* Trans. and ed. Anthony Pagden. New York: Orion Press, 1971.

Crane, Eugene R., and Reginald C. Reindorp, trans. and eds. *Chronicles of Michoacán.* Norman: University of Oklahoma Press, 1970.

Díaz del Castillo, Bernal. *The True History of the Conquest of New Spain.* Ed. A. P. Maudslay. London: Hakluyt Society, 1908.

———. *The Discovery and Conquest of Mexico.* Trans. A. P. Maudslay. Introduction by Irving Leonard. New York: Farrar, Straus, and Cudahy, 1956.

Durán, Diego. *The History of the Indies of New Spain.* Trans. Doris Heyden and Fernando Horcasitas. New York: Orion Press, 1964.

Fuentes, Patricia de. *The Conquistadors: First-Person Accounts of the Conquest of Mexico.* Norman: University of Oklahoma Press, 1993.

Lockhart, James. *We People Here: Nahuatl Accounts of the Conquest of Mexico.* Repertorium Columbianum, UCLA Center for Medieval and Renaissance Studies. Los Angeles: University of California Press, 1993.

López de Gómara, Francisco. *Cortés: The Life of the Conqueror.* Trans. and ed. L. B. Simpson. Berkeley: University of California Press, 1964.

Muñoz Camargo, Diego de. *Historia de Tlaxcala.* Ed. Alfredo Chavero. Mexico City: Secretaria de Fomento, 1892.

Pagden, Anthony, trans. and ed. *Hernán Cortés: Letters from Mexico.* New York: Orion Press, 1971.

SECONDARY SOURCES

Adorno, Rolena. "Arms, Letters, and the Native Historian in Early Colonial Mexico," in Rene Jara and Nicholas Spadaccini, eds. "Re/discovering Colonial Writing." *Hispanic Issues* 4 (1989): 201–24.

Baudot, Georges. *Utopia and History in Mexico: The First Chroniclers of Mexican Civilization.* Niwot, Colo.: University Press of Colorado, 1995.

Brundage, Burr Cartwright. *The Fifth Sun: Aztec Gods, Aztec World.* Austin: University of Texas Press, 1979.

Carrasco, David. *Quetzalcoatl and the Irony of Empire: Myth and Prophecy in the Aztec Tradition.* Chicago: University of Chicago Press, 1982.

Cerwin, Herbert. *Bernal Díaz: Historian of the Conquest.* Norman: University of Oklahoma Press, 1963.

Clendennen, Inga. *The Aztecs.* Cambridge: Cambridge University Press, 1991.

Davies, Nigel. *The Aztec Empire: The Toltec Resurgence.* Norman: University of Oklahoma Press, 1987.

Florescano, Enrique. *Etnia, estado y nación.* Mexico City: Aguilar, 1997.

Gardiner, C. Harvey. *Naval Power in the Conquest of Mexico.* Austin: University of Texas Press, 1956.

Gibson, Charles. *The Aztecs under Spanish Rule.* Stanford: Stanford University Press, 1964.

————. *Tlaxcala in the Sixteenth Century.* Stanford: Stanford University Press, 1967.

Gruzinski, Serge. *Painting the Conquest: The Mexican Indians and the European Renaissance.* Paris: Flammarion-UNESCO, 1992.

————. *Mexico and the Spanish Conquest.* New York: Longman, 1994.

Haskett, Robert. *Indigenous Rulers: An Ethnohistory of Town Government in Colonial Cuernavaca.* Albuquerque: University of New Mexico Press, 1991.

Hassig, Ross. *Aztec Warfare: Imperial Expansion and Political Control.* Norman: University of Oklahoma Press, 1988.

————. *Mexico and the Spanish Conquest.* New York: Longman, 1994.

Horn, Rebecca. *Postconquest Coyoacan: Nahua-Spanish Relations in Central Mexico, 1519–1650.* Stanford: Stanford University Press, 1997.

León-Portilla, Miguel. *Aztec Thought and Culture.* Ed. Jack Emory Davis. Norman: University of Oklahoma Press, 1963.

————. *Precolumbian Literatures of Mexico.* Trans. Grace Miguel León-Portilla. Norman: University of Oklahoma Press, 1974.

————. *The Aztec Image of Self and Society.* Trans and ed. Jorge Klor de Alva. Salt Lake City: University of Utah Press, 1992.

———. *The Broken Spears: The Aztec Account of the Conquest of Mexico*. 2nd ed. Boston: Beacon Press, 1992.

Marcus, Joyce. *Mesoamerican Writing Systems*. Princeton, N.J.: Princeton University Press, 1992.

Melville, Elinor G. K. *A Plague of Sheep: Environmental Consequences of the Conquest of Mexico*. Cambridge: Cambridge University Press, 1994.

Pastor Bodmer, Beatriz. *The Armature of Conquest: Spanish Accounts of the Discovery of America, 1492–1589*. Stanford: Stanford University Press, 1992.

Pollard, Helen Perlstein. *Tariacuri's Legacy: The Prehistoric Tarascan State*. Norman: University of Oklahoma Press, 1993.

Robertson, Donald. *Mexican Manuscript Painting of the Early Colonial Period*. Ed. Elizabeth H. Boone. 2nd ed. Norman: University of Oklahoma Press, 1992.

Santa María, Carmelo Saenz de. *Introducción crítica a la "Historia verdadera" de Bernal Díaz del Castillo*. Madrid: Consejo Superior de Investigaciones Científicas, 1967.

———. *Historia de una historia: Bernal Díaz del Castillo*. Madrid: Consejo Superior de Investigaciones Científicas, 1984.

Thomas, Hugh. *Conquest: Montezuma, Cortés, and the Fall of Old Mexico*. New York: Simon & Schuster, 1993.

Todarov, Tzvetan, and Georges Baudot, eds. *Récits aztèques de la conquête*. Paris: Ed. Seuil, 1983.

Warren, J. Benedict. *The Conquest of Michoacán*. Norman: University of Oklahoma Press, 1985.

Acknowledgments

Excerpt from *The Aztecs: The History of the Indies of New Spain* by Diego Durán, translated by Doris Heyden and Fernando Horcasitas. Copyright 1964, Orion Press. Reprinted by permission of Doris Heyden.

Excerpt from *Beyond the Codice: The Nahua View of Colonial Mexico*, edited by Arthur J. O. Anderson, Frances Berdan, and James Lockhart. Copyright 1976 by The Regents of the University of California. Reprinted by permission of University of California Press, Berkeley.

Excerpts from *Broken Spears*, by Miguel León-Portilla. Copyright 1962, 1990 by Miguel León-Portilla. Expanded and Updated Copyright 1992 by Miguel León-Portilla. Reprinted by permission of Beacon Press, Boston.

Excerpts from *The Chronicles of Michoacán*, translated and edited by Eugene R. Craine and Reginald C. Reindorp. Copyright 1970, University of Oklahoma Press. Reprinted by permission of University of Oklahoma Press, Norman.

Excerpt from *Codex Chimalpahin: Society and Politics in Mexico Tenochtitlan, Tlateloco, Culhuacan, and Other Nahua Altepetl in Central Mexico*, edited and translated by Arthur J. O. Anderson and Susan Schroeder. Copyright 1997, University of Oklahoma Press. Reprinted by permission of University of Oklahoma Press, Norman.

Excerpts from *The Codex Mendoza*, Frances F. Berdan and Patricia Rieff Anawalt. Copyright 1992 by The Regents of the University of California, Frances F. Berdan, and Patricia Rieff Anawalt. Reprinted by permission of the authors and University of California Press, Berkeley.

Excerpts from *The Conquistadors: First Person Accounts of the Conquest of Mexico*, edited and translated by Patricia de Fuentes. Translation copyright 1963 by Viking Press. Used by permission of Viking Press, a division of Penguin Putnam Inc.

Excerpts from *Hernando Cortés: Five Letters, 1519–1526*, edited and translated by J. Bayard Morris. Translation copyright, all rights reserved, 1969, 1991. Reprinted by permission of W. W. Norton & Company, Inc.

Excerpt from *Maya Conquistador*, by Matthew Restall. Copyright 1998 by Matthew Restall. Reprinted by permission of Beacon Press, Boston.

Excerpts from *We People Here: Nahuatl Accounts of the Conquest of Mexico*, Reportorium Columbianum, UCLA Center for Medieval and Renaissance Studies, Volume 1, by James Lockhart. Copyright 1993 by The Regents of the University of California. Reprinted by permission of University of California Press, Berkeley.

Index

261